FOOD HYGIENE IN THE CATERING AND RETAIL TRADES

To Marlene, Mark, Andrew and Paul

FOOD HYGIENE IN THE CATERING AND RETAIL TRADES

JOHN K. DAVENPORT, B.A., F.I.E.H.

Senior Assistant Environmental Health Officer
Stroud District Council

LONDON
H. K. LEWIS & CO. LTD
1982

Foreword

Some of the food eaten by man can and does make him ill and in a small percentage of cases such illness results in death. This fact has been known for many generations. The Bible describes some basic rules of food hygiene and prohibits the consumption of certain foods by the Jewish race. These laws were probably intended to give the Jews some protection from illnesses caused by parasites in meat and from diseased and moribund carcasses. The causal agents of much food-borne illness were shrouded in mystery for hundreds of years and only began to emerge when the existence of micro-organisms was discovered and their nature and patterns of behaviour were examined by pioneering microbiologists. Like other areas of science our knowledge of the origins and factors which are responsible for food poisoning and food-borne infection has steadily increased over the last 50 years. New micro-organisms responsible for illness after consumption of food contaminated with those micro-organisms are being discovered with increasing frequency so that types of gastro-enteritis, previously dismissed as digestive upsets or bilious attacks, are now diagnosed as resulting from a specific organism and are thus included in the statistics of food poisoning. In addition food is increasingly produced by methods of mass production and mass catering where any failure in hygiene techniques can create a risk to numbers of consumers. It is no wonder, therefore, that those statistics show no signs of diminution, indeed they show a considerable increase in recent years.

There is a legal obligation on all those who prepare food for sale to ensure that food is safe and fit for human consumption. Failure to do so can lead to prosecution by the Local Authority for offences under the Food and Drugs Act, 1955, and the Food Hygiene Regulations made under that Act. There is an increasing tendency also for proceedings under common law to follow food poisoning outbreaks and award of damages in such circumstances can result in a severe financial penalty to the food producer.

Central Government has a duty to produce legislation requiring food to be prepared under clean conditions. Such legislation exists and is reviewed periodically. The Department of Health and Social Security encourages local authorities to enforce such legislation and there exists throughout the United Kingdom a system of food inspection which rivals anything found elsewhere in developed countries. There is no doubt that this has a beneficial effect and gives considerable protection to the consumer. But it is at best a palliative. The real answer to the problem of food poisoning and food-borne illness is a thorough understanding by those who handle and prepare food of the nature and mechanism of food poisoning and the food hygiene precautions which need to be adopted to prevent such illness associated with food. Fortunately increasing information on the origins of food poisoning and food-borne disease is balanced by improved knowledge of the preventive measures needed to deal with such illnesses and it behoves all those who handle, prepare or produce food to keep abreast of recent developments in food hygiene.

Here then is a volume prepared by an Environmental Health Officer which is intended for the catering and retail trades and contains up-to-date information on the technology of food hygiene. It is admirably suited to its purpose and is a sound investment in terms of knowledge for those who wish to protect both themselves and their customers from outbreaks of illness caused by consumption of food which has resulted from negligence in the application of the rules of food hygiene.

I commend this book and hope that it will have some effect in reducing the misery caused to those who suffer illness resulting from the consumption of contaminated food.

H. L. Hughes, O.B.E., M.R.S.H., F.I.E.H.
Environmental Health Officer,
Department of Health and Social Security

Preface

Food Hygiene is an important subject that affects the lives of us all. Those who work in the food industry, handling, preparing and selling the nation's food, have a moral as well as legal duty to ensure that good standards of food hygiene prevail. It is the author's hope that this book will help them in their task.

This volume is intended to provide factual information and practical advice to all who hold a managerial or supervisory position in the catering and retail food trades. It is therefore intended for line managers, supervisors, senior catering and retail staff and hygiene officers. It is also hoped that local authority enforcement officers and students will find this book a useful source of reference.

In the preparation of this work I have received the help of many individuals and organisations and I am pleased to take this opportunity to acknowledge their assistance. In particular I wish to record my indebtedness to Mr Malcolm Smith, Senior Environmental Health Inspector, Gloucester City, who carefully read and commented on the whole of the typescript. This book has benefited considerably from his diligence and knowledge but the responsibility for any errors or omissions that remain rests entirely with the author. I am also grateful to Dr A. E. Wright, Consultant Microbiologist, Public Health Laboratory Service, for his comments on Chapters 2 and 3.

In addition my thanks go to my brother Mr Michael Davenport, for arranging the illustrations for this volume, and to Mr Steven Marshfield for a number of the photographs that are included.

I have also received valuable assistance from Mr H. Herbert and Dr P. J. Barlow of the University of Aston, Mr M. Wood of Bristol Polytechnic, Mrs P. Taylour of the Gloucestershire College of Arts and Technology and Mr R. Robinson, of Berni Inns.

Help, encouragement and general assistance has been forthcoming from many colleagues at Stroud Environmental Health and Planning Departments, especially Mr G. Critchley (now retired), Mr L. Scourfield, Mr T. H. Portlock and Mrs Gill Webb.

Many organisations and companies have kindly provided information and photographs including: The Automatic Vending Association of Britain; Cimex Ltd; G.K.N. Sankey Ltd; Henry Simon Ltd; I.C.I. Paints Division; Imperial Machine Co. (Peelers) Ltd; Machine Control Ltd; Mather and Platt Anti-Pollution Systems Ltd; The National Federation of Fish Friers; National Vendors; Nilfisk Ltd; Ozonair Engineering Co. Ltd; Rems Ltd; Sutcliffe Vending Services; The Take-away Food

Federation (U.K.) Ltd; Thorn Domestic Appliances (Electrical) Ltd; Ventron Technology Ltd; W. G. Sissons Ltd and Zoppas Catering Equipment Ltd.

I express my thanks to them all.

Swells Hill   J. K. D.
April 1981

Contents

Part 1

Chapter 1

AN INTRODUCTION TO FOOD POISONING AND FOOD HYGIENE IN BRITAIN

Food poisoning is always an unpleasant condition and can prove fatal for the more frail members of society. Each year many people become ill and a few die as a result of food poisoning, although it is a preventable condition. The underlying causes of food poisoning are ignorance and carelessness. Ignorance of the ways in which food poisoning organisms can enter the food chain at the farm, slaughterhouse, factory, shop or kitchen; and carelessness in failing to apply simple food hygiene measures wherever food is handled.

In an endeavour to prevent, or at least reduce, food-borne disease, legislation has been passed to promote good standards of food hygiene. The prevention of food poisoning has always been the prime motive in attempting to apply food hygiene standards, but it is not the only reason. There is a secondary consideration and this is to ensure that all food is produced, prepared and stored under clean conditions. This need not necessarily be related to any health risk. The consumer has the right to demand a high standard of cleanliness and organisation wherever the food that he will ultimately eat is prepared or held.

The success of efforts to improve food hygiene is difficult to measure. Perhaps the immediate reaction is to reach for the food poisoning statistics as a guide to trends of improving or declining food hygiene. Unfortunately this raises a number of problems.

TABLE I

Incidents of food poisoning and salmonellosis in England and Wales 1970–1979

	1970	1971	1972	1973	1974	1975	1976	1977	1978	1979
General outbreaks	194	207	153	186	208	247	245	223	214	217
Family outbreaks	641	545	473	603	383	328	372	328	365	325
Sporadic cases	4455	4941	3469	4729	3883	6501	5092	5273	6835	7413
All incidents	5290	5693	4095	5518	4474	7076	5709	5824	7414	7947

P.H.L.S. Communicable Disease Surveillance Centre, London, C.D.R. 1980/32 (unpublished) (for definitions of incidents, outbreaks and cases see Chapter 3, page 15).

Firstly, there are three main sources of food poisoning statistics: statutory notifications of clinical food poisoning, published by the Office of

Population Censuses and Surveys (O.P.C.S.); reports of medical officers of environmental health or local authorities to the Department of Health and Social Security (D.H.S.S.) concerning sporadic cases and outbreaks of food poisoning; and figures published by the Communicable Diseases Surveillance Centre (C.D.S.C.) of laboratory reports, which show isolations of food poisoning bacteria, including those from persons not clinically ill. The three sets of figures are not identical and indeed may indicate differing trends in food poisoning when considered in the short-term. However, if the three sets of data are viewed over a number of years, they show the same trend; a rise in the number of cases since 1972.

Cases of food poisoning and salmonellas reported to the O.P.C.S., P.H.L.S. & D.H.S.S.: 1970–79

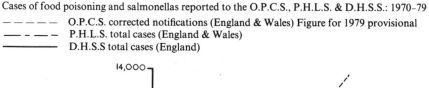

— — — — —   O.P.C.S. corrected notifications (England & Wales) Figure for 1979 provisional
— · — · —   P.H.L.S. total cases (England & Wales)
——————   D.H.S.S total cases (England)

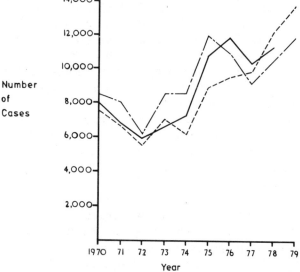

P.H.L.S. Communicable Disease Surveillance Centre, London, C.D.R. 1980/32 (unpublished)

The second problem with the food poisoning statistics is that they are not a measure of *all* cases of food poisoning. Most authorities agree that there are a considerable number of unreported cases, but obviously there is no way of determining what this number is or how it varies from one year to the next. All one can perhaps say is that the trend is in the wrong direction and, in absolute terms at least, that seven to eight thousand incidents of food poisoning a year is too many.

In addition the consumer is now better informed than ever before about the need for good food hygiene and is demanding higher standards than those that have prevailed in the past. Newspaper and television coverage of food poisoning outbreaks encourages a climate of food hygiene consciousness. The death of two elderly people in 1978 from botulism following the consumption of canned salmon aroused deep public concern about food safety in general and canned goods in particular.

A growing public awareness and concern about poor food hygiene conditions has been accompanied by developments in the field of enforcement. 1974 saw the reorganisation of local government and in many cases the setting up of specialist food hygiene sections within the local Environmental Health Department. With this reorganisation came a sharp upturn in prosecutions for contraventions of the Food Hygiene Regulations, and much fresh thinking on ways to encourage compliance with the spirit, as well as the letter of the law. A food hygiene advisory service, separate from its enforcement section, was introduced by one local authority, whilst night-time patrols, food hygiene improvement areas and 'extended' inspections were among the innovations introduced in other areas.

This increased public awareness and enforcement activity has acted as a catalyst in the food trade, with many undertakings, both large companies and individual food traders, striving to achieve the very highest standards. Such food premises have justly earned public respect for their consistently hygienic approach to the sale and preparation of food.

TABLE 2

General outbreaks of food poisoning and salmonellosis in England and Wales 1970–1979

Organism	1970	1971	1972	1973	1974	1975	1976	1977	1978	1979
Salmonellae	138	163	103	128	145	134	124	126	143	138
Clostridium perfringens	31	29	29	30	42	69	84	78	38	53
Staphylococcus aureus	18	8	8	6	7	15	13	6	11	4
Bacillus cereus	0	2	4	16	10	20	13	8	10	4
Other/unknown	7	5	9	6	4	9	11	5	12	8

P.H.L.S. Communicable Disease Surveillance Centre, London, C.D.R. 1980/32 (unpublished).

The food poisoning scene itself is not static and the last 10 years have seen interesting developments in the nature of food poisoning incidents in Britain. Infections due to salmonellae remain the most important problem, with organisms of this group of bacteria being responsible for the vast majority of cases that occur.

TABLE 3

Human isolations of common salmonella serotypes 1979

Serotype	Isolations	Rank order
S. typhimurium	3259	1
S. hadar	2477	2
S. virchow	859	3
S. enteritidis	787	4
S. agona	648	5

P.H.L.S. Communicable Disease Surveillance Centre, London, C.D.R. 1980/42 (unpublished).

However, there have been changes in the serotypes responsible for salmonella infections. *S. typhimurium*, traditionally by far the commonest serotype found, is now rivalled by *S. hadar*. In 1971 the Public Health Laboratory Service recorded only 31 isolations of *S. hadar* but by 1979 this figure had risen to 2,480. Outbreaks of *S. hadar* are particularly associated with the consumption of poultry, especially very large turkeys, which require extreme care in preparation and cooking.

Compared with salmonellae, *Clostridium perfringens* and *Staphylococcus aureus* food poisoning are responsible for a small, but fairly constant number of incidents. However, an increasing number of 'new' or recently recognised forms of food poisoning are now being notified. The 1970s saw the first notifications of *Bacillus cereus* food poisoning in Britain. Many cases have followed, usually as a result of the consumption of fried or reheated rice. *Vibrio parahaemolyticus*, a common cause of food poisoning in the East, was unknown in this country until 1972 but is now isolated in a small number of incidents each year.

Two other 'new' forms of food poisoning are perhaps related to changes in eating habits. The increased consumption of smoked mackerel has brought with it a growing number of reports of scombrotoxin fish poisoning. Whilst the habit of eating raw red kidney beans in salads has led to cases of poisoning due to an as yet undiscovered toxin in the uncooked beans.

In addition to food poisoning, the extent to which *Campylobacter jejuni/coli* is responsible for illness, sometimes food-borne, is being increasingly recognised. In 1979 a milk-borne outbreak of campylobacter enteritis occurred, involving over 2,000 children and adults, probably resulting from a failure in a pasteurisation plant. A full discussion of the food poisoning agents mentioned is given in Chapter 3.

Unfortunately, the law on food hygiene has not kept pace with this changing scene and neither does it take fully into account current knowledge concerning the spread of food poisoning. The first food hygiene regulations came into operation in 1956 when the symptomless excretor or carrier was considered the greatest danger and only minor changes have been made in the law since that time. Thus, the regulations are preoccupied with the condition of the food handler; availability of washing facilities, 'now wash your hands' notices, prohibition of smoking *etc.* It is not suggested that these things do not matter—of course they do—but we now know that the main danger arises from the raw food itself.

The most effective way of dealing with the salmonella problem is at the farm and, in particular, the compulsory treatment of animal feeding stuffs to eliminate this source of infection. Perhaps the other single most effective means of preventing food poisoning is good temperature control of protein foods. However, the provisions of the existing Food Hygiene Regulations relating to temperature control are so weak as to be virtually valueless. The Milne Committee, which investigated the Aberdeen typhoid outbreak, made the point that all cold meats should be displayed at below 4.5°C (40°F). In what could be considered a spirit of constructive common sense they observed that because of difficulties in small shops the necessary legislation could not be introduced immediately, but amendments should be made as soon as possible. That was in 1964. Could that committee have possibly envisaged that 17 years and over seventy thousand food poisoning incidents later there would still be no effective temperature control legislation in the United Kingdom?

It is to be regretted that no general revision of food hygiene legislation is planned to deal with the real deficiencies of the existing regulations. But whilst the law is important, and can set *minimum* standards, *good* standards will only be achieved when all understand the principles of food hygiene and are committed to putting them into practice. It is the author's hope that this volume will assist food trade management in this task and help enforcement officers to monitor its success.

Chapter 2

INTRODUCTION TO BACTERIOLOGY

Although chemical food poisoning does occur in Britain it is rare, and almost all the cases of food poisoning notified are due to the contamination of food with bacteria or their toxins. In order to apply food hygiene rules and systems effectively, it is essential to understand something of the nature of bacteria and their requirements for growth and multiplication.

2.1 THE NATURE, SIZE AND SHAPE OF BACTERIA

Bacteria are minute single-celled organisms invisible to the naked eye. They vary in size from $0.5\,\mu m$ to 70 or $80\,\mu m$ ($1\,\mu m = 1/1,000\,mm$).

They are to be found almost everywhere; in the air, in water, in soil *etc.* and most of them are harmless. Indeed some are beneficial and may even be used in the production of food, such as cheese and yoghurt. However, some bacteria are pathogenic to man and can cause illness, including food poisoning. Disease-producing bacteria are known as pathogens.

Bacteria are classified according to their shape. Four basic shapes exist:

Cocci—spherical in shape.
Bacilli—rod-shaped.
Spirilli—spiral-shaped.
Vibrio's—comma-shaped.

2.2 THE STRUCTURE OF BACTERIA

All bacteria have the same basic internal structure regardless of their shape. This structure is illustrated in Fig. 1.

The cell wall retains the characteristic shape of the bacterium and contains the cell membrane which controls the entry and exit of substances to the organism. In addition some bacteria possess an outer capsule, the function of which may be to protect the cell from destruction by harmful substances. Certain bacteria are capable of movement in liquids by the rhythmic motion of hair-like processes, or flagellae.

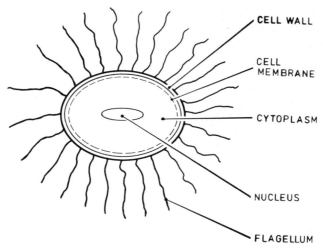

Fig. 1 Structure of a bacterium

In order to make bacteria more visible under the microscope they are often stained before examination. Various methods are used but in 1884 the Danish bacteriologist Hans Christian Gram, whilst working in Berlin, discovered a staining process that not only made bacteria more visible but also allowed them to be divided into two distinct classes. Basically gram-staining, as it is known, consists of staining bacteria on a microscope slide with gentian violet and iodine. This causes the cells to turn black. The slide is then washed with spirit and counter-stained with safranin pink. The result is that gram positive (g +ve) cells appear purple and gram negative (g −ve) pink. The difference is probably due to variations in the structure of the cell wall and is important when considering the destruction of bacteria, as chemical agents may affect gram positive cells differently to gram negative cells.

2.3 GROWTH AND MULTIPLICATION OF BACTERIA

Bacteria multiply by simple division, known as binary fission. One bacterium divides into two and two into four and so on. The time that this division takes, the generation time, can be very short; under ideal conditions twenty minutes or less. Thus, in twelve hours a single bacterium could produce 70 billion progeny! Whilst comparatively large numbers of food poisoning bacteria are required to cause illness it can be seen that such numbers can develop rapidly under certain conditions. Good food hygiene practice avoids the preparation and storage of food under such conditions.

The opportunity for pathogenic bacteria to multiply to a dangerous level in food depends on the time available for bacterial growth and the environmental conditions that exist. The most important environmental factors influencing growth are the nature of the food; the prevailing temperature; the availability of water and oxygen and the acidity or alkalinity of the food (the pH level). The significance of these factors is discussed in the following paragraphs.

2.3.1 Time

Given a suitable environment, bacterial cells will grow until they reach the right size for division.

In the multiplication of bacteria four growth-rate phases can be observed, as shown in Fig. 2.

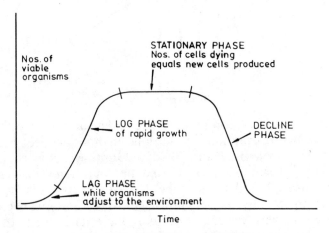

Fig. 2 Growth phases of bacteria

Lag phase
This phase can last several hours, during which little or no multiplication occurs. It is a period when the cells adapt to the environment and eventually grow in size. They will be relatively few in number at this stage and therefore may be more easily destroyed. The more suitable the medium on which the bacteria are growing the shorter will be the lag phase. (For the significance of lag phase in the cooling of cooked food see 9.3.2 page 126.)

Log phase
During this phase bacteria multiply rapidly until the maximum number that can be supported by the medium is reached. If the logarithm of the number of bacteria is plotted on a graph, against time, a straight line is usually obtained; hence the name, log phase. It is this phenomenal logarithmic multiplication that can quickly give rise to dangerous levels of bacteria in food held at warm temperatures.

Stationary phase
The number of cells reaches a maximum as the food supply is depleted and the amount of waste products increase rapidly. Eventually a stable

situation is reached when the number of cells dying approximately equals the number of new cells produced.

Decline phase
As the environment becomes less ideal, due to lack of nutrient and the build-up of toxic wastes, so the numbers of cells decline. This decline will continue as the bacteria die, unless they are transferred to another suitable medium when the multiplication process starts again.

2.3.2 Food
Bacteria require suitable food to provide the basic elements for cell construction and energy. Enzymes are secreted to break down complex foods into simple organic compounds which can be incorporated into cell components. The types of enzyme produced by bacteria vary and this influences the foodstuffs on which they will grow successfully. Proteolytic bacteria break down proteins; lipolytic bacteria can utilise fats and so on. The waste products produced by bacterial enzymes can be used to identify the bacteria present. For example, some bacteria are able to break down sugars and produce acid and gas, whilst others can decompose proteins and produce ammonia or hydrogen sulphide. These differences can be extremely useful to the microbiologist when examining bacteria.

2.3.3 Temperature
The speed at which bacteria will grow and multiply is greatly influenced by temperature. All bacteria have an optimum temperature at which they will multiply most effectively. In addition there is a maximum and minimum temperature above or below which they will not multiply. For convenience bacteria are divided into three groups, depending on the temperature conditions they prefer.

Psycrophiles
These bacteria favour relatively cool conditions and have an optimum temperature growth range of 10-15°C (50-59°F). They will grow between 3-20°C (37·5-68°F) and indeed growth may occur down to temperatures as low as −5°C (23°F). As will be appreciated such bacteria can be a problem in refrigerated storage.

Mesophiles
This group includes most bacteria pathogenic to man. The optimum temperature for mesophiles is near to that of body heat, 37°C (98·4°F). Their growth range is 10-45°C (50-113°F) and this obviously includes the normal ambient temperatures of kitchens, store rooms *etc*. Adequate refrigerated storage of susceptible foods will prevent the multiplication of mesophilic bacteria.

Thermophiles
These bacteria prefer relatively high temperatures and their optimum temperature is normally 45–55°C (113–131°F) and their growth range between 30–65°C (86–150°F).

2.3.4 Water

Nutrients are absorbed through the cell wall in solution and therefore moisture must be present for bacterial growth to occur. The amount of water available in food, or in a solution, can be referred to in terms of water activity or Aw. Pure water has an Aw of 1·0, and would provide no nutrient for bacterial growth. Bacteria normally require a high Aw, whereas yeasts and moulds will survive a lower Aw. If the Aw is below 0·6 few micro-organisms can grow.

Solutions of salt and sugar exert osmotic pressure on the cell, causing it to lose water and dehydrate. This osmotic pressure is the basis of food preservation through the use of sugar in jam and other preserves, and in the salting of meat. A few bacteria have adapted to resist high osmotic pressures and some others particularly prefer an environment with a high salt level; these are called halophilic (or salt-loving). *Staphylococcus aureus* is a halophile.

2.3.5 Oxygen

Some bacteria require atmospheric oxygen to grow whilst others will only grow in the absence of air. Those that require molecular oxygen are known as aerobes, whilst anaerobes will only thrive in the absence of atmospheric oxygen. Some bacteria are adapted to survive in both situations and are known as facultative bacteria. Facultative anaerobes prefer aerobic conditions but will grow in the absence of air, whilst facultative aerobes grow best in an anaerobic environment.

2.3.6 pH (acidity or alkalinity)

The acidity or alkalinity of a solution is expressed numerically by the pH scale of 0–14. pH 7 is neutral. Acid conditions exist from 0–7 and alkaline from 7–14. Micro-organisms will only grow and multiply within a certain pH range. Most micro-organisms require reasonably neutral conditions between pH 5–9; however, some will tolerate conditions more acid or more alkaline than this. The inhibiting effect of acid is utilised in the pickling of food.

2.4 SPORES (ENDOSPORES)

Two genera of rods, bacilli (aerobic) and clostridia (anaerobic), are able to produce spores. Spores are resting bodies whose production is stimulated by unfavourable conditions, especially the lack of moisture. They are formed to ensure the survival of the bacterium if conditions become extreme. Because they are formed from within the vegetative cell (the normal bacterial cell) they are also called endospores. Endospores should not be confused with mould spores, which are involved in reproduction.

After the endospore forms, the vegetative cell slowly disintegrates. The spore contains sufficient material to form a new cell and can itself withstand drought conditions and often very high temperatures (see 3.1.6). When the environment becomes favourable the spore coat splits and a new vegetative cell emerges, able to recommence multiplication. Spores cannot reproduce and in the case of food poisoning bacteria only give rise to illness if they are allowed to germinate in a suitable food.

Some spores can remain viable for very long periods of time.

2.5 TOXINS

Certain bacteria responsible for food poisoning produce poisons, known as toxins. Toxins can be divided into exotoxins and endotoxins. Exotoxins are excreted by the cell as the bacterium grows; staphylococcal food poisoning and botulism are caused by exotoxins. Endotoxins are released on the death of a cell or during sporulation, as they form part of the cell structure. *Clostridium perfringens* is an example of a food poisoning agent where endotoxins are responsible for illness.

The term enterotoxin will also be encountered in works on food poisoning. It simply means a toxin which causes gastro-enteritis.

Some toxins are extremely heat resistant and able to survive periods of boiling, *e.g.* the enterotoxin produced by some strains of *Staphylococcus aureus*.

2.6 PHAGE TYPING

Bacteriophages are parasitic viruses that are found attached to certain bacteria. As the type of bacteriophage is specific to certain bacteria the laboratory identification of a phage type can be used to identify the strain of bacteria very precisely. Phage typing can be used for some salmonellae and staphylococci, and may give an indication of their likely source.

2.7 OTHER MICRO-ORGANISMS

Although bacteria are the most common cause of food poisoning other micro-organisms can be important in the food industry and these include:

2.7.1 Viruses

Viruses are the smallest micro-organisms, being 10–300 nm (nm = 1/1,000,000 mm) and can only be viewed under an electron microscope. They are metabolically inert but are able to enter living cells and in such an environment multiply. Viruses are responsible for many diseases including the common cold and influenza. Little is known about the transfer of virus infections by food although such a method of spread may occur in poliomyelitis and other conditions (see 3.2.2).

2.7.2 Yeasts

These are single-celled organisms and are larger than bacteria. They are mainly saprophytic, living on decaying plant material. Yeasts are used in several food processes because of their ability to ferment sugars to produce carbon dioxide and alcohol, *e.g.* beer, wine and bread making.

2.7.3 Moulds

These are also mainly saprophytic organisms but are multicellular, and easily observed with the naked eye. Mould growth is not infrequently seen on stale bread and other foods (see 3.2.5).

2.7.4 Protozoa

Protozoa are simple single-celled animals that are found in ponds, streams, soil-water and the sea. Most species are harmless but some are responsible for disease. Amoebic dysentery is a disease that can be food-borne and is caused by the protozoan parasite *Entamoeba histolytica*. It is a condition that is rarely encountered in Britain.

2.8 THE DESTRUCTION OF MICRO-ORGANISMS

Micro-organisms can be destroyed by various means including heat and chemicals. See Chapter 6 for details.

Chapter 3

FOOD POISONING AGENTS, FOOD-BORNE DISEASES AND VEHICLES OF INFECTION

The term food poisoning describes an illness that follows the consumption of food contaminated by certain micro-organisms, their toxins or other poisonous substances. The symptoms are usually gastro-intestinal; vomiting and/or diarrhoea being common. In the case of bacterial food poisoning illness may be due either to an infection, or an intoxication. Infection occurs when living pathogenic bacteria are consumed and they set up a gastro-intestinal infection. Usually the infection remains localised but occasionally it becomes systemic, with the pathogens invading the bloodstream. In a true food poisoning infection, such as salmonellosis, the symptoms will take some time to occur, as the bacteria will first need to multiply and become established in the gastro-intestinal tract. This delay between the consumption of contaminated food and the onset of symptoms is known as the incubation period. The length of the incubation period will vary with the susceptibility of the patient and the number of organisms consumed. A food poisoning intoxication follows the consumption of food containing bacterial toxins (see 2.5) or other poisonous substances. Since this form of food poisoning does not involve the multiplication of bacteria in the alimentary canal, the onset of symptoms is more rapid, *i.e.* the 'incubation period' is shorter.

An outbreak of food poisoning involving many people can be very dramatic and will make headline news but food poisoning incidents do not always involve large numbers of people. The Public Health Laboratory Service define the various occurrences of food poisoning thus:

A general outbreak—two or more related cases or excretors in persons of different families.
A family outbreak—two or more related cases or excretors in persons of the same family.
A sporadic case—one case which, as far as was ascertained, was unrelated to other cases.
An incident—any one of these occurrences.

In 1979 sporadic cases in England and Wales accounted for 62% of all cases reported to the Communicable Disease Surveillance Centre.

3.1 BACTERIAL FOOD POISONING

3.1.1 Salmonella

Organisms of the Salmonella group are the most common cause of food poisoning in Britain. The genus *Salmonella* is divided into different sub-groups or serotypes. There are approximately 2,000 known serotypes and most can cause illness in man and animals. Serotypes are often named after the person who first recognised them or the place where they were first isolated, thus *S. stanley* and *S. heidelberg*. *S. typhimurium* (*typhimurium* means mouse typhoid) has always been the most commonly isolated serotype and this remains the case although others, particularly *S. hadar*, are becoming increasingly important.

Salmonellae are gram-negative facultative bacilli and although they are not spore-forming they can survive drying and freezing for consider-able periods.

Symptoms

Salmonellosis is a true infection and the main symptoms are fever, head-ache, aching limbs and diarrhoea. Sometimes the patient also suffers abdominal pain and vomiting. The duration of the illness is normally between 1 and 8 days and in the very young, the old or chronically sick it can be a serious condition and on occasions fatal. Certain serotypes, *e.g. S. cholerae suis* and *S. virchow*, are particularly virulent and are able to invade the bloodstream causing septicaemia, multiple abscesses in the organs and sometimes endocarditis (inflammation of the heart valves).

The incubation period is 12–48 hours or sometimes even longer.

Growth temperatures

Maximum 45°C (113°F).
Minimum 6·7°C (44°F).
Optimum 37°C (98°F).

Ecology

Salmonellae are widely distributed throughout the world, their common habitat being the intestinal tracts of mammals, birds and reptiles. Salmon-ellosis is a zoonosis; a disease that may be naturally transmitted be-tween animals and man, and in Britain the main reservoirs of salmon-ella infection are the food animals, principally poultry, pigs and cattle.

Salmonellosis is a particular problem in countries where food animals are intensively raised. The intensive farming of animals involves stock being kept in very confined spaces and sharing drinking and feeding facilities that can easily become fouled. Shortage of space also tends to produce stress in animals and this may enhance the excretion rate, so leading to an increased risk of cross-infection. In such circumstances any inadequacy in husbandry provides numerous opportunities for infection to pass from one animal to another.

In modern intensive animal husbandry the waste products and remains of animals are recycled as fertilisers and feeding stuffs. The importation of inadequately heat-treated or contaminated bone, meat and bone, and fish meals have resulted in salmonella contaminated feeding stuffs being given to food animals. In this way serotypes previously unknown in Britain have been introduced into the country. In 1931 only 5 salmonella serotypes were known to be involved in food poisoning outbreaks in England and Wales. In 1938 only 7 different salmonellae were recorded in the 72 reported outbreaks but by 1967 over 100 different serotypes were known to be involved in food poisoning in Britain. *S. agona* provides a good example of an organism introduced to this country through imported animal feed. Although 1978 saw its decline in importance, prior to that year it had climbed steadily up the league table of salmonellae responsible for human infection. The introduction of *S. agona* has been traced back to the use of infected Peruvian fish meal in livestock feeds.

With the presence of salmonellae in animal feed it is not difficult to see how easily food animals can be infected. Neither is such infection easy to spot as tests show that when given contaminated feed, animals usually develop a latent and not a clinical infection.

Of all the farm animals, cattle are most likely to suffer clinical illness following the consumption of contaminated feed. *S. dublin* is the serotype that is specifically adapted to cattle and is responsible for many cases of bovine salmonellosis, but other salmonellae do cause infections in cattle. The pig is the natural host of *S. cholerae suis*, although other serotypes are more common in pigs in Britain. Contaminated animal feed has resulted in many pigs becoming carriers of infection and the disposal of pig slurry on grazing land can result in a further spread of the disease.

In both cattle and pigs the infection may be passed on to healthy animals during transport to the market or slaughterhouse. Further cross-infection can occur in the abattoir lairage and during the slaughtering and dressing process.

In poultry, clinical disease due to salmonella is rare. In the past *S. gallinarum* (fowl typhoid) and *S. pullorum* (bacillary white diarrhoea) caused heavy losses in the poultry industry, although neither is a human pathogen. These conditions have now been controlled but poultry may be sub-clinically infected by many other serotypes and as these rarely cause loss of stock the incentive to eliminate them is reduced. Some serotypes have now become well established in the breeding flocks and are passed from generation to generation. The infection travels to the poultry packing station with the birds and during transport, slaughter and evisceration contamination of non-infected carcases may occur. A survey of four English processing plants revealed that 35% of carcases were contaminated by the end of the process.

The rate of salmonella infection in sheep is low and they are rarely associated with human salmonellosis.

A further complication concerning salmonellosis in food animals involves the use of antibiotics. In the past, antibiotics were extensively used for growth promotion in pigs and poultry and strains of bacteria resistant to those antibiotics appeared. During the short-term use of antibiotics in medical or veterinary treatment the growth of resistant bacteria in the digestive tract is favoured; however, when the treatment ceases the flora of the gut quickly returns to its normal composition. But when small quantities of antibiotics are administered over a long period, for prophylaxis or growth promotion, it has been found that resistant strains remain long after treatment has ceased. Furthermore resistant strains of the normally harmless intestinal organism *E. coli* have been shown to transmit this resistance to pathogens, including salmonellae. The growth of resistance among pathogens limits the choice of antibiotics available for the treatment of human disease. In 1969 the Joint Committee on the Use of Antibiotics in Animal Husbandry and Veterinary Medicine recommended the abandonment of medical antibiotics for growth promotion, although it approved the use of 'non-medical' antibiotics for this purpose. The problem of drug resistance of salmonellae, especially *S. typhimurium*, continues and is a very worrying factor in the salmonella story.

Salmonella is not only associated with food animals. Surveys have indicated that 1% of town dogs and 1·4% of cats, suffer from sub-clinical salmonella infection. Other pets in which infection has been recorded include tortoises and terrapins. Wild animals too can be sufferers and carriers of the disease. The life style of rats and mice mean that they are particularly liable to come into contact with salmonella. There are also reports of human infection originating from wild birds which had access to food preparation areas.

Poor personal hygiene can result in an infected food handler passing a salmonella infection to others. For this reason handwashing after visiting the lavatory is an essential requirement. Besides acute and convalescent cases there are those whose symptoms are mild and are therefore not associated with any illness. These ambulant cases are particularly dangerous, as are symptomless excretors or carriers who pass the organisms in well-formed stools. However, in the developed world the salmonella carrier rate is low and the principal reservoir of infection remains the food animals.

3.1.2 *Clostridium perfringens* (*welchii*)

Clostridium perfringens is the second most common cause of food poisoning in Britain. It is a gram-positive anaerobic bacillus, which is able to produce spores, some of which can survive very high temperatures. Illness results from an enterotoxin released in the intestine by living bacteria, that have been consumed. This is different to *Cl. botulinum* food poisoning, where the enterotoxin is pre-formed in the food (see 2.5). There are five known types of *Cl. perfringens* and they are classified by the toxin they produce. Types A and C are known to cause human illness although type C is rarely found in this country.

Symptoms

These usually consist of abdominal pain and diarrhoea. Vomiting is rare although nausea is not uncommon. It is a relatively mild condition and does not usually last more than 24 hours. The incubation period varies between 8 and 22 hours.

Growth temperatures

Maximum 50°C (122°F).
Minimum 10°C (50°F).
Optimum 45°C (113°F).

Ecology

Cl. perfringens is found in the bowel of animals, birds and man. In such a habitat it will spore readily and the spores are passed out and onto the soil or into the sewerage system. Spores will survive in soil or dust for a very long time and if vegetation or water sources are contaminated, infection of food animals is likely. Contaminated animal products may result in human infection, and soil adhering to vegetables is another potential source of *Cl. perfringens* in food preparation areas.

Very large numbers of this organism are required to cause human illness. The toxin is released in the intestines, as a result of sporulation. The spores themselves are harmless and cannot reproduce until suitable conditions of moisture and warmth exist, when they will germinate and form vegetative cells capable of multiplication. Some strains of *Cl. perfringens* are heat-resistant and the spores will survive boiling for up to four hours, whilst the spores of heat-sensitive strains will be rapidly destroyed by cooking.

This type of food poisoning is often associated with reheated meat and meat products. *Cl. perfringens* is an anaerobe so it will only multiply in the absence of air and thrives at the bottom of a stockpot or in the centre of a meat pie or rolled joint. As cooking proceeds oxygen is driven off, so producing ideal anaerobic conditions. The spores of heat-resistant strains will survive even quite high cooking temperatures and if the dish is allowed to cool, spore germination will occur at about 50°C (122°F). The growth and multiplication of vegetative cells then occurs and as the generation time of this organism is very short, perhaps 10–12 minutes at around 45°C (113°F), a dangerous level of contamination can be quickly built up (see 9.3.2—precautions to be taken when cooking, cooling and reheating meat dishes).

3.1.3 *Staphylococcus aureus*

In 1979 the organism *Staphylococcus aureus* was found to be responsible for 328 cases of food poisoning in England and Wales. It is a non-motile gram-positive coccus. Under the microscope the organisms have the appearance of clusters of grapes. There are several hundred types of *S. aureus* but only those that produce an enterotoxin cause food poisoning. Four types of enterotoxin are recognised, A, B, C and D, and all enterotoxin-producing strains are coagulase positive (*i.e.* they will coagulate oxalated blood plasma). However, not all coagulase-positive strains produce enterotoxin. *S. aureus* is a facultative anaerobe and is quite salt-tolerant. It can also withstand freezing and drying for long periods.

Symptoms
S. aureus food poisoning is an intoxication and not a true infection. The toxin is formed in the contaminated food and therefore the symptoms appear quite rapidly after consumption; usually between 1 and 6 hours. Severe vomiting and prostration usually occur and on occasions this is accompanied by diarrhoea. Recovery is often swift, the duration of the illness normally being about 24 hours, but some cases are quite severe, occasionally lasting a week or more.

Growth temperatures
  Maximum 47°C (116°F).
  Minimum 6·7°C (44°F).
  Optimum 35°C (95°F).

It is reported that toxin is produced at an appreciable rate between 15·6–46·1°C (60–115°F) with optimum toxin production between 21·1–36·1°C (70–97°F).

Ecology
S. aureus is a commensal of the body, its most common habitats being the nose, throat, boils and other skin lesions. It can also be found in the pores of the skin. Various surveys have shown that large numbers of people carry *S. aureus* in their noses (up to 80%) and on their hands (up to 44%). Although not all the organisms concerned would be from enterotoxin-producing strains, the potential for the contamination of food directly by food handlers is considerable. The widespread existence of *S. aureus* is one of the reasons why coughing and sneezing over food is a dangerous, as well as objectional habit. The prevalence of the organism in cuts and abrasions emphasises the need to keep all skin lesions covered with suitable waterproof dressings.

At least 10^6 organisms/gram (*i.e.* 1 million/gram) of foodstuff, are required to produce sufficient toxin to cause illness. Under normal conditions *S. aureus* grows slowly compared with food spoilage organisms. Therefore, food will usually become obviously unfit before a dangerous level of toxin has built up. However, as *S. aureus* is salt-tolerant it can develop more rapidly than most other competing organisms in cured meats and other foods with a high salt content. Food poisoning following the consumption of such food, particularly cold cooked meats, is therefore often due to this organism.

S. aureus is quite easily destroyed by heat, *e.g.* 60°C (140°F) for $\frac{1}{2}$ hour will kill the organism, but the toxin is very heat-stable and will survive periods of boiling. For this reason it is sometimes impossible to recover the organism from patients' stool specimens as cooking may have destroyed the staphylococci, whilst the toxin that caused the illness remains unaffected by the process.

S. aureus can also be responsible for mastitis in cows and the consumption of untreated milk from affected animals is a potential hazard.

3.1.4 *Bacillus cereus*

Bacillus cereus was not recognised as a cause of food poisoning in Britain until the early 1970s. Since this time it has been implicated in many outbreaks and associated with several foods, but most notably with fried or boiled rice. It is a gram-positive aerobic spore-forming bacillus that produces a toxin. Two distinct toxins are known to cause illness and a serological typing scheme exists for *B. cereus*.

Symptoms
Large numbers of organisms are required to cause illness, perhaps $> 10^6$/gram (*i.e.* over 1 million/gram) of food. The onset of illness is very sudden and in Britain the main symptom is vomiting with some abdominal pain. In Europe and the United States a different syndrome is more common and the main symptoms are abdominal pains and diarrhoea.

The incubation period in Britain varies between 1 and 6 hours and in Europe and the United States between 8 and 16 hours.

Growth temperatures
  Maximum 48°C (119°F).
  Minimum 10°C (50°F).
  Optimum 28–35°C (82–95°F).

Ecology
B. cereus is a common soil organism and is also found on vegetation, and many raw and processed foods. Surveys have indicated that *B. cereus* is found on 80–90% of rice. Outbreaks of *B. cereus* food poisoning associated with restaurants and takeaway premises have followed the storage of rice at warm ambient temperatures. The boiling of rice will not destroy all the spores present and if the rice is held in a warm kitchen, rather than in a refrigerator, the spores will germinate. This germination will be followed by the rapid multiplication of vegetative cells and the production of toxin. Counts of 2×10^9/gram of *B. cereus* have been

found in rice stored at incorrect temperatures. The rapid cooling of any unused boiled rice to below 20°C (68°F) is essential.

Other aerobic spore-forming bacilli have been implicated in food poisoning incidents, notably *B. subtilis*. *B. subtilis* has been suspected as a food poisoning agent in incidents in Britain, Australia and New Zealand during recent years. In Australia and New Zealand the symptoms are said always to include a burning or peppery taste in the mouth followed by nausea or vomiting. Diarrhoea is rare, and the incubation period is 1–4 hours. (See also 11.2.2.)

3.1.5 *Vibrio parahaemolyticus*

This organism is responsible for 60–70% of outbreaks of food poisoning in Japan. It was first reported in Britain in 1972 and a number of other incidents have occurred in this country since that date. It is a halophile (*i.e.* salt tolerant) and is usually associated with raw or lightly cooked seafood.

Symptoms
The illness is a true infection and the patient suffers fever, vomiting, profuse diarrhoea and abdominal pain. The symptoms usually persist for 2–5 days. The incubation period is 2–48 hours.

Ecology
V. parahaemolyticus is an organism found in coastal waters. Although it has been isolated in the seas around Britain and in locally caught sea creatures, it is much more common in the warmer waters that prevail around Japan. The organism is generally killed by thorough cooking.

3.1.6 *Clostridium botulinum*

The consumption of food containing toxin produced by the organism *Clostridium botulinum* gives rise to the very serious condition known as botulism. There have only been 8 recorded incidents in Britain, the most recent during the summer of 1978. On that occasion four people became ill after eating contaminated canned salmon and two of them died.

Cl. botulinum is a gram-positive spore-bearing anaerobic bacillus. There are six types, A–F, of which four are known to cause illness in man. Most outbreaks are associated with types A, B and E, but occasionally type F is involved. Botulism follows the consumption of minute quantities of toxin, which have been produced in the food as the organisms grow. The toxin is easily inactivated by heat, *e.g.* 80°C (176°F) for 30 minutes or a few minutes' boiling. However, the spores are very heat-resistant and high temperatures are utilised by the canning industry to ensure their destruction. The following combinations of temperature and time give some indication of the extent of heat treatment necessary to destroy *Cl. botulinum* spores in a food.

100°C for 360 minutes.
105°C for 120 minutes.
110°C for 36 minutes.
115°C for 12 minutes.
120°C for   4 minutes.

Most strains of *Cl. botulinum* are putrefactive and their growth, especially in meat products, will give rise to gas production and decomposition. This does provide some safeguard and no-one should be tempted to sample suspicious food. However, on occasions infected foods, particularly vegetables, show no change in appearance, odour or taste.

Symptoms
The toxin is absorbed in the small intestine and paralyses the involuntary muscles. The symptoms are therefore quite different to those that occur in other forms of food poisoning. Headache, dizziness and tiredness is followed by hoarseness of the voice and blurred vision. The fatality rate is high (65% in the United States), paralysis of the respiratory centres being the usual cause of death. If the patient recovers, convalescence is slow. Gastro-intestinal symptoms may occur early in the course of the illness but these are short-lived, with diarrhoea being followed by constipation. It seems likely that the diarrhoea may be due to other organisms present in the food. An antitoxin is available but must be administered early if it is to be effective. The incubation period is 12–36 hours.

Growth temperatures
Types A and B
  Maximum 48°C (118°F).
  Minimum 10°C (50°F).
  Optimum 35°C (95°F).
Type E
  Maximum 45°C (113°F).
  Minimum 3·3°C (38°F).
  Optimum 30°C (86°F).

Ecology
Most serotypes are saprophytic living in the soil and on rotting vegetable matter. The organism is found in both cultivated and virgin soil, although it only occurs in certain parts of the world. It may be present on the surface of vegetables but it will not grow in such a situation as it is a strict anaerobe. However, pickling, canning and smoking can reduce the free oxygen to a level at which growth and toxin production can occur. Because toxin production does not occur below 4·5 pH botulism is associated with low to medium acid foods. When foods with a pH of 4·5 or above are canned they must be subjected to a 'botulinum cook' sufficient to destroy any spores present. Despite the tragic cases in 1978

the commercial canning industry has a very good record but home canning, as quite widely practised in the United States, has been responsible for several outbreaks of botulism involving foods such as runner beans, corn and asparagus.

The curing of meat in brine also inhibits the growth of *Cl. botulinum*. The amount of salt required to prevent growth of the organism varies with the composition of the food and the temperature. Sodium nitrate may also be used in the curing of meat and inhibits the growth of the organism. A number of outbreaks have occurred in France following the consumption of inadequately cured bacon.

Cl. botulinum type E differs from other types in two important respects. Firstly, it is found in marine mud and the intestines of fish, and secondly, it will grow and produce toxin at very low temperatures, down to $3\cdot3°C$ ($38°F$).

Cl. botulinum type E has been found in the sea around Japan, Russia and in the Great Lakes in N. America. This type has been responsible for illness mainly following the consumption of fish or fish products (see 14.6).

3.1.7 *Escherichia coli*

E. coli is a normal inhabitant of the intestine, but some strains are enteropathogenic and cause diarrhoea in infants and occasionally in adults. The incubation period is believed to be between 12 hours and 3 days and the principal symptom is prolonged diarrhoea with blood and mucus in the stools. The optimum growth temperature for *E. coli* is $10°C$ ($50°F$).

Other coliforms are able to give rise to symptoms similar to those that occur in cases of salmonellosis.

3.1.8 Streptococci

Streptococci cause a variety of diseases which can vary clinically, depending on the portal of entry. These include scarlet fever, streptococcal sore throat and puerperal fever. But certain streptococci are also known to produce typical symptoms of food poisoning, *i.e.* vomiting, diarrhoea and abdominal pain. It seems likely that a toxin is formed in food if it is heavily contaminated with streptococci. The symptoms are usually mild and the incubation period is thought to be 1–4 days.

3.1.9 Other bacteria implicated in food poisoning

Heavy contamination of food with organisms not normally associated with food poisoning can give rise to symptoms of diarrhoea, abdominal pain and vomiting. The range of bacteria implicated in such incidents is wide and includes *Proteus*, *Pseudomonas*, *Yersinia enterocolitica* and *Aeromonas hydrophila*.

3.2 NON-BACTERIAL FOOD POISONING

Many other agents besides bacteria can give rise to food poisoning. Some of these agents are micro-organisms, others are chemicals, which have been accidentally incorporated in food.

3.2.1 Chemical food poisoning

Chemical food poisoning is, fortunately, unusual in Britain but when it does occur the consequences can be very serious. Any number of chemicals may contaminate food due to careless handling or through the mistaken identification of substances.

The ingestion of food contaminated by heavy metals will result in the rapid onset of symptoms. The period between consumption and illness can vary between 5 minutes and a few hours, with the patient often complaining of a metallic taste to the food. Examples of metallic poisoning include zinc poisoning following the storage of acid food in galvanised iron containers, and antimony poisoning from acid food held in poor-quality enamelware (see also 3.4.2, 10.2.2 and Chapter 15 page 189).

The correct and clear labelling of cleaning materials and other chemicals used in food premises is very important. Many incidents have resulted from the incorrect identification of chemicals. The pesticide sodium fluoride has been confused with baking powder, with disastrous results. The consumption of food contaminated with organo-chlorine insecticides results in violent convulsions, whilst sweating, nausea and vomiting follow poisoning with the organo-phosphorous group of insecticides.

Certain poisonous vegetables and fungi are sometimes accidentally used in food preparation. The mistaken collection of poisonous fungi for edible mushrooms can result in serious illness or even death. The Death Cap (*Amanita phalloides*) is highly toxic and the mortality rate amongst those who consume it is very high. Other poisonous mushrooms include the Fly Agaric (*Amanita muscaria*), the False Blusher (*Amanita pantherina*) and the Destroying Angel (*Amanita virosa*), all of which cause serious illness.

In 1959 a small outbreak of solanine poisoning occurred following the consumption of a batch of imported potatoes. The alkaloid, solanine, can develop in the potato skin and will cause illness. In this particular batch the solanine levels were very high.

Certain fish are known to be highly toxic on occasions. Ciguatera poisoning from the consumption of fish caught in inshore waters of the Caribbean and Pacific, is quite common in that part of the world. The larger barracuda is the fish most often implicated, although many other species are involved. Ciguatoxin can cause death due to respiratory failure with the symptoms of lip and tongue numbness developing up to 30 hours after ingestion. Ciguatoxin is not harmful to the fish and is not destroyed by cooking. Carnivorous fish acquire the toxin through the food chain, involving the consumption of smaller herbivorous fish which in turn feed on the dinoflagellates which produce the toxin. Another potentially deadly condition is tetradon, or puffer poisoning. This condition can follow the consumption of fish of the order *Tetraodontiformes* which includes puffers and porcupine fish. The ovaries, skin and intestines of such fish are highly toxic and on occasions the musculature can also contain the poison. A member of this order of fish, the fugu fish, is considered a delicacy in Japan. In Japanese restaurants trained personnel remove the parts most likely to be toxic but none the less deaths do occur. The fatality rate is very high where illness occurs and there have been reports of death within 17 minutes of consumption of the fish. In 1975 attempts were made to introduce this deadly delicacy to Britain but firm action by a London Environmental Health Officer resulted in the surrender of supplies for destruction. (See 11.2.4 Chinese Restaurant Syndrome.)

3.2.2 Viruses

It would appear that, on occasions, viruses able to cause intestinal illness can be food-borne. Viruses cannot multiply in food but only in living tissue and would normally be easily destroyed during cooking. However, in December 1976 an extensive outbreak of gastro-enteritis, presumed viral, occurred following the consumption of cockles from Leigh-on-Sea. Over 800 cases were reported and it seems likely that the source of the virus was various sewage outfalls in the Thames estuary. The cockles had been cooked by steaming, although subsequent investigations revealed that the methods used did not raise the cockles to a sufficiently high temperature. Following the outbreak the local Environmental Health Department insisted on more effective heat treatment of the cockles as well as other improvements in handling methods.

3.2.3 Shellfish poisoning

Apart from gastro-intestinal illness due to the consumption of shellfish contaminated with food poisoning bacteria or viruses, two other conditions are of interest. Firstly an erythematous or allergic reaction to shellfish protein, the symptoms of which are a rash and sometimes asthma.

More seriously, paralytic or neurotoxic illness can occur following the consumption of bivalves such as mussels. This is known as paralytic shellfish poisoning or P.S.P., and its cause is the concentration of large numbers of dinoflagellate protozoans in bivalve shellfish, due to their filter feeding mechanism. These protozoans are a component of plankton and contain a powerful neurotoxin. During the summer months, conditions exist which allow a rapid proliferation or bloom of the dinoflagellate population. The condition in humans is a serious one, as the toxin causes paralysis, and can be fatal. The 'incubation period' is between $\frac{1}{2}$ and 3 hours, and a characteristic symptom is a tingling of the tongue and mouth, almost as soon as they come into contact with the shellfish.

In 1968, 78 people in the north-east of England were affected by P.S.P. after consuming locally collected mussels. The outbreak was found to be due to the dinoflagellate *Gonyaulux tamarensis*. Annual monitoring of mussels since the outbreak has shown that their toxicity reaches a peak in June. Only 10 outbreaks of P.S.P. have been recorded in Britain since 1828 and all have been associated with mussels (see also 3.4.3).

3.2.4 Scombrotoxic fish poisoning

The first reported cases of scombrotoxic fish poisoning in Britain occurred at Ipswich in October 1976, although outbreaks have been known in the United States and Japan for many years. Since 1976 incidents have been reported from all over Britain, with 37 incidents occurring in 1979 involving over 160 people.

The name of this form of poisoning has been derived from the families of the fish that have usually been associated with the condition, *i.e.* the families *Scomberesocidae* and *Scombridae*, which include tuna, bonito and mackerel. Smoked mackerel is involved in 90% of incidents in Britain and this coincides with the increasing popularity of this fish. However, in 1979 and 1980 a number of incidents occurred involving non-scombroid fish, particularly sardines.

The exact cause of the condition is not known but illness is usually associated with high levels of histamine in the flesh of the fish. Histamine is not the toxin responsible for illness, but it is a good indicator of the likely toxic condition of the fish. The action of certain bacteria, normally occurring in the gut of the fish, converts the free amino acid, histadine, to histamine. Fresh fish contains less than 1 mg of histamine per 100 grams of flesh, whilst most fish examined following incidents of scombrotoxin poisoning have histamine levels in excess of 25 mg/100 grams of flesh. Such histamine levels indicate some degree of spoilage, as they will not arise in fresh fish. However, the spoilage may be insufficient to be detected by the consumer.

The toxin is not destroyed by heat even at canning temperatures. Freshly opened canned mackerel and sardines have been involved in sc ombrotoxic poisoning.

Symptoms occur between 10 minutes and 2 hours after the consumption of the fish and include a burning in the mouth, reddening of the skin, headache, dizziness, diarrhoea and sometimes vomiting.

The most important preventative measure is to ensure that fish are adequately refrigerated at all stages of distribution and sale. 4°C (39°F) should be regarded as the maximum temperature for the storage of fish (see 14.2).

3.2.5 Illness associated with the consumption of moulds

Little attention has been paid in the past to the dangers of eating food contaminated by moulds. However, it is now known that foods containing mycotoxins (the toxic products of moulds) can adversely affect the health of humans.

Certain strains of the moulds *Aspergillus flavus* and *Aspergillus parasiticus* produce aflatoxins, substances able to induce acute and chronic liver disease (*i.e.* mycotoxins). Aflatoxins have been detected in many foods including maize, ground nuts and tree nuts. They are also found in animal feed and if ingested by food animals can subsequently be detected in milk and meat products. The aflatoxin-producing fungi are ubiquitous and can infect crops during growing, harvesting or storage. Crops in tropical regions are more likely to be contaminated, as high humidity and a high temperature favour toxin production.

Aflatoxins were thought to be responsible for a serious outbreak of acute hepatitis in India in 1974, when 106 people died following the consumption of maize known to be infested by mould.

Ergotism is another potentially fatal condition that follows the consumption of grain, usually rye, infested by the mould *Clavicepts purpurea*.

Other mycotoxins, potentially harmful to human health, may sometimes be found in food and this is an area of food safety that will justifiably receive more attention in future years.

3.3 FOOD-BORNE DISEASES

Food poisoning is not a precise term. It is normally used to include accidental chemical poisoning as well as illness following the consumption of food in which pathogens have been allowed to grow and multiply. However, food can also transmit other diseases caused by micro-organisms that will grow very little or not at all in food. Such diseases are often easily carried by food because the number of organisms required to cause illness (the infective dose) is much lower than in true bacterial food poisoning.

Many of these diseases can be transmitted in other ways, particularly through unsatisfactory water supplies. Because of the existence of good water and sewerage systems in Britain, diseases such as typhoid and cholera are rare. Incidents that do occur often involve people returning from parts of the world where the sanitation and water supply is primitive.

3.3.1 Typhoid

The bacterium *Salmonella typhi* is responsible for typhoid and the sources of infection are the faeces and urine of patients or carriers. Typhoid is often water-borne but it can be transmitted by food and has been associated in particular with milk and shellfish. The incubation period is 1–3 weeks and the symptoms include a prolonged fever, prostration, rose-coloured spots on the body, with intestinal symptoms not being prominent until the second or third week of fever.

A particularly worrying feature of typhoid and to a lesser extent paratyphoid, is that some of those who contract the disease become chronic carriers; 2–3% of cases in typhoid. Carriers of *S. typhi* usually excrete the organism intermittently and may go for weeks without passing typhoid organisms, and so are difficult to trace. Chronic infection is often centred on the gall bladder, especially if gall stones are present and removal of the gall bladder can sometimes correct the situation. A urinary carrier is rarer but potentially more dangerous. Typhoid organisms do not usually lodge in the genito-urinary tract unless some abnormality exists. It is possible for a person to remain a carrier, following infection, for the rest of his life. The most notorious carrier was 'Typhoid Mary'. She contracted the disease in 1901 and, in her career as a cook, she worked in many kitchens and left a trail of typhoid victims across the United States. She was eventually traced and permanently detained.

3.3.2 Paratyphoid

The causal organism is *Salmonella paratyphi* of which there are three types, A, B and C.

The disease can take on two distinct forms. *S. paratyphi* can give rise to an enteric fever with symptoms similar to typhoid but with a much lower fatality risk. In other cases the symptoms can be quite mild, producing local inflammation of the gastro-intestinal tract. In such cases the symptoms are those normally associated with food poisoning.

The incubation period is 1–3 weeks for enteric fever and 1–10 days for gastro-enteritis.

3.3.3 Cholera

Cholera is usually water-borne although various foods have been implicated. It is characterised by the sudden onset of vomiting and diarrhoea which can rapidly lead to dehydration and collapse. The severity of the illness varies enormously, with mild cases showing only diarrhoea, but on occasions the fatality rate can reach 75%. The causal organism is *Vibrio cholerae* and the source of infection is the faeces of patients and convalescents. The incubation period is 1–5 days.

3.3.4 Bacillary dysentery

Bacillary dysentery is caused by bacteria of the genus *Shigella* (dysentery bacillus). Four sub-groups exist: *Sh. dysenteriae*, *Sh. flexneri*, *Sh. boydii* and *Sh. sonnei*. Man is the only host of these organisms but they can survive for some time outside the body. The main symptoms of the disease are diarrhoea and fever although vomiting can occur. Bacillary dysentery is usually transmitted through close personal contact and can spread very quickly in communities such as schools and institutions, especially where personal hygiene is suspect. It can, however, be food-borne. The incubation period is 1–7 days.

3.3.5 Brucellosis

The organism *Brucella abortus* is responsible for abortion in cattle and in man a condition sometimes known as Undulant Fever. The principal symptoms in human brucellosis are intermittent fever, headache and weakness. The disease may last for a long period, in some cases for several years.

Those working in close contact with animals or meat are particularly at risk, *e.g.* farmers, veterinarians and meat inspectors. However, some cases occur following the consumption of untreated milk from infected cows. Pasteurisation destroys the organism and The Milk (Special Designation) Regulations, 1977, were introduced to ensure that all milk not intended for heat treatment should be from herds accredited as brucella-free. There is evidence to show that the Brucella Accreditation Scheme, which involves the regular veterinary testing of cattle for brucella and the disposal of reactors, is bringing about a considerable reduction in human brucellosis.

3.3.6 Infective hepatitis (hepatitis A)

A virus infection that is normally transmitted through close personal contact by the faecal–oral route. Epidemics have been related to contaminated milk and other foods, especially bivalve shellfish. In 1978 an outbreak involving 41 cases occurred in Britain and was associated with the consumption of mussels. The symptoms include fever, nausea and stomach discomfort, followed by jaundice. One of the difficulties in tracing the vehicle of infection in cases of infective hepatitis is the long incubation period of from 15 to 50 days.

3.3.7 Campylobacter enteritis

Campylobacter is a generic name for a group of small vibrio-like bacteria. One type has for many years been known to cause abortion in cattle and ewes, but it was only in the late 1970s that *Campylobacter jejuni/coli* was recognised as the cause of human illness. Indeed it has been found that campylobacter can be isolated from about 7% of people suffering from diarrhoea, making it the commonest bacterium associated with diarrhoea in Britain.

In man the first sign of infection is often the onset of flu-like symptoms. This is followed by abdominal cramps and foul-smelling and frequently blood-stained stools. In some cases these symptoms are so severe that they result in admission to hospital. The abdominal pain often persists after the diarrhoea has ceased and symptoms can last up to three weeks. The incubation period is probably between 2 and 10 days.

Campylobacter jejuni/coli has been isolated from many farm and domestic animals and it seems clear that the organism is widely spread in the animal kingdom. Most human infection probably results from direct contact with farm animals or pets, or even through handling raw meat or poultry. However, there is evidence which indicates that campylobacter enteritis can be food-borne. Untreated milk has been the medium for transmission in several outbreaks and in one large incident over 2,000 people were infected after the consumption of pasteurised milk, following a failure in the heat-treatment process.

3.4 VEHICLES OF INFECTION

Certain foods are frequently associated with food poisoning whilst others rarely so. Food poisoning bacteria require a suitable medium in which to grow and produce sufficient numbers or toxin to cause illness. As bacteria need a relatively high Aw (see 2.3.4) and many food poisoning organisms are proteolytic, food poisoning incidents are usually associated with animal protein foods, *i.e.* meat, poultry, fish, eggs and dairy products. However, on occasions other foods prove to be the vehicles of infection. For example, fried rice is the commonest food implicated in outbreaks of *Bacillus cereus* food poisoning.

Table 4 gives details of food implicated in outbreaks between 1973 and 1976.

3.4.1 Meat and poultry

Meat and poultry in particular are commonly implicated in food poisoning incidents. About 75% of incidents in Britain, where the cause is

TABLE 4

Foods implicated in 484 general and family outbreaks of bacterial food poisoning and Salmonella *infection in England and Wales (1973-1976)*

Food		Number of outbreaks	Percentage of outbreaks
Meat—beef, pork, ham *etc.*		207	43
Poultry—chicken, turkey		149	31
Rice	60		
Milk and cream	37		
Sweets, cakes and trifles	14	128	26
Seafood	13		
Vegetables	2		
Eggs	1		
Pancake rolls	1		
Total		484	100

From Outbreaks and Surveillance Studies by R. J. Gilbert and Diane Roberts (1979) *Health and Hygiene*, Vol. 3, No. 1.

traced, relate to the consumption of meat or poultry. Not only are such foods good media in which bacteria may grow but the living food animals themselves are a principal source of salmonella infection and, therefore, food produced from them can easily become contaminated.

3.4.2 Fish and fish products

As fish are cold-blooded animals the organisms that cause fish diseases rarely affect human beings. Furthermore, most fish are caught well out to sea and therefore away from serious pollution. For these reasons fish is not a common cause of food poisoning but that is not to say that dangers do not exist. Some fish are caught in rivers and coastal areas where the water can be contaminated by human sewage and industrial waste. The Minamata incident in Japan illustrated, in a tragic way, the dangers of discharging toxic industrial waste into water used as a fishing ground. Between 1953 and 1960 methyl mercury poisoning affected the population around Minamata Bay, causing paralysis, convulsions and death. A long time passed before the cause was realised to be the combination of organic and mercurial effluents, causing a build-up of methyl mercury in locally caught marine animals.

Cl. botulinum type E has been found to be a natural contaminant of some fish and given inadequate processing or storage, sufficient toxin could develop to cause botulism in a consumer. Fish can also cause illness because of the presence of ciguatoxin, tetrodotoxin or through the increasingly commonly recognised scombrotoxic poisoning (see 3.1.6, 3.2.1 and 3.2.4).

The handling of fish exposes the product to the dangers of cross-contamination from the food handler and working environment. Indeed, most incidents involving fish stem from contamination that has occurred during filleting or the making up of fish dishes.

3.4.3 Shellfish

Shellfish have been the vehicle for a number of differing infections and conditions (see 3.2.2, 3.2.3 and 3.3.6). Problems occur when shellfish layings are contaminated by the discharge of sewage or when a bloom of toxic dinoflagellates occurs during the summer months. The greatest danger arises from the consumption of bivalve molluscs such as oysters, mussels and scallops. Unlike gastropod molluscs (the periwinkle and whelk) bivalves are filter feeders and during feeding filter out of the water bacteria as well as food material. This means that bacteria present in the water can become concentrated in the shellfish. Under favourable conditions the European flat oyster (*Ostrea edulis*) may concentrate up to six times the levels of faecal bacteria present in the surrounding water.

Vibrio parahaemolyticus has been demonstrated to be widely distributed in coastal waters around Britain and in locally gathered shellfish. However, the numbers of this organism found are usually low and most incidents of *V. parahaemolyticus* food poisoning have followed the consumption of imported shellfish; prawns from the Far East being a particular problem.

3.4.4 Milk and dairy products

Although milk contains sufficient nutrients to make it an ideal medium for bacterial growth it is only infrequently implicated in food poisoning in Britain. The main reason for this good safety record is that over 95% of liquid milk is pasteurised. This heat treatment destroys not only food poisoning bacteria but the organisms that cause tuberculosis and brucellosis as well. Cases of food poisoning traced back to milk relate almost entirely to untreated milk (see 3.3.7).

Raw milk from cows suffering from mastitis can give rise to a particular danger, as the condition is sometimes due to a staphylococcal infection. Staphylococcal food poisoning following the consumption of untreated mastitic milk is therefore a possibility.

Cream is another product rarely associated with illness in Britain, although it is a common cause of staphylococcal infection in the United States. There is no legal requirement for the heat treatment of cream in this country, although all major manufacturers do pasteurise their product.

The manufacture of cheese usually involves considerable handling and the ultimate low pH of the product is relied upon to prevent the growth of harmful organisms. However, there is evidence to suggest that the necessary low pH is not always attained, perhaps because failure of the lactic acid starter organisms sometimes occurs due to the presence of antibiotics in the milk. The risk of pathogen survival is greater in soft than in hard cheese but in all cases the use of heat-treated milk to produce the cheese does much to reduce the potential dangers.

3.4.5 Eggs and egg products

Like milk, eggs can provide a good medium on which bacteria can grow. Any salmonellae present in faecal material may contaminate eggs through cracks in the shell or as the eggs are broken out. Bulked liquid egg has in the past proved a particular hazard and the Liquid Egg (Pasteurisation) Regulations, 1963, were introduced to eliminate this source of salmonellae. Dried egg products receive varying forms of heat treatment during processing. The heat treatments applied are not always sufficient to kill salmonella and the risk of cross-contamination is present when such products are used in the kitchen or bakery.

Duck eggs pose an additional danger as ducks are much more likely than hens to suffer from salmonella infection of the oviduct. In such circumstances eggs may be laid containing the pathogenic bacteria. For this reason duck eggs require a minimum boiling time of ten minutes.

3.4.6 Bakery products

Although bread, cake and pastry have an Aw too low to allow bacterial growth, some of the fillings and decorative materials used in bakery goods can support the development of pathogens. The fresh and imitation creams used are the most likely vehicles of infection, but custards can give rise to similar problems if good hygiene practice is not observed. Samples of custard-filled vanilla slices have been found to contain the organism *Bacillus cereus*.

Desiccated coconut is used as a decoration for cakes and confectionery and in the early 1960s was responsible for several outbreaks of paratyphoid. Improved hygiene in the country of origin rectified the situation, and the product has given little cause for concern since.

3.4.7 Ice cream

Prior to the introduction of The Ice-Cream (Heat Treatment *etc.*) Regulations, 1959, which made the pasteurisation of ice cream mandatory, the product was associated with food-borne disease. The most famous example being an incident in Aberystwyth in 1947 when ice cream infected by a typhoid excretor resulted in 210 cases and 4 deaths. The ice cream industry now has an excellent record with the last recorded case attributable to ice cream occurring in 1954.

3.4.8 Vegetables

Vegetables are not often associated with food poisoning incidents, and between 1965 and 1976 only 7 outbreaks of food poisoning were traced to vegetables. However, the potential for infection or for cross-contamination to other foods exists. A survey carried out in the Netherlands in 1976 revealed that 103 samples (11%) of vegetables contained $> 10^4$ *E. coli* per 100 grams. These 103 samples were examined for the presence of salmonellae and 23 proved positive. Faecal streptococci were also found in 14% of the samples taken. Vegetables can be contaminated by soil-borne organisms, such as Clostridia, whilst the use of polluted water for irrigation is another danger. Most vegetables are cooked and this is an important safeguard, but all vegetables to be eaten raw require thorough washing, ideally in a hypochlorite solution of 40–50 p.p.m.

Watercress has, on at least one occasion, been viewed as a possible vehicle for typhoid. Certainly the purity of the water supply in watercress beds is important. Watercress has been responsible for cases of liver fluke infestation in humans (fascioliasis). Cattle and sheep are the normal primary hosts of the liver fluke, *Fasciola hepatica*, and the life cycle of the fluke involves the freshwater snail *Limnea truncatula*. If infested snails have access to watercress beds, liver fluke cercariae can become encapsulated on the watercress and pass on the infestation to a consumer. To prevent the access of snails, watercress beds require careful construction and cattle and sheep should be excluded from adjoining grazing land.

In recent years a number of incidents of vomiting and diarrhoea have occurred following the consumption of uncooked red kidney beans (*Phaseolus vulgaris*). In most of these cases the beans were soaked for 24

Bacterial food poisoning and campylobacter enteritis

	Usual incubation period	Duration	Vomiting	Diarrhoea	Abdominal pain	Other symptoms
Salmonella	12–48 hrs or longer	1–8 days	Variable	++/++++	+	Fever almost always present
Cl. perfringens	8–22 hrs	12–24 hrs	±	++	++	No fever
Staph. aureus	1–6 hrs	6–24 hrs	+++	++	+	Prostration, but no fever
B. cereus (a) in Britain	1–6 hrs	12–24 hrs	+++	+	+	
(b) in Europe and U.S.A.	8–16 hrs	6–24 hrs	−	++	+	
V. parahaemolyticus	2–48 hrs	2–5 days	++	++	++	Fever, diarrhoea profuse
Cl. botulinum	12–36 hrs	death 1–8 days or slow recovery		±		Headache, dizziness, tiredness, hoarseness, blurred vision and respiratory failure
Enteropathogenic E. coli	12–72 hrs	1–7 days	±	++		Blood and mucus in stools
Campylobacter enteritis	2–10 days	up to 3 weeks		+++	+++	Stools foul-smelling and often blood-stained

hours at warm ambient temperatures before being served raw in a salad, but on other occasions they were subject to light cooking. Although moderate growths of *Bacillus* spp. were found following some of the incidents, in others there were no traces of known bacterial pathogens. It is thought that illness was probably the result of a toxic protein in the beans, and that such toxin is normally destroyed by thorough cooking. Certainly red kidney beans should be properly cooked before they are eaten, and this information could usefully be carried on packets of such beans.

3.5 IF FOOD POISONING OCCURS

If suspected cases of food poisoning occur among customers or staff it is essential that the circumstances are reported and investigated quickly and efficiently. A prompt investigation may prevent further cases of illness and will mean that the cause of the outbreak is more likely to be revealed. For these reasons the local Environmental Health Department should be telephoned at once, using the emergency number if the problem occurs outside office hours.

Any suspected food should, of course, be withdrawn from sale and if possible, a list made of people to whom such food had been supplied. Suspected food must not be destroyed but retained for the investigating Environmental Health Officer, along with cans or other packaging. The search for the remains of suspect food may involve retrieving scraps and containers from the dustbin. In catering premises it is very good practice to retain daily a small portion of each food served, so that it can be examined in the event of an outbreak. Each sample should include a quantity of any sauces, creams and gravies used and should be kept in a refrigerator for 72 hours before disposal.

The collection of certain information prior to the arrival of the Environmental Health Officer will greatly assist the investigation. The names and addresses of all staff, including those away from work, and the reason for their absence will be required; as will details of the methods of preparation, storage and/or cooking of foods and, in the case of catering premises, menus for the appropriate days.

When the investigation commences all staff will be interviewed and asked about their state of health. It is likely that faecal and perhaps urine specimens will be required from all food handlers, as well as from those who have become ill. There is sometimes a reluctance to provide such specimens but the serious nature of the situation must be explained to all and it made clear that the investigation is to prevent further cases and not to cast blame on an individual food handler.

Chapter 4

FOOD PREMISES: LAYOUT, CONSTRUCTION, SERVICES AND EQUIPMENT

The physical environment can make an important contribution to the level of hygiene achieved in food premises. In this chapter layout, construction, services and equipment are considered as they affect the hygiene of all catering and retail premises. Such aspects relating to specific types of food business are dealt with in Part 2.

4.1 LAYOUT OF FOOD PREMISES

Sufficient space to carry on the business efficiently and hygienically is a prime requirement for all food premises. One of the underlying causes of poor hygiene in many food premises is the inadequacy of space, whether for food preparation or storage. Too often incompatible food handling operations are carried on side by side, because there is insufficient space to arrange the work so that cross-contamination is less likely. Inadequate storage space manifests itself in food and equipment being held in passageways and on staircases, thus causing accident hazards and making cleaning more difficult. All food premises should be planned to allow sufficient space for current usage with, ideally, some room for future expansion.

The use that is made of the available space is also important. Where food preparation is carried out the premises should be designed to allow a smooth flow from the raw to the finished product. Care should be taken to physically separate the handling of cooked and uncooked foods. In the case of retail premises stock should progress smoothly from goods reception through the storage area, to retail display.

Sanitary accommodation should be conveniently situated but separated from the rest of the premises by an intervening ventilated space. All doors leading from this space should be self-closing.

4.2 CONSTRUCTION

4.2.1 Floors

The choice of the correct flooring for a food premises is vital. A considerable proportion of the cleaning time spent in catering and retail establishments is spent cleaning the floor. It is therefore essential that spillages and other accumulations can be removed from the floor without difficulty. Furthermore the floor can be subjected to impact, heavy loads and the erosive effect of moisture and chemicals. Unsuitable floors will quickly start to wear or even break up, causing additional cleaning and maintenance problems. One further consideration that can make the choice of flooring material difficult, is the frequent need to combine ease of cleaning with good non-slip properties. It is also recognised that cost may be an important constraint, although penny-pinching in this area may soon be regretted.

It is impossible to recommend one particular flooring for all catering and retail applications, as the problems and requirements of individual situations need to be considered. But as a general guide, for heavy duty food preparation areas, one would consider ceramic or quarry tiles, polymer flooring and vinyl/aluminium oxide sheet. Whilst in light duty dry areas the choice may also include terrazzo, vinyl and thermoplastic tiles.

In areas where spillages frequently occur and large volumes of water are required for cleaning, floors should be properly drained. The use of channels for this purpose is not recommended as the cast-iron gratings with which they are covered are very difficult to clean. Instead the floor should be sloped to properly trapped drainage gullies situated at strategic points. A fall of one inch in 10 feet towards a drainage point is usually sufficient.

The principal flooring materials both traditional and modern are considered below. (See also 13.1.2—butchery floors.)

Concrete
Concrete is cheap and can be hardwearing in dry areas. It is chemically attacked by acids, alkalis, fats and oils and tends to dust. Concrete floors are also cold and can be slippery when wet. The old treatment to eliminate dusting is to treat the surface with sodium silicate, but the effect does not last long and modern proprietary seals are likely to be more successful. In particular, two-part polyurethane seals are very tough and protect the concrete from a wide range of chemical attack.

Granolithic concrete is concrete incorporating granite chippings or crushed granite. It is harder wearing than ordinary concrete and more resistant to chemicals, although it is still subject to attack by acids, fats and oils.

Bituminous cement

Cement and aggregate are mixed with a bituminous emulsion to give a warm, flexible and water-resistant flooring. The disadvantages of this type of flooring are that depressions will form if it is loaded heavily, and like concrete it is attacked by acids, fats and oils.

Mastic asphalt and pitchmastic

Mastic asphalt is bitumen asphalt to which has been added suitable mineral fillers, *e.g.* crushed granite. It is laid hot and gives a smooth, waterproof surface. It does not suffer from dusting and resists acids and alkalis, although it will be softened by heat as well as by fats and oils. It is not suitable for heavy loads.

Pitchmastic is a similar material made from coal-tar pitch with added fillers of sand, granite dust *etc.* It has similar properties to mastic asphalt although its resistance to fats and oils is better.

Ceramic tiles

Ceramic tiles are hardwearing and resistant to chemical attack. If a non-slip surface is required, tiles incorporating carborundum should be chosen, rather than grooved tiles which are difficult to clean. When using tiles it is essential that the bedding and jointing materials used are as impervious and resistant as the tiles themselves. Rubber latex cements, waterproof polyester or epoxy cement may be used for this purpose.

Quarry tiles

Quarries have a good resistance to water, oils and acids but may be affected by alkalis. They are reasonably non-slip and have been used successfully in kitchens and other heavy duty areas for many years. The considerations concerning jointing and bedding applies as for ceramic tiles.

Polymer flooring

Most polymer flooring is based on derivatives of epoxy, polyester and polyurethane resins. They possess the advantages of resisting wear, chemical attack and impact. As they are laid in large areas the flooring can be jointless, and coving and drainage channels be incorporated at the time of laying. Furthermore, the use of appropriate fillers will produce a non-slip surface.

However, such flooring is very expensive and its suitability in the particular premises in question must be determined. It is always advisable to examine any proprietary flooring under working conditions before deciding on its suitability. The key to the success of polymer flooring is thoroughness in sub-floor preparation, and the care and skill with which the components are mixed and laid. Such work should only be undertaken by specialist flooring contractors.

Many polymer applications involve the use of strong solvents and it is necessary during floor reconstruction to protect food from the risk of tainting.

Epoxy resin flooring may be in the form of a trowel-applied mortar to a depth of 6 mm. Such trowelled resin can incorporate various aggregates, for example granite or quartz. Self-levelling epoxy resin is applied as a 3 mm layer and incorporates finer fillers giving a smoother finish.

Polyester floorings share most of the properties of epoxy resins although they are not quite so resistant to chemical attack. They are usually laid to a depth of 6 mm and glass fibre is often incorporated in the mix to reduce the tendency of the resin to shrink on hardening.

Polyurethane resins are very hard and very resilient. They are often laid as a series of thin layers with the total thickness rarely exceeding 2 mm.

Thermoplastic tiles

Thermoplastic tiles are made from asbestos or other mineral fillers bound with asphalt or resins. Given the correct adhesive, they can be applied to many different types of sub-floor. They are not suitable in areas where they are subject to heavy traffic or where they are exposed to oil and grease or frequent washing with water.

Vinyl tiles and sheet

These are similar to thermoplastic tiles but the binder used is polyvinyl chloride (P.V.C.). Vinyl tiles are harder wearing and more resistant than plain thermoplastic tiles. Tiles having a minimum thickness of 3·2 mm should be specified. Heavy duty vinyl sheet may also be used and this can be welded to give large areas of jointless flooring. Like all vinyl flooring it can be slippery when wet and to overcome this problem vinyl sheet incorporating aluminium oxide filler is available and is very good in medium to heavy duty areas.

Terrazzo

This attractive flooring consists of coloured marble chippings set in white Portland cement. Terrazzo can be attacked by acids, alkalis and fats although fillers can be added to increase its resistance.

Rubber

Although rubber flooring is quiet and warm to stand on, it becomes very slippery in areas where spillage of water, oils or fat occur.

Wood

A wooden floor surface, whether hardwood or softwood, is unsuitable in food premises as it is pervious to moisture, grease and bacteria (see Fig. 4). Dirt will also be found to accumulate in the joints between the blocks or boards. In existing premises a hardwood floor may be acceptable in storage areas where no open food is kept and in such cases the floor should be treated with a two-part polyurethane seal.

4.2.2 Walls

The general requirement for all walls in food premises is that they should be smooth, impervious and easy to clean. As with flooring the final choice of finish should depend on the particular situation of the wall. In areas where heavy contamination of wall surfaces is likely then surfaces that can be frequently and easily washed should be chosen, *e.g.* glazed tiles or impervious wall cladding. Ideally, such surfaces should extend from floor to ceiling although treatments to 1·8 m (6 ft) will be satisfactory in many situations. Where general contamination of the walls is unlikely, splashbacks of tiles or wall sheeting should be provided behind sinks, working surfaces and other possible areas of local contamination.

Walls should be light coloured to show up dirt and coved at their junctions with both floor and ceiling. Where trolleys are in use, plastic crash rails can be fitted to protect the wall finish and external angles be fitted with metal edging strips.

Hollow partition walls should be avoided as they may provide harbourage for pests.

Glazed wall tiles
These provide an excellent hygienic wall surface as long as porous grouting material is not used. The wall surface to which the tiles are to be fixed must be dry and even. If the tiles are not carried to the full height of the room the top course should be finished with a rounded edge tile to prevent the lodgement of dirt.

The main disadvantages of glazed wall tiles are their tendency to crack if too near a heat source and their susceptibility to impact damage.

Glazed masonry blocks
Glazed masonry blocks may be used in the construction of a food premises and will provide a surface similar to glazed ceramic tiles. The glazed surface is thermoset into the block and damage to that surface is not easily remedied.

Metal sheeting
Stainless steel sheeting is very durable and can provide a hygienic wall finish. Stainless steel is, however, very expensive and care must be taken with bedding and jointing to avoid any build-up of food debris behind the sheets. Food quality aluminium is also suitable for wall lining.

Proprietary wall cladding
Many different proprietary wall cladding materials are available. They will usually provide a satisfactory surface although, as with other materials, jointing is very important. Such cladding should be applied

directly to the wall surface with a suitable adhesive. The fixing of wall sheeting on battens is not recommended as the cavity provides a potential harbourage for pests. If rigid P.V.C. sheeting is used the joints may be sealed with a silicone sealant or stainless steel cover straps. Examples of P.V.C. sheeting include Cobex, Darvic and Duraform.

Polypropylene sheeting has the advantage that its joints can be welded to give a joint-free finish. It also possesses good impact and chemical resistance. Propylex is the trade name of polypropylene sheeting produced by British Celanese Ltd.

Sheets constructed of glass reinforcement impregnated with polyester resin are also available, *e.g.* Stericlad.

Polymers
Polymers can be applied direct to existing wall surfaces, either with suitable aggregates or incorporating glass fibre reinforcement.

Polyester or epoxy resin may be used and the finish can be applied over existing bricks, tiles *etc*. Polymers give a good impervious surface that is resistant to both impact and chemical attack. Unfortunately such wall treatment is expensive.

Paints
Good quality washable paints are suitable for use in many food premises where the walls are not subjected to heavy wear or frequent contamination. In heavy duty areas paints have a very short life and flaking paintwork can pose a contamination hazard.

Polymer resin-based paints do provide a fairly tough resistant surface, provided the manufacturer's instructions are adhered to. If polymer paints are to be used the paint manufacturer should be consulted, as some are unsuitable for application in food premises as they may impart flavours and odours to certain foods. Two-part epoxy and polyurethane paints are not suitable for use on plaster.

When using any paint, surface preparation is all important. Except in the case of chlorinated rubber paint, the surface must be free of dampness before painting is commenced. Chlorinated rubber paints will stand immersion in water and frequent hosing down. Besides being suitable for wall surfaces they can be used to good effect on the external surfaces of machinery used in wet areas.

Where mould growth is a problem an antifungal wash should be used during preparation (*e.g.* bleach). Mould-inhibiting paints are available, both emulsion type and oil-based products. The antifungal agents used in such paints must be able to extend their action into the layer of dust that may develop on the wall surface, otherwise this will become a source of nutrient for developing fungi. Only non-mercurial and non-toxic mould-inhibiting paints should be used in food premises.

Most paints contain strong-smelling solvents and sensible precautions must be taken when using paints in existing food premises. Useful advice on precautions to be taken as well as information on different paint types is to be found in *Code of Practice 'Food Quality' Paints*, produced jointly by I.C.I. and Marks and Spencer, and available from the Dulux Trade Group, I.C.I. Paints Division, Wrexham Road, Slough, SL2 5DS.

4.2.3 Ceilings

Ceiling height is very important. If the ceiling is too low, problems will be experienced with ventilation; if it is too high, the ceiling will be very difficult to clean. In fact cleaning the ceiling is never the easiest of tasks, and so its surface should be smooth, to make the removal of adhering dirt more manageable. An absorbent plaster is normally the best surface and this can be emulsion-painted when discolouration occurs. Gloss paint should not be used on ceilings as it encourages condensation.

Suspended ceilings should be avoided in food premises as they provide a potential harbourage for pests. Neither are roof lights recommended as they can make temperature control very difficult during the summer months.

4.2.4 Doors and windows

These should be of simple design to minimise the lodgement of dust. Doors should be fitted with finger-plates to allow easy cleaning and kicking-plates to prevent damage to the base of the door.

Window-sills can be steeply sloped to prevent them being used as shelves.

4.2.5 Lifts

Where goods lifts are used it is important that their internal surfaces are easily cleaned. Easy access to the base of the lift shaft is important as dirt and food debris can accumulate in this area, which may become a focus for insect and rodent infestation.

4.3 SERVICES

4.3.1 Lighting and electrical supply

Adequate artificial lighting is essential in any food business. Good light-ing not only aids efficiency, it enables cleaning to be carried out thoroughly. The lighting layout should be carefully considered at the planning stage of any new food premises, and light fittings placed in positions related to equipment, working surfaces *etc.*

Fluorescent lighting gives a more evenly distributed light, producing fewer shadows than tungsten lighting as well as being cheaper to run.

Recommended levels of illumination in specific situations are given in the *Code for Interior Lighting* published by the Chartered Institution of Building Services, which should be consulted (some details are given in Part 2). The level of illumination is important but so is the avoidance of glare. Glare may be caused by excessive contrast or if the light source is directly visible. All light fittings should therefore be provided with shatterproof diffusers.

Electrical wiring should be in conduits, preferably chased into the wall. Where frequent wet cleaning is necessary the conduit should be water-resistant or the wiring be in Pyro. All switches should be flush fitting and easy to clean. Ideally, proximity switches, that can be operated without touching, should be fitted.

It is a very useful arrangement to incorporate a mains switch to isolate all electrical equipment except refrigerated and frozen food storage plant. This allows for repairs to be carried out without the need to switch off refrigeration equipment.

4.3.2 Ventilation

Adequate ventilation makes the working environment more comfortable and reduces the amount of cleaning necessary by preventing any build-up of steam, volatiles and heat. Natural ventilation is widely used and is appropriate in many situations. Louvred windows are a particularly controllable means of natural ventilation. In large retail stores or where quantities of heat, steam and fume are produced during cooking, natural ventilation will be inadequate. In such cases some form of mechanical ventilation is necessary. The simplest system is the use of an extract fan to draw air out of the premises, with replacement air finding its way into the building via gaps around doors and windows. In such an extract system there is no control over the inlet air and draughts are set up, due to the negative pressure induced by the fan. An alternative is the plenum system, whereby fresh air is forced in through high-level inlets, by the use of fans, and stale air leaves via low-level outlets. In this way the source of air supply can be chosen and if necessary filtered and heated. Furthermore the building is under a slight positive pressure so draughts are minimised.

In a balanced system, inlet and outlet fans are used and such a system is often operated in conjunction with air-conditioning.

In restaurant kitchens and takeaway premises, where vapours containing fats and oils need to be dealt with, some form of grease filter is necessary in the extraction system. A number of different grease filters are available. One very efficient unit comprises a corrugated eliminator, where controlled air turbulence cools the air below the dew point of the vaporising oil. The oil condenses on the surface of the eliminator and runs to a collecting tray, which can be periodically emptied. The filter cells are easily removable for cleaning. An alternative grease filter system is available that utilises disposable fibreglass elements.

Such grease arresting systems are necessary to reduce the possibility of cooking odours causing a nuisance to nearby residents. Grease filters also prevent the build-up of oil and fats in the ventilation trunking and so minimise a difficult cleaning problem and reduce a serious fire risk. In any event extract ducting must have accessible cleaning apertures of not less than 15×15 cm (6×6 inch) at 2 m (6 ft) intervals.

Where problems of nuisance from cooking smells are likely, consideration should be given to the installation of an activated carbon filter unit for odour removal. Such units must be protected from contamination by grease and dust through the provision of efficient grease and particulate filters, otherwise the carbon cells will quickly become clogged. The activated carbon unit must not be situated directly over a cooking point, as the temperature and relative humidity are likely to be too high for efficient operation of the unit. A minimum distance of 6 m (20 ft) from a cooking source is recommended and this will also allow any remaining fatty vapours to condense on the ducting before they reach the carbon unit. Cells of activated carbon will need replacement from time to time, depending on the levels of odour concentration with which they are expected to deal.

An alternative to an activated carbon unit is the incorporation of a small ozone generator in the extraction system. Ozone is a form of oxygen containing three oxygen atoms in each molecule compared with the normal two. This additional atom readily becomes detached from the molecule and acts as a powerful oxidising agent which is very effective in dealing with oxidisable odours. As with activated carbon filters an extraction system incorporating an ozonator must be carefully designed and include efficient grease removal equipment. The initial cost of an ozone generator is rather higher than that of an activated carbon unit but the expensive regeneration of the carbon plates is eliminated.

Air reconditioners are now increasingly in use. These draw polluted air in at their base and remove dust and other pollutants before discharging the purified air. They work on the principle of electrostatic filtration and some also incorporate a carbon filter. Their use can be very beneficial but does not dispense with the need for adequate through ventilation.

4.3.3 Drainage

The satisfactory drainage of any premises is a fundamental requirement, and in food premises it is particularly important that the drainage system is well designed, well constructed and sufficient for its needs. All new drainage works must be undertaken under the supervision of the local authority and it is particularly important to have sufficient access points to allow rodding to be carried out in the event of a blockage.

In premises where large quantities of greasy water are disposed of via the drainage system it may be necessary to install a grease interceptor to prevent a build-up of congealed fat, which might eventually obstruct the drain. In such a grease trap the fat is solidified by the cooling action of a comparatively large quantity of water contained in the unit. A perforated tray is provided at the base of the interceptor and this can be lifted to remove the congealed fat. An airtight double sealed cover must be provided to the fitting.

The cleaning of grease traps is an unpleasant job and consequently one that is frequently neglected. A grease interceptor is available that is designed to be charged with an enzyme powder which breaks down any grease in the waste water, so avoiding the need to manually remove it.

Grease traps should only be provided where a definite need for them arises.

4.3.4 Refuse storage and disposal

The type of refuse storage adopted is largely determined by the collection system operated by the local authority. If dustbins are used a sufficient number, conforming to the relevant British Standard (B.S. 792: 1947 and B.S. 1577: 1949) are required, and close-fitting lids are essential. The dustbins should be stored on a concrete or paved area which can be hosed down easily.

Plastic or paper refuse sacks, being disposable, are more pleasant to handle than the traditional dustbin, but if not protected can be damaged by roaming animals. Wire guarded holders are available for such sacks or a caged enclosure can be constructed for their storage.

In premises that generate a large quantity of rubbish, bulk refuse containers are a considerable improvement on large numbers of small dustbins. However, the local authority must be equipped with special vehicles for their emptying. Alternatively private contractors will provide large refuse skips, which are removed when full and replaced with an empty skip. If this latter system is adopted only skips provided with proper covers should be used and it should be ensured that the contractors thoroughly clean the container after emptying it and before returning it to the food premises. In some premises it may be economically worthwhile to install a waste compactor and so reduce charges for refuse collection. When using a compactor a metal liner is fitted into a plastic sack. This allows bottles, cans and other sharp objects to be compacted without perforating the sack. The liner is withdrawn just before the sack is completely filled. A ram compacts the refuse to one-fifth or less of its original volume.

4.4 EQUIPMENT

All equipment likely to come into contact with food should be non-absorbent and readily cleansable. Food equipment should be free of cracks, grooves and corners where dirt can accumulate. Whenever new equipment is to be purchased it should be carefully examined for the absence of such dirt traps. Machinery should be easily dismantled to allow thorough cleaning, and details of the cleaning stages should be shown on an instruction plaque.

Traditionally, wooden equipment and surfaces have been used exten-

Fig. 3 Refuse compactor in use. (*Reproduced by courtesy of Imperial Machine Co.* (*Peelers*) *Ltd*)

sively in the food trades but wood is porous and can absorb moisture, blood and bacteria (see Fig. 4). Wood also has a tendency to crack. It is therefore not a suitable material for surfaces that come into contact with open food. Where wood is used for table legs or as shelving it should be treated with polyurethane varnish.

Wood is, of course, the traditional material for butchers' chopping blocks although synthetic blocks are now available (see 13.2.1).

The stainless steel used in the food industry is low in carbon. 18/8 stainless steel is often specified and this grade contains 18–20% chromium and 8–12% nickel. Stainless steel comes in a variety of different finishes including satin finish and mirror finish. It is impervious, very durable and well suited for use in the food industry. It is protected by a self-repairing surface film of chromium oxide. The use of harsh abrasives will destroy this protective film and allow pitting of the metal to commence.

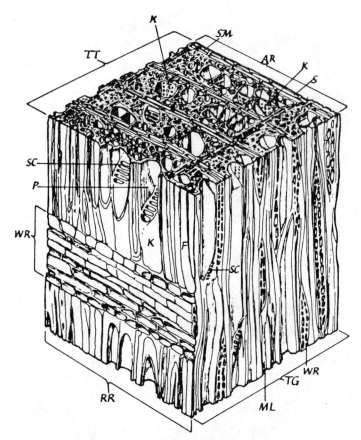

Fig. 4 Diagrammatic representation of the structure of hardwood. (*Taken from 'Catering Science and Technology' by Magnus Pyke*)

TT = Minute portion of the top surface of a stump or end surface of a log.
RR = Surface cut parallel to the radius (the centre of the tree is to the right) and the vertical plane.
TG = Surface cut at right angles to the radius or tangentially within the log.
WR = Wood rays, strips of short horizontal cells extending in a radial direction.
P   = Pores.
SC = Grating separating pores.
F   = Wood fibres, the strength-giving elements of hardwoods.
K   = Thin places or pits in the wood fibres and vessels allowing the passage of sap from one cavity to another.
AR = Annual ring.
S   = Early wood or spring wood.
SM = Late wood or summer wood.
ML = Middle lamella, a thin layer cementing together the cells in wood.

4.4.1 Cutting boards

Synthetic materials are increasingly being used in roles traditionally reserved for wood. In particular for that important piece of equipment, the cutting board. Hard synthetic rubber pads have been used for this purpose for some time and they have the advantage over wood that they will not crack, split or swell, neither will they absorb fat or moisture. After an extended period they can be resurfaced by sanding. However, such boards suffer from the disadvantage that they warp in hot water. Whiteside boards are an example of synthetic rubber cutting surfaces.

Certain grades of P.V.C. sheeting, *e.g.* Darvic H.P., are suitable for use as cutting boards, but they cannot be disinfected by heat and chemicals must be used. Polypropylene boards, however, can be subjected to hot water without any warping and are therefore suitable for cleaning in a dishwasher or 'sterilising' sink.

The Cookley board is an example of a polypropylene cutting board. It is reversible and is fitted with anti-slip reversible feet; a very useful feature. Cookley boards can be impressed with a colour symbol to reduce

Fig. 5 Stainless steel mobile sink. (*Reproduced by courtesy of W. and G. Sissons Ltd*)

the risk of cross-contamination; red for raw foods, green for cooked food and blue for fish. See Appendix B for manufacturer's details.

4.4.2 Tables and worktops

Stainless steel tables should be the first choice in food preparation areas. They should have tubular legs sealed at their feet. Worktops can be provided with 150–300 mm upstands to the rear to reduce soiling of wall surfaces.

Good quality laminated plastic (*e.g.* Formica) work and table tops are also suitable in many situations. However, they are not a suitable surface for cutting food on, as they score easily and they can also be damaged by placing hot containers on them.

If working surfaces and tables can be mounted on lockable castors it will allow them to be easily moved for cleaning.

4.4.3 Sinks and wash hand basins

Sinks should be constructed of 18/8 stainless steel. Galvanised, enamel and stoneware sinks are less easily cleaned, the last two being subject to chipping. Mobile stainless steel sinks are available and can be very useful in catering.

Wash hand basins should be provided in convenient positions. They must not be too large otherwise they may be used as sinks or storage shelves. Spray taps are recommended and ideally these should be foot or knee operated. Liquid soap should be provided and paper towels or hot-air hand dryers. Automatic roller towels have a tendency to stick and all too often are seen to have run out, leaving a soiled and wet end of material, which food handlers might be tempted to use. In addition the law requires a nailbrush to be provided at the wash hand basin.

All sinks must be provided with a sufficient supply of hot and cold water and basins with hot and cold water or warm water at a suitably controlled temperature.

Chapter 5

REFRIGERATION

The operation of an effective system of temperature control is the single most important contribution a caterer or retailer can make to the prevention of food poisoning. Refrigeration is an important aspect of temperature control and this chapter deals with the effects and mechanics of refrigeration, as well as the practical use of refrigeration equipment.

The low temperature storage of food is employed for two reasons. Firstly, proper refrigerated storage will prevent the growth of food poisoning bacteria and secondly, it will reduce spoilage and slow down the loss of food quality. Thus, good refrigeration is necessary for both public health and quality control reasons. Although these are separate considerations they cannot be divorced when discussing the storage of food at low temperatures.

5.1 THE EFFECTS OF REFRIGERATION ON FOOD

All raw animal and vegetable products begin to decay from the moment they are slaughtered or harvested. Chemical and bacteriological changes occur that will affect the quality of the food and ultimately spoil it. These processes can be slowed down by the use of refrigeration.

The chemical changes are due to the action of enzymes within the food cells. During the life of the plant or animal these enzymes were essential for growth but following harvesting or slaughter they become destructive in action. Although enzymic action is retarded by low temperatures many enzymes will continue to operate at temperatures well below 0°C (32°F). For this reason most vegetables are blanched before being frozen, as this heat treatment destroys the enzymes present.

Low temperatures also reduce bacterial activity. All micro-organisms have an optimum temperature at which maximum growth and multiplication will occur. As the temperature drops below this optimum, so the growth of the organism will slow down until the temperature falls below the minimum growth temperature for the species concerned (see 2.3.3). Below this temperature growth will cease and indeed, microbial cells may begin to die.

Food poisoning bacteria will not grow at temperatures below 3·3°C (38°F) although some growth of psycrophilic spoilage bacteria may occur at temperatures as low as −5°C (23°F). Certain psycrophilic moulds can also develop at sub-zero temperatures, and prove a nuisance in refrigerated stores.

Temperatures of below 0°C (32°F) will kill or irreversibly inactivate large numbers of micro-organisms. As the temperature of the food drops so the water within it begins to freeze. This results in a concentration of salts within the liquid that remains unfrozen. As the ice advances the salt concentration increases and unfrozen water is drawn out of the cells by osmosis. Thus, micro-organisms are killed or damaged by a drop in Aw (see 2.3.4), dehydration and, perhaps, the physical action of the ice crystals. The number of organisms that die will vary with the nature of food being frozen and the susceptibility of the different species of micro-organisms. Gram-negative species are considered more sensitive to freezing than gram-positive species, salmonellae being more easily destroyed by freezing than other food poisoning bacteria. However, freezing cannot be relied upon as a means of destroying pathogens. Even salmonellae have been recovered from egg and meat products after they have remained frozen for two years. Furthermore, clostridia spores and staphyloccocal enterotoxin are very resistant to cold.

The rate of freezing will also affect the survival of bacteria as they suffer greatest damage at temperatures just below freezing point. The critical temperature range appears to be between −1°C (30°F) and −5°C (23°F) and the longer bacteria are held between these temperatures the more will die. It would therefore appear that slow freezing is desirable but although this might reduce the bacterial loading of the food, slow freezing would also result in more mechanical and enzymatic damage and a poorer quality product. In addition, if the freezing process is slow, some growth of bacteria may occur before the food becomes frozen. Frozen food manufacturers therefore freeze food quickly, passing through the critical range as rapidly as possible.

Frozen food should be stored at −18°C (0°F) or below. During storage at such temperatures more bacteria will die, with the highest death rate occurring during the first month of storage, when the most sensitive bacteria are killed. Thawing will see a further reduction in bacteria, especially as the temperature passes through the range −5 to −1°C (23 to 30°F). Organisms that survive thawing will require time to recover from the damage caused by the freezing/thawing process before they can commence growth and multiplication. Psycrophiles will eventually become active and as these are spoilage organisms, badly handled frozen food will usually sour before it can become toxic. Nevertheless, thawed food should be treated just as carefully as fresh food and not held in the danger zone of 10–65°C (50–150°F) (see 9.3.2).

5.2 THE REFREEZING OF FOOD

Should a refrigeration unit fail it will take several hours for even small packets of frozen food to thaw out. This is because of the considerable heat that is required to change ice to water before any significant rise in food temperature occurs. If the temperature of the products remains below 3·3°C (38°F) food poisoning bacteria will not have had an opportunity to multiply. A favourable judgement may therefore be made in the case of food still partially frozen, especially if suitable freezing equipment is available on the premises. The advice of the local Environmental Health Officer should be sought in such cases. However, the refreezing of thawed food in frozen food storage cabinets cannot be recommended. Such equipment is not designed to freeze food quickly and if used for this purpose the quality of the food will be considerably diminished. Furthermore, the shelf life given by the 'star marking' of frozen food packs will no longer be appropriate (see also 12.4).

The storage of ice cream is regulated by The Ice Cream (Heat Treatment *etc.*) Regulations, 1959, which prescribe that the maximum storage temperature for this product shall be 2·2°C (28°F). If the temperature rises above this level the ice cream must be re-pasteurised before sale.

Should an interruption in electricity supply be anticipated the freezers should be switched to 'fast freeze. and the thermostats on frozen food storage cabinets be lowered for several hours before the power cut is expected. The doors and lids of all refrigerated cabinets should be kept shut whilst the power is off and open display cabinets covered with aluminium foil to retain the cold air. If this is done and the cabinets are kept well stocked, it will be many hours before the frozen food begins to soften.

Should frozen food be subjected to inappropriate temperatures over a long period the following indicators will be seen.

(1) Food will be welded together and a solid accumulation of ice may be seen in the packs. This is caused by thawing and refreezing.
(2) Green vegetables will become yellow and eventually khaki with the development of unpleasant odours and sliminess. Such changes are due to the proliferation of lactic acid bacteria.
(3) Meat and pastry products will sour.

5.3 THE LEVELS OF REFRIGERATION

The term refrigeration refers to any lowering of the temperature below the prevailing ambient level. In the storage of food three main levels of refrigeration are recognised.

(a) *Cellar storage*
This is the storage of food in a naturally cool room where the temperature is only a little below that outside. Cellar storage is appropriate for fruit and vegetables and deterioration of the food continues but at a slower rate than would otherwise be the case.

(b) *Chilled storage*
Chilling is an imprecise term but is usually taken to mean the maintenance of a temperature just above freezing point, usually between 1–5°C
(34–41°F). Such temperatures will significantly slow down the microbial
and chemical changes in the food and therefore increase its storage life.

Some foods can be damaged by chilling, *e.g.* bananas and apples, and
optimum chilled storage conditions vary for different foods. The important factors are temperature and relative humidity (r.h.) and these two
are related. If the r.h. is too low there will be moisture loss in the food
whereas too high an r.h. encourages the growth of micro-organisms and
speeds up spoilage.

(c) *Frozen storage*
As has already been indicated −18°C (0°F) is generally accepted as the
maximum temperature required for the long-term storage of frozen
food. But an even longer storage life can be attained at the lower temperatures of −25°C (−13°F) to −29°C (−20°F), and many manufac-
tures of frozen foods maintain such temperatures in their distribution
stores.

5.4 THE MECHANICS OF REFRIGERATION

Two types of refrigeration unit are in common use, the vapour compression system and the vapour absorption system. Both utilise liquid refri-
gerants that boil at near ambient temperatures; each system being based
on the principle that a boiling liquid takes in latent heat from its sur-
roundings.

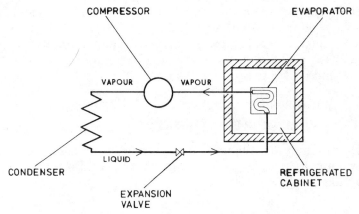

Fig. 6 Vapour compression system

5.4.1 Vapour compression system

This is the type of equipment normally used in commercial units and
consists of three main components:

(a) *An evaporator*
The liquid refrigerant passes into the evaporation chamber via an expansion valve, which regulates the pressure drop in the system. A partial vacuum is maintained in the evaporator by the action of the pump. The change in pressure causes the refrigerant to vaporise, extracting heat from the food stored in the cabinet. In small units the evaporator coils are built into the walls of the cabinet, so lowering its temperature. In larger equipment and cold rooms the evaporator may be surrounded by brine-filled pipes, with the cooled brine being circulated to effect refrigeration. A further variation is the use of a fan to blow the air in the chamber over the evaporator or surrounding brine coils.

(b) *A compressor*
This is a pump operated by an electric motor. It compresses the refrigerant gas received from the evaporator. This high pressure vapour is discharged to the condensor.

The compressor is thermostatically controlled and responds to temperature rises in the cabinet.

(c) *A condenser*
In the condenser the vapour is cooled by air or water and the vapour gives up its latent heat, turning to liquid. The condenser consists of a number of vanes or, in a large unit, a series of water-filled cooling coils. In food freezers the condenser is often fan-cooled with air being forced over the vanes from a grille at the base of the cabinet.

5.4.2 Vapour absorption system

This system has no moving parts and is therefore silent. It is operated by the application of gentle heat and its use is mainly restricted to small refrigerators. Ammonia in water is the refrigerant and hydrogen gas is used to charge the low pressure side of the system, so that the pressure throughout the plant is uniform. The refrigerant is heated by gas or electricity and ammonia gas is released. This passes to an air-cooled condenser where it liquefies. The liquid ammonia then evaporates, removing heat from the cabinet. An absorber is incorporated in the system and this separates the ammonia and hydrogen gases.

5.5 REFRIGERATION EQUIPMENT AVAILABLE

5.5.1 Chill cabinets and coldrooms

These units are designed to hold food at chill temperatures, *i.e.* between 1-5°C (34-41°F). The domestic refrigerator fits into this category and such cabinets are used for the short-term storage of perishable foods. Chill cabinets are invaluable for storing food at safe temperatures and chilled storage space should not be taken up with foods which do not require refrigeration, *e.g.* U.H.T. milk.

Chill cabinets should not be used to cool hot food as this is likely to damage the unit and adversely affect other food stored in the appliance.

5.5.2 Blast chillers and rapid cooling cabinets

These cabinets are specifically designed to lower the temperature of a quantity of hot food in a very short time. For example one unit will reduce the temperature of up to 68 kg (150 lb) of food from 65°C (150°F) to 4°C (40°F) in 2 hours. Such rapid cooling will do much to reduce food poisoning risks when food is not to be consumed immediately after cooking (see 9.3.2).

Rapid cooling equipment is essential when a cook/chill system is operated (see 9.1).

5.5.3 Blast freezers

Blast freezer units are designed to rapidly freeze either hot precooked food or uncooked food down to temperatures of −20°C (−5°F) or below.

5.5.4 Frozen food storage cabinets (conservators)

Frozen food storage cabinets are not intended to be used for freezing unfrozen food but merely to store food that is already in a frozen state. Food frozen in such cabinets will be of poor quality because of the long period necessary to accomplish the process. Furthermore, the introduction of unfrozen food into a storage cabinet will increase the temperature of the frozen food already being stored and will have a deleterious effect on its quality.

B.S. 3739 specifies the operating temperatures required for cabinets to meet the criteria laid down in the 'star marking system', details of which are given in Fig. 7.

The frozen food compartment in the normal domestic refrigerator may be rated as one, two or three star depending on its operating temperature. A frozen food storage cabinet is usually three-star rated, and should comply with B.S. 2501. Sectional walk-in frozen food store rooms should be constructed in accordance with B.S. 2502. Whilst open-topped display/sales cabinets are covered by B.S. 3053.

5.5.5 Food freezers

To receive the four-star symbol of a food freezer (see Fig. 7) a unit must, in successive periods of 24 hours, be capable of lowering the temperature of a specified weight of food from 25°C (77°F) to −18°C (0°F) without affecting the frozen food already stored in the cabinet.

5.5.6 Warning devices and defrost systems

Frozen food storage cabinets and freezers incorporate an electricity supply light which indicates that the supply is switched on. An additional worthwhile precaution is to tape across the electric plug to prevent the

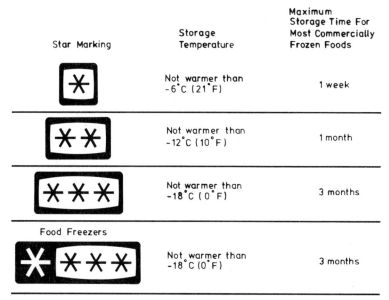

Star Marking	Storage Temperature	Maximum Storage Time For Most Commercially Frozen Foods
✳	Not warmer than -6°C (21°F)	1 week
✳✳	Not warmer than -12°C (10°F)	1 month
✳✳✳	Not warmer than -18°C (0°F)	3 months
Food Freezers ✳✳✳✳	Not warmer than -18°C (0°F)	3 months

Fig 7. The star marking system for refrigeration equipment

appliance being accidentally disconnected or switched off. Most frozen food cabinets and freezers are also fitted with a temperature safety light which illuminates should the cabinet temperature fall unduly. This light can be supplemented by an audible warning unit, battery powered so that it is independent of the mains supply.

Many frozen food cabinets and freezers incorporate an automatic or semi-automatic defrosting system. Semi-automatic systems require a button to be pressed to initiate the defrost cycle and when defrosting is complete the refrigeration unit will operate again. In such a system the frozen food must be removed from the cabinet during defrosting.

With an accelerated defrosting system the cycle commences following the operation of a push-button control but the process is speeded up by the provision of a heat source in the evaporator walls. In such a system the stored frozen food does not need to be moved. Similarly, frozen food can be left *in situ* with an automatic defrost system. In such cases the unit cuts out automatically when defrosting is necessary and cuts in again when the defrost cycle is completed. The water produced is evaporated by the heat from the compressor.

5.6 THE PRACTICAL USE OF REFRIGERATION EQUIPMENT

Certain rules should be followed wherever refrigeration equipment is used, and these are given below. Open-topped storage/display cabinets pose additional problems which are considered in 12.2.9.

(1) When delivered, frozen food should be frozen and should not be accepted unless it is.
(2) The delay between receiving frozen food and placing it in refrigerated storage should be kept to a minimum.
(3) Good stock rotation of frozen food is essential.
(4) Unfrozen food should not be placed in frozen food conservators.
(5) Cabinets should be regularly defrosted and serviced.
(6) The door to a refrigeration appliance should not be left open except when loading or unloading is being carried out.
(7) Walk-in coldrooms should be provided with an inner curtain to reduce cold air loss.
(8) Food should not be stored on the floors of walk-in coldrooms but on pallets to allow air circulation beneath the products.
(9) Refrigeration equipment should not be overstocked, otherwise the circulation of air will be impeded.
(10) Frozen food should always be covered to prevent evaporation and drying.
(11) Food should be placed so that cross-contamination will not occur in the cabinet (see 9.3.1).
(12) All frozen food and chill storage cabinets should be fitted with a thermometer which will give an early indication of any rise in temperature, but see also 5.7 on the difficulties of temperature assessment of frozen or chilled food.

5.7 MEASURING THE TEMPERATURE OF FROZEN AND CHILLED FOOD

It is difficult to measure accurately the prevailing air or product temperature in a refrigeration cabinet. With an automatic defrost cabinet the air temperature fluctuates up and down and in any unit the temperature across the cabinet will vary noticeably. The measuring of product temperature is also much more difficult than might be imagined and accurate measurement requires laboratory type techniques. Details of a reference method of temperature measurement as well as a practical, but less accurate method, can be found in the U.K.A.F.F.P. *Code of Recommended Practice for the Handling of Quick Frozen Food.* The main difficulties encountered in assessing product temperature are the selection of a representative sample of packages and the need to ensure intimate contact between the thermometer and the food being examined.

Chapter 6

CLEANING AND DISINFECTION IN FOOD PREMISES

6.1 THE IMPORTANCE OF CLEANING

Thorough cleaning will reduce the risk of food contamination. This is the overriding reason why cleaning in the food industry must be properly carried out. Furthermore, a clean and tidy environment is good to work in and will encourage efficiency and care in those who handle food. Thus, good cleaning can make a very positive contribution towards food hygiene and the avoidance of food poisoning. Most people will accept the need for the absolute cleanliness of equipment and surfaces that come into contact with food. However, many do not realise the danger in allowing a build-up of dirt in other parts of the premises where direct contact with food is unlikely. For example, the floor can be a major reservoir of bacterial contamination. Bacteria can only survive in association with dirt particles and minute aerosol droplets of moisture. The critical size of such particles is a minimum of $10-12\,\mu m$. Dust particles of this size eventually fall to the ground but are easily lifted again by convection currents and may be deposited on other surfaces or on food itself. Thus, thorough cleansing of all parts of the food room is essential.

6.2 THE IMPORTANCE OF DESIGN AND OPERATION IN REDUCING CLEANING PROBLEMS

Before considering in detail the various cleaning methods available it is important to realise that the design of both premises and equipment, and the operational methods employed, have a fundamental impact on cleaning efficiency. Chapter 4 considers the problems and some of the solutions in designing and equipping food premises. However, most retail and catering businesses have to utilise existing buildings which may fall very far short of the ideal. In such cases considerable thought and ingenuity may be necessary to reduce the cleaning difficulties imposed by the structure.

The part that efficient ventilation can play in reducing the need for cleaning should not be overlooked. Much of the dirt and discolouration of paintwork found in kitchens could be eliminated if the ventilation efficiency was matched to the inevitable production of heat, humidity and volatiles from food. The methods of cooking employed will affect the amount of cleaning required. Deep fat frying always poses cleaning problems, whereas a change from open saucepans to pressure steaming will reduce the production of dirt and condensation (see 4.3.2 ventilation).

The use of a modern doormat system, such as the 'Matador' produced by Cimex International, can help to reduce the amount of dirt brought into the building by pedestrian traffic. Such a mat is constructed of strips of rubber which scrape dirt from the shoes and this dirt falls through the mat and into a well.

An alternative is the use of rubber-backed cotton interception mats, provided by a servicing contractor who replaces the used mat with a clean one at regular intervals.

6.3 DRY CLEANING METHODS AND EQUIPMENT

There are many parts of the food premises that require efficient dry cleaning. The traditional broom has its uses in areas outside the building but it can cause additional cleaning problems when used within the premises. As it does not collect all the dust that it dislodges the broom will inevitably cause dirt to accumulate on other horizontal surfaces with the consequent need for difficult high level cleaning.

To reduce the risk of spreading dust during cleaning operations other items of equipment have been developed to replace the brush and broom. With the need to prevent cross-infection being so vitally important in hospitals, impregnated mops are often used in wards and other areas to prevent the spread of dust and bacteria. Some modern mops are made of synthetic materials that build up static electricity during use, so attracting and holding dust.

6.3.1 Mechanical dry cleaning

Labour can represent 70-80% of cleaning costs and therefore it makes sense, whenever possible, to equip cleaning staff with well-designed mechanical equipment.

(a) *Vacuum cleaners*

Dirt is sucked into the machine in a powerful stream of air. The air is filtered and the dirt trapped. The design of a vacuum cleaner poses a problem of how to balance the efficiency of the filter to the power of the motor. If the filter is too efficient the airflow at the nozzle will be much reduced. If the filter is inefficient the dust will pass out of the machine. In addition powerful motors mean heavy equipment, which reduces manœuvrability and ease of working. A good vacuum cleaner may draw 80 cubic feet of air per minute, but the use of extension pipes will reduce this through leakages and air friction against the tube walls. The use of long extensions therefore requires a powerful motor and inevitably heavy equipment. Flow velocity can be increased by restricting nozzle size.

Fig. 8 High level vacuum cleaner in use. (*Reproduced by courtesy of Nilfisk Ltd*)

Various fittings are available for difficult cleaning jobs. These include extensions with an angle brush to clean girders, radial nozzles for dealing with pipework and provided with either bristles (for loose dust) or serrated edges (for sticky dust).

(b) *Vacuum sweepers*

These are necessary where the suction of a vacuum cleaner is insufficient on its own to dislodge dirt. Dirt trapped in carpet pile is a common example. In such a case some form of mechanical agitation of the dirt is necessary to dislodge it and allow its collection in the air stream. This action may be achieved with revolving brushes or a rotating beater.

6.4 WET CLEANING

As useful as dry cleaning methods may be, much of the cleaning undertaken in the food retail and catering trades will require the application of a water-based cleaning system. Such cleaning will involve at least three stages and sometimes four:

  (a) the *physical* removal of gross contamination;
  (b) the *chemical* removal of the remainder of the visible dirt *e.g.* fat films, as well as the majority of the micro-organisms;
  (c) the rinsing of the article in clean water,
      and when necessary,
  (d) disinfection to reduce still further the bacterial loading.

6.4.1 Detergents

Wet cleaning involves the use of detergents. A detergent is a substance which, when added to water, greatly enhances its cleansing power. That many different substances are able to do this will be apparent, indeed the number of detergents available has grown dramatically over recent years. Companies producing cleaning agents have proliferated and new detergent products are constantly appearing on the market. This situation is often made even more confusing by the literature that advertises the various detergents available. The glossy pamphlets may be very eye-catching and the claims they make enticing, but they often do little to assist in the rational choice of a product to deal with a particular cleaning problem.

Some detergents are designed to deal with very specific cleaning jobs and are extremely limited in their application. In the food retail and catering trades it should not be necessary to use large numbers of different detergents. Indeed a positive effort should be made to restrict the detergents used to three or four suitable products. In this way those using them are less likely to be confused over the appropriate dilutions and methods of application.

It is not possible to give detailed information on all the detergents available but it is hoped that this section will assist in the selection of suitable products. Attention will be drawn to the main requirements for detergents, the principal categories of detergents available and some of their properties. With such information it should then be possible to discuss product selection in an informed manner, with representatives of reputable manufacturers.

A modern detergent is likely to be a complex mixture of chemical cleaners in addition to sequestering and other water conditioning agents. The 'ideal' detergent has not yet been formulated and cannot reasonably be expected in the future. A product that is ideal in one situation may be unsuitable in another. Many have constructed lists of the qualities of such an 'ideal' detergent for use in the food industry. Such a check list does have a value in drawing attention to the type of requirements that need to be met by a detergent used in the food trade. A detergent should:

(1) be readily soluble in water
(2) not form scum or scale in hard water
(3) have good wetting properties to evenly cover the equipment being cleaned
(4) be able to emulsify fats and oils
(5) have the ability to dissolve food material, and ensure that the dirt remains dispersed in the water and is not re-deposited
(6) be easily rinsed away
(7) be non-toxic and non-corrosive.

There are two modes of detergent action that assist in dirt removal. Firstly chemical action, whereby the structure of the dirt is attacked to render it soluble or dispersible throughout the detergent solution. This is the main action of the 'inorganic' detergents. Secondly the reduction of the surface tension of the solution to enable it to penetrate the dirt and so lift it from the surface. This is known as surface activity and is the main action of the so-called 'organic' detergents, which for this reason are also known as surfactants. The terms inorganic detergents and surfactants will be used in this chapter.

Inorganic detergents
Inorganic detergents often consist of strong alkaline powders which have good emulsifying properties and the ability to dissolve food solids. Their main drawback is that they are corrosive and may cause damage to equipment and hands. They are also adversely affected by hard water but do not foam readily and are often therefore the basis of dishwashing detergents. The most important inorganic detergents include:

(a) Alkalis
(1) *Caustic soda (Sodium hydroxide)*. Caustic soda is useful where a very strong cleaner is required as it has excellent emulsifying and dispersing properties. Unfortunately it is corrosive to the skin and metals, especially aluminium and zinc. When used in hard water it precipitates

calcium and magnesium salts. Caustic soda has the advantage of possessing bactericidal properties.

(2) *Sodium metasilicate.* This is also good for emulsifying fats and dispersing proteins and is much less corrosive than caustic soda.

(3) *Sodium carbonate* (soda ash). This is also less corrosive than caustic soda but produces scale in hard water.

It should be noted that many inorganic detergent powders will incorporate a water softening agent which will maintain the salts of hard water in solution so reducing scale and allowing more effective cleaning.

(b) Acids
These are rarely used in the food trade but are useful against inorganic soils such as hardness scale. Hydrochloric and phosphoric acids are two of the commonest acids used in cleaning but they are, of course, highly corrosive and an inhibited form is usually used.

Surfactants (organic detergents)
Surfactants are usually produced as a by-product in the oil industry and possess very important properties. They are often very effective in removing food soil and many are not affected by hard water. They are rarely corrosive and are therefore easily handled. Many surfactants do, however, foam very freely and are not suitable for use in mechanical washing systems.

Classification of surfactants is usually achieved by dividing them into anionic, cationic, non-ionic and amphoteric products. This classification relates to the predominant electrical charge, if any, carried by the ions or particles making up the chemical structure of the detergent. If the predominant charge is negative then it is an anionic detergent, if it is positive then it is a cationic detergent. Non-ionic detergents are products that carry neither a positive nor negative charge. Amphoteric compounds give rise to either positive or negative ions depending on the conditions in which they are used. In acid conditions they usually behave as cationic and in alkaline conditions as anionic. The important point to note when choosing detergents is that indiscriminate mixing can cause problems. Because anionic and cationic detergents carry opposite charges any mixture of the two would result in much reduced detergency. Non-ionic detergents can be successfully mixed with anionics and some cationics but even here care is needed and advice from a reputable manufacturer should be sought.

Some of the principal properties of the various classes of surfactants are given below:

(a) Anionic surfactants
This is the largest group of surfactants. Being negatively charged they can be mixed with soap which is also anionic. Anionic surfactants are sometimes mixed with a hypochlorite to give a combined detergent/ disinfectant product, known as a sanitiser.

Anionic detergents are affected by water hardness and so water conditioners are usually added to them. They also have a tendency to froth excessively and so are not used in machine dishwashing.

(b) Cationic surfactants
The most important group of cationic surfactants are the quaternary ammonium compounds (Q.A.C.s). These are rather poor detergents but have very useful bactericidal properties and are therefore considered in more detail in section 6.5.2.

Some Q.A.C.s foam readily, others do not. They are not affected by hard water and may be mixed with selected non-ionic surfactants to produce a combined detergent/disinfectant product (*i.e.* a sanitiser).

(c) Non-ionic surfactants
These are not affected by water hardness and foam less readily than anionics. They are often blended with anionics to produce a detergent with acceptable foaming characteristics.

(d) Amphoteric surfactants
Amphoteric surfactants are mainly used in acid solutions where they act as cationics and exhibit bactericidal properties.

6.4.2 Foam cleaners

Foam cleaners are becoming more frequently used in food businesses. Foam cleaning has been applied in large food manufacturing premises for some while, but combined detergent/disinfectant foam products are now available in small aerosol packs. Foam cleaning does have certain advantages over more traditional wet cleaning methods. The foam provides visual evidence that the cleaning and disinfecting product has been evenly applied. Splashing is eliminated, therefore stronger chemicals may be used and as the foam slowly collapses so a fresh film of detergent/ disinfectant is continually brought into contact with the soiled surface, lifting even tenacious dirt from the surface, to be completely removed by later rinsing.

6.4.3 Scouring powders

These products are used to remove stubborn soil, *e.g.* burnt-on food residue from cooking utensils. They consist of a detergent and an abrasive to which is frequently added a hypochlorite.

6.4.4 Equipment for wet cleaning systems

(a) Manual equipment
Mops. The traditional soft woven cotton strand mop is still to be found in food premises. Its main drawback is that unless it is frequently and thoroughly cleaned, disinfected and dried it merely becomes an additional source of contamination. Damp, inadequately cleaned mops are marvellous breeding grounds for bacteria and their later use spreads the

contamination far and wide. If mops are to be used they must be washed and disinfected daily, and stored in as dry a condition as possible. Detachable mop heads can be boiled.

The key to the efficiency of any mop is the extent to which it can be wrung dry. Mops work by capillary attraction and therefore as they become wetter they also become progressively less efficient. The use of a mechanical mop wringer instead of the perforated cone, so often seen, is therefore to be preferred.

Much more commonly seen now than the 'string' mop is the sponge mop. Here again the efficiency of the squeezing device is very important. Two sponge types are used, cellulose and polyurethane. Cellulose sponges are light brown in colour and peppered with irregular holes. The cellulose becomes stiff when dry. Such mops are very hard wearing but are subject to bacterial attack and rot if left wet for long periods. They should be washed out after use and rinsed with a hypochlorite solution.

Polyurethane sponges may be any colour and contain very uniform size holes. They remain soft, even when dry. This type of sponge is not affected by bacteria, but is much less hard wearing than cellulose.

Cloths and brushes. Unfortunately, the cleaning cloths used in many food premises are little more than dirty rags liberally used to spread contamination around the premises. Non-disposable cleaning cloths should be viewed with extreme suspicion as they are fertile breeding grounds for bacteria. Many disposable cloths are available and these should be used in food businesses. (See 6.5.2 page 71, self-disinfecting cloths.)

Similarly brushes should be chosen with care. Brushes made from wood and natural fibres will not stand up to disinfection by heat and brushes constructed of inorganic materials capable of heat disinfection should be chosen. Such brushes are more expensive than the traditional equipment but do have a much longer life.

Equipment for the application of detergents etc. A variety of hand-operated spraying devices are available for the application of detergents and disinfectants. Some detergent/disinfectants are now being marketed in ready-to-use aerosol cans and can be used for localised cleaning jobs (see 6.4.2).

(b) Mechanical equipment
Mechanical scrubbers and scarifiers. A considerable array of mechanical equipment is available to aid cleaning, especially floor cleaning. There are machines available for sponging, scrubbing, shampooing and scarifying, most with built-in water and detergent tanks. Such machines may operate a one-, two- or three-brush system. The more complicated the equipment the heavier the machine, and the more maintenance it is likely to demand. However, the simple single-brush machine does have the disadvantage that it tends to swing round due to motor torque and therefore requires continual correction by the operator. The two-brush

machines and the Cimex 'torqueless' three-brush system have been devised to overcome this problem.

The attempted removal of heavy grease in, for example, butchery areas will sometimes result in the brushes of a scrubbing machine becoming blocked. In such a case wire scarifying brushes, available for some machines, need to be used.

Suction drying. Dirty detergent left on the floor following cleaning will cause streaks to form. Suction dryers are available to overcome this problem by removing residual water and detergent. The vacuum is operated through a narrow nozzle and a squeegee blade is fitted to assist in drying. Unfortunately, such equipment tends to be large, heavy and expensive, and its economic application is limited to the larger premises.

Mechanical wall cleaning. Cimex produce a machine that can be used for wall washing as well as floor sponging. It is provided with a telescopic handle giving a reach of five metres. The suction removes water from the wall without drip and so ensures very rapid drying.

The water and detergent tanks of all mechanical cleaning machinery must be drained and cleaned daily, and the equipment itself cleaned and dried.

Pressure jet cleaners. High pressure jet cleaners can be useful for inaccessible areas where dirt is particularly tenacious and cannot be removed by brushing. Such equipment is not suitable for loose dirt, where a low pressure flat jet is more appropriate. If high pressure jet cleaners are to be used the premises need to be designed with this in mind to avoid damage to the electrical system and other equipment.

6.5 DISINFECTION

British Standard 5283 1976: *Glossary of Terms Relating to Disinfectants* defines disinfection as a process intended to remove or destroy a sufficient number of micro-organisms to a level that will neither pose risk to health or damage perishable foods.

The point has already been made, but bears repeating, that thorough cleaning is always necessary but additional disinfection is only useful in certain circumstances. A specific disinfection stage should only be included in the cleaning routine when a positive advantage can be gained from it. Disinfection may provide a useful safeguard against the dangers of cross-contamination between raw and cooked foods. Working surfaces and equipment that come into contact with raw meat and poultry or cooked protein foods can benefit from disinfection after use.

6.5.1 Disinfection by heat

High temperatures will destroy bacteria if applied for a sufficient time. The time : temperature ratio is very important—the longer the bacteria are exposed to heat the lower the temperature required to achieve their destruction. Bacteria may be broadly divided into groups classified as heat-sensitive or heat-resistant, but it should be remembered that the susceptibility of individual cells, even within such groups, varies considerably. Heat disinfection, therefore, needs to cater for the most heat-resistant cells present.

The destruction of bacterial cells using wet heat (hot water or steam) is achieved by the coagulation and denaturing of the cell and enzyme proteins. Dry heat destroys cells by dehydration and oxidation.

Disinfection by heat includes the following methods:

(a) Boiling for 10 minutes will kill all vegetative cells and all but the most heat-resistant spores. This is a very useful method for disinfecting knives, cloths *etc.*

(b) The immersion of utensils in water of 82°C (180°F) for at least 30 seconds is a very useful means of disinfection. This process will destroy non-sporing bacteria and is the means of disinfection incorporated in the 'sterilising' sink and dishwashing machines.

(c) Steam disinfection gives good results but is rarely suitable for use in the retail and catering trades.

(d) Dry heat is used for the disinfection of laboratory equipment. A temperature of 160°C (320°F) must be maintained for 1 hour. This method is best reserved for laboratory use.

6.5.2 Chemical disinfection

There are a number of popularly held misconceptions about the use and efficiency of chemical disinfectants. The first is that such chemicals should be liberally applied wherever food or drink is prepared or sold. Undoubtedly, much of the chemical disinfectant used is unnecessary. Disinfectants are not normally required for the general cleaning down of walls, floors *etc.* Here, what is essential is that the cleaning is carried out conscientiously, using an appropriate detergent. This will, in itself, prevent the build-up of large bacterial populations.

When disinfection is felt to be a useful additional safeguard, disinfection by heat should be chosen wherever possible. It is more reliable than chemical agents and generally cheaper to apply.

The second great myth concerning chemical disinfectants is that they are a miracle product and one quick wipe with a cloth soaked in a solution will ensure bacterial decontamination. Unfortunately, this is not the case and those responsible for the use of chemical disinfectants must be aware of the proper procedures and the limitations of such products.

To be effective the disinfectant must come into intimate contact with the cell wall of the bacterium. The chemical may cause the cell contents to leak from the bacterium or allow foreign substances to enter the cell. The chemical therefore interrupts the essential functions of the cell. It may interfere with enzymes required for vital cell processes, prevent metabolic activity essential for growth or interfere with the reproductive processes of the cell.

Bacteria will show a range of sensitivity to a particular disinfectant, some being more easily destroyed than others. The most resistant cells are very important as they may be unaffected by the process. This form of 'selection' can give rise to the multiplication of resistant cells.

No one chemical agent is effective against all organisms and manufacturers talk about the spectrum of a disinfectant. This is the range of bacteria against which a particular disinfectant will be of value. Gram-negative and gram-positive bacteria often react differently to chemical disinfection and this is presumably due to differences in the construction of their cell walls. Bacterial spores are very difficult to destroy with chemicals except by the use of highly corrosive agents which have limited practical application.

The practical application of chemical disinfectants
A number of important practical points must be taken into consideration when using chemical disinfection:

(a) Has the disinfectant the right spectrum to deal with the bacteria likely to be encountered?

(b) Hard water will inactivate some disinfectants. The suitability of the product for use with the water available should be ascertained.

(c) The action of most chemical disinfectants is reduced by the presence of organic matter (*i.e.* dirt and food soil). It is therefore essential that items to be disinfected should be cleaned first. For this reason the value of products advertised as combined detergent/disinfectants or sanitisers is doubtful, except in situations where gross soiling is not encountered.

(d) Disinfectants can be inactivated if mixed with incompatible detergents. Some are also inactivated by cork, rubber, nylon, cellulose sponge mops and certain plastics. Therefore, some knowledge about the disinfectant and its limitations is essential.

(e) Disinfectant mixtures deteriorate with time; they should be made up to the correct dilution daily. 'Topping up' an existing solution is unsatisfactory.

(f) The period of time the chemical agent is in contact with the surface is important. A minimum of 2 minutes is necessary for effective disinfection.

(g) Chemical disinfection will not take place in the absence of water. The surface to be treated must be effectively wetted.

(h) To prevent the survival of bacteria resistant to a particular agent, it is worth while employing two disinfectants and alternating their use every 3–4 months.

Commonly available chemical disinfectants

Sodium hypochlorite. Chlorine is a powerful germicide and possesses a very wide range of action against many bacteria, including some spores. Sodium hypochlorite is the most common chlorinating agent used and is usually sold in a solution having 10% available chlorine. (Some cheaper products may only have 4–5% available chlorine.) Half a fluid oz (approximately ½ egg cup full) in 2 gallons will give a disinfecting solution of 150 p.p.m. of chlorine, if made from a solution having 10% available chlorine.

Hypochlorites are often used in the food trade because of their wide spectrum and cheapness, but they do have limitations. They are anionic and therefore must not be mixed with cationic detergents. They are easily inactivated by organic matter, and for this reason should only be applied *after* thorough cleaning has taken place. Hypochlorites lose strength during storage and corrode metal surfaces. These last two problems are overcome by the use of chlorinated trisodium phosphate (C.T.S.P.) which is produced in stable crystalline form. The C.T.S.P. crystals are dissolved to give a buffered hypochlorite solution which is non-corrosive and safe to handle.

Hypochlorite must never be mixed with acid materials as poisonous chlorine gas will be given off.

Trade names include Brobat, Domestos and Chloros.

Iodophors. Iodine is the active constituent in iodophors. Iodine possesses similar bactericidal properties to chlorine although it is less sporicidal. The iodine is incorporated in a surface active agent which may be anionic, cationic or non-ionic, and such products therefore possess detergent as well as disinfectant properties. Iodophors are considerably inactivated by organic matter but are usually unaffected by other materials.

Trade names include Wescodyne and Biothene.

Quaternary ammonium compounds (Q.A.C.s). As explained in 6.4.1 Q.A.C.s are cationic detergents which possess bactericidal properties. They are now commonly used in the food trade but are more expensive than hypochlorites and more limited in their range of bactericidal activity. Some bacteria are able to survive in Q.A.C. solutions.

Unlike most other disinfectants that work following absorption by the bacterial cell, Q.A.C.s do not appear to penetrate the cell wall but interfere with essential cell functions from outside. As a group they are incompatible with anionic detergents and some are inactivated by organic material, soap, water hardness, nylon, cellulose sponge and some plastics.

Trade names include Deogen and Microl.

Phenolic disinfectants. There are several different types of phenolic disinfectants available all of which are anionic. These include:

(a) Black fluids. These are produced from crude coal tar cresol and are sticky and strong smelling. They have been largely superseded by more refined products.

(b) White fluids (lysol). These are emulsions of cresol in soap solution. Like hypochlorites and iodophors, they have a wide range of antibacterial activity but are much less easily inactivated by organic material. Their main drawbacks are that they are strong smelling and poisonous. This restricts their use in food premises to the disinfection of drains *etc*.

Trade names include Izal and Clearsol.

(c) Chlorinated phenol disinfectants. The addition of chlorine to phenols increases their bactericidal action without increasing corrosiveness or the poisonous nature of the product. This allows lower concentrations to be used. However, chlorinated phenols have a more restricted range of antibacterial activity than phenols and are more readily inactivated by organic matter.

Trade names include Dettol.

(d)˙ Complex phenols. This group is related to the chlorinated phenols and is used to secure personal hygiene. Hexachlorophene is probably the most commonly used product in this field, and is often incorporated in toilet soaps and barrier creams. Such products do have some merit in reducing the risk of staphylococcal infection. Hexachlorophene incorporated in soap is transferred to the skin during washing and remains active on the skin for several hours.

Amphoteric surfactants. These detergents possess a narrow range of germicidal properties. They are inactivated by organic matter, hard water, cellulose sponge and nylon.

Pine disinfectants. These are chlorinated phenols with the addition of pine perfume which acts as a deodorant. The smell makes their application limited in food premises and their danger is that they may be used to cover up unpleasant odours when what is really required is thorough cleaning.

The self-disinfecting cloth. This is a relatively new product and is marketed under the name Wipex (see Appendix B). It is a non-woven man-made cloth onto which is bonded a blend of cationic disinfectants. The chemicals are released as the cloth is used and so is a blue dye incorporated in stripes on the product. The presence of the blue stripes indicates that the disinfectant is still active and when the stripes fade the cloth is disposed of, although as a precaution a reserve of disinfectant will remain.

Self-disinfecting cloths are most effective as a second stage when physical cleaning has already been carried out. Their great advantage is their simplicity in use, avoiding the need to make up chemicals to the correct strength.

Choice of chemical disinfectants. Because of the range of disinfectants available the choice of a suitable product can be very difficult. The only 'officially' recommended disinfectants are the Approved Chemical Agents listed under the provisions of Regulation 27 (6) (a) of the Milk and Dairies (General) Regulations, 1959. This relates to products suitable for dairy use but can also be used as guidance in other food premises. A British Standard exists for pine fluids which a number of products meet.

Another useful source of information on the suitability of a disinfectant for use in connection with food is the Directory of the British Association for Chemical Specialities. This publication also names the main active ingredient of many disinfectants. The Association's address is given in Appendix A.

6.6 THE STORAGE AND CARE OF CLEANING EQUIPMENT

Cleaning equipment and materials must be kept away from food and food utensils, so avoiding the danger of cross-contamination or odour taint. The facilities required will vary with the size of the premises but in a large business a separate room for the storage of mops, buckets and mechanical cleaning equipment will be necessary and should be provided with a deep sink. Such a room should be well ventilated and not subjected to high temperatures from an adjoining boilerhouse.

After use mops, brushes and other cleaning equipment should be washed out and then disinfected, by heat or with a weak hypochlorite solution. All such equipment should be dried before storage.

6.7 THE ORGANISATION OF CLEANING

Good cleaning costs money, inadequate cleaning is expensive! Many reputations have been damaged following an outbreak of food poisoning or a prosecution for unhygienic conditions. It is unfortunate that such events are necessary to make some people hygiene conscious. Cleaning is so often looked on as a non-productive and therefore separate and secondary part of the food business. When cleaning is viewed in this light it is seen as a necessary evil to be done only because the law dictates it shall be. Such a negative attitude results in cleaning staff with little reason for pride in their work, which inevitably produces a superficial cleaning job.

A much more positive approach is necessary and must originate from top management. Those in the most senior positions must be seen to be committed to the very highest standards of food hygiene. Cleaning must be treated as an integral part of the retail or catering process and must be programmed into the whole business operation. The vital requirement is that cleaning should be systematic. A system must be instituted that ensures that all parts of the premises and all equipment are cleaned as often as is necessary. Such a system should prescribe exactly who is responsible for cleaning each item or surface, how the cleaning is to be carried out and who will check that the cleaning has been completed. In other words, for all but the very smallest food business a cleaning schedule should be drawn up. Some examples are given at the end of this

Chapter. This may seem a great length to go to in order to achieve a clean working environment but experience has shown that it is essential if a high standard of hygiene is to be maintained at all times.

The requirement that all food handlers 'clean as they go' should be incorporated in any cleaning schedule as this time-honoured principle reduces any build-up of contamination.

6.8 CLEANING CONTRACTORS

If staff 'clean as they go' and this is backed by a systematic cleaning scheme, dirt and grease will not build up to such an extent that it becomes a major undertaking to remove it. However, if for any reason routine cleaning is neglected for a while, the task to restore conditions to the standard necessary may be beyond the capabilities of the staff available. In such circumstances it is possible to call on the services of a specialist cleaning contractor who is equipped to undertake the necessary 'deep clean', as it is often known. Such work can be carried out at night, when the premises are closed and may also include such particularly difficult cleaning operations as the removal of scale from sanitary fittings, the removal of carbon deposits from cooking appliances and the cleaning of ventilation canopies and trunking. (See Appendix A for address of the Contract Cleaning and Maintenance Association.)

6.9 THE ASSESSMENT OF CLEANING EFFICIENCY

It is part of management's function to ensure that cleaning is being properly carried out. This requires a frequent inspection of all parts of the premises. Such an inspection must be systematic to ensure that nothing is left out. Particular attention should be paid to areas beneath and behind equipment where there may be a tendency to skimp the cleaning; a small torch is essential for this purpose. Light switches, door handles and control knobs must not be forgotten, as food handlers come into frequent direct contact with these.

Such a visual examination will give a very good picture of the hygiene standard achieved but a more objective and easily comparable assessment is sometimes valuable. Such assessments, based on the detection of bacteria present, may reveal that equipment, although it appears visually clean, has not been properly cleansed or disinfected. There are now a number of techniques available to allow such assessments to be made and these may also be valuable as health education tools, as the results of inefficient cleaning can be demonstrated to staff. The various systems are described below. Sources of proprietary products are given in Appendix A.

Plate count
This is the principal method used in food hygiene laboratories such as those of the Public Health Laboratory Service. It gives a very good

indication of bacterial contamination, but the equipment, expertise and time necessary for such tests is only likely to be available to the very largest concerns.

Contact plates

These are small plastic petri dishes on which a grid is marked in square centimetres. The special design of the plates allows them to be filled with agar to the top of the lip and a grip on the base of the plate is used to hold it, whilst the face of agar is pressed onto the surface to be sampled. Incubation is then carried out and the resulting bacterial colonies can easily be counted and by reference to the grid can be referred to as so many colonies/sq. cm.

Agar sausage

These are artificial casings filled with agar media suitable for the growth of bacteria. The end of the sausage is cut off with a flame-sterilised knife. The cut face of the sausage is pressed against the surface to be examined and is contaminated with any bacteria present. A sterilised knife is again used to cut off this contaminated slice of agar and it is tipped onto a petri dish, with contaminated surface uppermost. Another sample can then be taken with the freshly exposed surface. The samples then require incubation and this may be achieved in an incubator or even by sealing the petri dish in a plastic bag and storing in a warm office. The number of colonies present can then be counted. In practice it has been found that the agar sausage technique is rather cumbersome.

Dip slides

This very convenient and simple method of bacteriological assessment of hygiene equipment has been developed from medical use for detecting bacteria present in urine samples. The small microscope-type slides are coated on both sides with agar. On the one side with Plate Count Agar and on the other with MacConkey Agar No. 3, which allows the identification of coliform bacteria, which appear as violet red colonies. A finger grip provided on the slides makes it a very simple operation to 'swab' any desired surface, and the slides are then replaced in the sterile plastic bottles provided. Incubation takes 1–2 days and incubators designed for domestic yoghurt making can be utilised for this purpose and are very cheaply obtained.

One manufacturer gives the following guidance for the assessment of the number of colonies found:

1–9 very slight growth
10–20 slight growth
20–100 moderate
100 heavy.

P.G.C. system

This system involves the use of a ready prepared pack consisting of a sterile swab and a tube containing a red gel. The swab is dipped in a reagent, a wire template placed on the work surface and the area within the template is swabbed. The swab is inserted in the red gel and incubation carried out. If the red gel shows a colour change to yellow during an 8-hour incubation period the surface is deemed to have been inadequately cleaned. An alternative kit designed to reveal coliform bacteria, thus indicating faecal contamination, is also available.

This is a very simple system designed to be used by unskilled staff and no attempt is made to quantify the degree of contamination found.

Millipore swab test kit

This is another very convenient method of assessing cleaning efficiency. The test kit consists of two parts: a swab in a container of sterile diluent, and a separate plastic holder in which is placed an absorbent pad impregnated with a dehydrated nutrient medium and marked with graph-like squares. The surface is swabbed and the swab replaced in the diluent container which is shaken. This releases the micro-organisms. The absorbent nutrient pad is then placed in the diluent and during incubation colonies of micro-organisms develop on the pad.

The graduations on the pad make counting easy. There are test kits available for 'total counts', coliforms, or yeasts and moulds. The main drawback of Millipore kits is their comparatively high cost.

6.10 SAFETY AND THE USE OF BACTERIOLOGICAL PLATES, SLIDES *etc*

Great care must be exercised when handling petri dishes *etc.* on which micro-organisms are growing. On no account should viable colonies be taken into food rooms. If it is desired to use such colonies in a health education exercise they should first be rendered harmless. This can most easily be achieved by spraying the petri dish *etc.* twice with a proprietary brand of hair lacquer and this also has the effect of preventing the drying out of the agar.

Petri dishes, slides *etc.* containing cultures should, ideally be disposed of by incineration but failing this they may be autoclaved at 15 lb for 15 minutes or soaked overnight in a 3% lysol solution or sodium hypochlorite, diluted to give 200 p.p.m. of available chlorine, before their ultimate disposal.

CLEANING SCHEDULES

An example of a kitchen cleaning schedule is included but it is not intended to be complete.

Kitchen cleaning schedule

WORK AREA/ EQUIPMENT	METHOD	FREQUENCY	RESPONSIBLE PERSON
FLOOR (Quarry tiled)	1. Remove spillages immediately.	As necessary.	Kitchen staff present.
	2. Clear area of as much movable equipment as possible.		
	3. Clean with freshly prepared solution of .... The solution should consist of 2 measures/gallon of warm water.		
	4. The sponge mop provided should be used after first rinsing in clean water.	As required but a minimum of 3 times per day following peak periods.	Kitchen porter.
	5. Pay particular attention to areas beneath equipment and around table legs *etc.*		
	6. Rinse with fresh water where necessary (this will depend on detergent type) and mop dry.		
WALLS (Ceramic tiles)	1. Spillage to be removed immediately.	As necessary.	Kitchen staff present.
	2. Clean with freshly prepared solution of .... The solution should consist of 2 measures/gallon of warm water.	Lower portions of walls weekly, upper parts at intervals of 3 months.	Kitchen porter.
	3. Pay particular attention to areas subject to contact with hands, *e.g.* around light-switches.		

Work Area/ Equipment	Method	Frequency	Responsible Person
Working Surfaces (Laminated plastic)	1. Clean with freshly prepared solution of .... The solution should consist of 2 measures/gallon of warm water.		
	2. Pay particular attention to surfaces used for preparation of raw meat and poultry.		
	3. Such surfaces described in 2 above should be disinfected after cleansing by the application of a fresh solution of .... The solution should consist of one measure/$\frac{1}{2}$ gallon of water. This should be applied with a clean disposable cloth and a contact time of 2 minutes allowed before rinsing with clean water and drying.	All surfaces should be cleaned after completion of food preparation process.	Kitchen staff present.
	4. Supporting stands to be scrubbed to remove food soil, using .... solution as in 1 above. Any food deposits seen on surrounding walls, water service pipes *etc.* should be removed.	Twice weekly.	Kitchen porter.
Sinks	. 1. Scrub sink, splashback and draining boards with a freshly prepared solution of .... The solution should consist of 2 measures/ gallon of warm water.	Three times a day at end of busy periods.	Kitchen assistant.
	2. Supporting stands to be scrubbed to remove food soil using .... solution		

WORK AREA/ EQUIPMENT	METHOD	FREQUENCY	RESPONSIBLE PERSON
	as in 1 above. Any food deposits seen on surrounding walls, water service pipes *etc.* should be removed.	Twice weekly.	Kitchen porter.
	3. Clean taps with disposable cloth and a solution of	Daily.	Kitchen assistant.
WASH HAND BASIN	1. Clean with a freshly prepared solution of .... The solution to consist of 2 measures/gallon of warm water.	As required but a minimum of 3 times a week.	Kitchen porter.
	2. Clean taps with disposable cloth and a solution of	Daily.	Kitchen assistant.
CROCKERY CUPBOARDS	1. Remove all crockery *etc.* from cupboard. 2. Brush out any loose dirt. 3. Clean with freshly prepared solution of .... The solution to consist of 2 measures/gallon of warm water.	Monthly.	Kitchen porter.
OVENS	1. Remove shelves and clean separately. 2. *Interior* (a) Pre-heat oven to 65°C (150°F) and turn off. (b) Spray with .... oven cleaner. (c) Let solution stand for 5 minutes. (d) Loosen carbonised food soil with stiff brush. (e) Remove loosened soil with damp cloth. (f) Rinse with fresh water. (g) Wipe with weak solution of sodium bicaronate and leave to dry.	At least twice weekly dependent on use.	Kitchen assistant.

Work Area/Equipment	Method	Frequency	Responsible Person
	3. Clean exterior paying particular attention to controls, service pipes, hinges *etc*.	Twice weekly.	Kitchen assistant.
Grille	1. Scrape loose soil from surfaces as soon as equipment is cool enough to work on. 2. While surface is still warm spray with .... oven cleaner and allow to penetrate the soil. 3. Scrape off the loosened soil and rinse with wet cloth. 4. Empty and wash scrapings pan.	Daily.	Kitchen assistant.
	5. Supporting stands to be scrubbed to remove food soil using solution of .... The solution should consist of 2 measures/gallon of warm water.	Twice weekly.	Kitchen assistant.
Can opener	1. Remove from socket and scrub with a solution of .... 2. Rinse in hot clean water and air dry.	Daily.	Kitchen assistant.

Chapter 7

PEST CONTROL

There are several important reasons why food premises should be kept free of pests. Firstly, certain pests are known to be vectors of disease. It is impossible to quantify the precise importance of pests in the spread of food-borne disease but rats, mice, cockroaches, flies and Pharaoh's ants can carry food poisoning bacteria. For this reason their presence in food premises cannot be tolerated, and the law requires that all possible steps be taken to keep food premises free of infestation. Besides the health and legal implications, pests damage and contaminate large quantities of food each year, resulting in waste and loss of profit. Rats and to a lesser extent mice damage the fabric of the building and can also attack water, gas and electrical services, sometimes with disastrous consequences. Furthermore, an infestation can result in the loss of a good reputation should the public become aware of the presence of pests, such as mice or cockroaches, on food premises. For these reasons the responsible food trader will take all possible steps to prevent pests gaining access to his premises and in the event of an infestation occurring to ensure that the pests are speedily and safely eliminated.

Pest control, especially in food premises, requires skill and training and this chapter is not intended to equip those in the catering and retail trades to undertake this work themselves. Indeed, they would be unwise to attempt such a course of action, particularly when poisons or insecticides are likely to be required. The wise course of action is to seek professional assistance from the local Environmental Health Department or a reputable pest control operator (see 7.5).

The aim of this chapter is to show how infestations can be avoided by good hygiene and proofing works and to provide the background information necessary to enable an appreciation of the complexities of pest control in food premises.

7.1 GENERAL PRINCIPLES OF PEST CONTROL

In pest control, prevention is better than cure, and so food premises should be constructed and maintained so as to reduce the chance of pests gaining access. Once inside a building pests require food, moisture and harbourage. Retail and catering businesses should be so run as to deny these essential requirements to any pests that are present. Scrupulous hygiene is therefore necessary as even small accumulations of food soil will provide sufficient nutrient for pests to survive. Whenever possible, food should be covered or stored in containers and sources of water, such as dripping taps and leaking waste pipes, should be eliminated. Keeping stock tidy not only makes cleaning easier but it reduces the number of hiding places available for pests. When goods are stored on pallets these should not be placed against walls but a space left behind them to allow for cleaning and inspection. A regular inspection of the building for signs of infestation should be a standard procedure in all food premises and will mean that any problems are quickly spotted.

Should an infestation occur, then a survey to determine the species involved and the size and extent of the problem is essential. The right treatment can only be formulated in the light of this information as it is necessary to know something of the biology and habits of the pest, as well as its distribution within the premises in question.

Once treatment has been carried out its effectiveness should be monitored. If the control method employed is unsuccessful then the reasons must be determined and appropriate measures taken. Reasons for unsuccessful treatments include: reinfestation from elsewhere; treatment poorly carried out; resistance of the pest to the pesticide used; or even sabotage of the treatment by staff or others.

This then is the pattern, whatever the pest: survey—treat—monitor.

7.2 RODENT PESTS

Rats and mice consume large quantities of food but contaminate even more with their urine and faeces. They can transmit food poisoning as well as the serious condition leptospirosis (Weil's disease). Mice may also pass on the eggs of the tapeworms *Hymenolepis nana* and *H. diminuta* in their droppings.

The incisor teeth of rodents grow throughout their life and must be continuously worn down by gnawing. As the enamel on the outer surface of the teeth is very hard they can cause great damage by gnawing through wood, water pipes or even electricity cables.

Three rodent species commonly infest premises in Britain: the common rat, the ship rat and the house mouse. Occasionally the long-tailed field mouse, *Apodemus sylvaticus*, enters buildings, particularly during colder weather.

The common rat (Rattus norvegicus)
The common rat is usually brown in colour with a grey underbody. For this reason it is sometimes called the brown rat, but this can be misleading as colour variations do occur and black common rats have been found. It weighs 100–500 grams (4 oz–1¼ lb) and its tail is shorter than the combined length of its body and head. The common rat can be found anywhere where food and shelter are available and frequently takes up residence in drains and sewers. It is good at burrowing and can climb, although it is not such an adept climber as the ship rat.

The ship rat (Rattus rattus)
The ship rat is mainly black although occasionally brown forms are found. It is smaller than the common rat, weighing 100–300 grams (4 oz–12 oz) and has a tail that is longer than the combined length of its head and body. The ship rat does not inhabit sewers but is found in buildings, especially in port areas. It is a particularly good climber and frequently infests the upper floors and roof spaces of premises.

The house mouse (Mus musculus)
A small animal weighing up to 30 grams (1 oz) and usually brown in colour with a grey underbody. A frequent pest in food premises.

Rats and mice are nocturnal in habit and although omnivorous prefer a cereal diet. Rats require a constant supply of water but as long as their food is not too dry mice do not need to drink at all.

The common rat exhibits 'new object reaction' to a marked degree. New object reaction is the tendency to avoid any objects that are recognised as new in the environment. This habit is very important in relation to rodent treatment, as it means that 3–5 days will usually elapse before a common rat will feed freely from bait. New object reaction is not so marked in the ship rat and is absent in the house mouse, which is an inquisitive animal and tends to examine new objects.

The phenomenal breeding rate of rats and mice should be noted as it is one reason why they are such successful and serious pests. A female rat can produce up to 5 litters in her lifetime, with each litter containing between 2 and 14 young, whilst mice can produce 6 litters with 2–13 young in each.

7.2.1 Survey of evidence of rodent infestation

The presence of rats or mice should be quickly detected in a well-run food business. When evidence of infestation is found a detailed survey should be carried out to determine the extent of the infestation, the rodents' means of access, any nesting sites on the premises, the sources of food and the species present. The survey should ideally include adjoining premises as pests do not respect boundaries. It is very unusual during such a survey to see live rodents and so other evidence must be sought.

Droppings
The pellets of a common rat are usually dark brown or black in colour, up to 20 mm ($\frac{3}{4}$ inch) long, and when fresh have a glazed appearance. Ship rat droppings are a little smaller than those of the common rat and are slightly curved in shape. Rat droppings dry out in 2–3 days and become hard. Very old droppings are discoloured and covered in dust. Mouse droppings have the appearance of common rat droppings but are much smaller.

From an examination of the droppings it is possible to determine which species is present, whether the infestation is recent or longstanding and from the number of droppings the probable size of the infestation. Certainly if two or three distinct sizes of droppings are present it does indicate that families are being raised and that the infestation is likely to be heavy.

Runs and smears
Because rats and mice live in areas where dirt and grease is to be found their bodies quickly become covered with a greasy film. When a rat or mouse rubs against a wall or other surface he tends to leave a smear of dirt and grease. With the constant use of a particular route rodents will quickly produce distinctive smears against walls and pipes or around roof timbers that they have negotiated. These latter marks in roof spaces are known as loop smears.

Holes and gnawing
Rats will produce holes with a diameter of about 80 mm ($3\frac{1}{4}$ inch) and mice 20 mm ($\frac{3}{4}$ inch) diameter holes. Gnawing around doors and door posts may occur in an effort to gain access but gnaw marks may also be seen on pipework, cables *etc.*, as constant gnawing is essential if the rodent is to limit the growth of his incisors.

Damage to food
Damage to food and food packaging is a fairly obvious sign of infestation.

Footprints and tailmarks
These can sometimes be seen in dusty areas. Flour can be used as a tracking powder to determine whether rodents are still active in the area.

7.2.2 Treatment of rodent pests

Poisoning
This is the most common way of dealing with rodent infestations and usually the most effective. There are two basic types of poisons available: acute or single dose poisons and the chronic poisons.

Acute poisons act rapidly after consumption and should prove fatal after the rodent has eaten bait on only one occasion. They do, however, possess two major drawbacks. Firstly, their toxicity is such that they must be used with extreme care and can rarely be recommended for use in food premises. Secondly, should a rodent consume a non-fatal dose of poison it will be reluctant to consume any further bait. This reaction is known as 'poison shyness'. This second problem is reduced by prebaiting with plain unpoisoned bait when dealing with a rat infestation. Prebaiting is continued until the new object reaction of the rats is overcome and they are feeding freely, usually between 3 and 6 days. Only then is the unpoisoned bait removed and the poisoned bait laid. Prebaiting is less important when dealing with mice, who do not exhibit new object reaction. A acute poison treatment should always be followed by further baiting with a different unpoisoned bait to determine whether any survivors remain. If the treatment has not been fully effective a different acute poison should be used in the follow up treatment. In the past many different acute poisons have been used, some of which are now prohibited under The Animals (Cruel Poisons) Act, 1962. Only 4 acute poisons are now approved for rodent control and all must be used with great care.

(1) Zinc phosphide
This is a dark grey powder that gives off the poisonous gas phosphine when wet. It is not suitable for use in food premises.

(2) Norbormide
This poison interferes with the blood supply. It is only suitable for use against rats as it is harmless to mice. In the concentrations used it is very safe as it will not harm domestic or farm animals. It is available as a ready-mixed bait containing 0·5% norbormide and at this concentration is not effective against the ship rat. Unfortunately it has not always given good results in practice.

(3) Alpha-chloralose
This is a narcotic drug that affects the metabolic processes of warm-blooded animals, slowing down respiration, reducing blood pressure and lowering body temperature. In small animals heat may be lost so quickly that death occurs. Alpha-chloralose is used against mice. The chance of mice recovering from a dose of the poison is increased at higher temperatures and where other food is available. For these reasons the use of alpha-chloralose is not recommended where the ambient temperature is 18°C (65°F) or higher or where an alternative food supply exists.

(4) Fluoracetamide
This is a highly toxic poison and its use is restricted to the baiting of sewers and certain warehouses by trained personnel.

Chronic or multiple dose poisons need to be consumed on several occasions over 2–3 days to be lethal. This is a significant safety factor and one reason why chronic poisons are to be preferred in food premises. However, it must be remembered that warfarin and other chronic poisons are approximately as poisonous to man and domestic animals, weight for weight, as to rodents and should be carefully handled.

With the exception of calciferol all the chronic poisons are anticoagulants and interfere with the mechanism for the production of pro-thrombin, which is necessary to ensure adequate blood clotting. Rodents poisoned by an anticoagulant may die following minor damage to blood capillaries through cuts and abrasions or by spontaneous haemorrhages induced by the poison. Animals that have had, or are about to have, litters are especially vulnerable. The antidote to anticoagulant poisoning is vitamin K, as this restores the prothrombin content.

There are 5 anticoagulants available in Britain and, against non-resistant rodent populations, all are equally effective. The 5 are warfarin, coumatetralyl, chlorophacinone, diphacinone and difenacoum.

In 1958 rats resistant to warfarin appeared on a Scottish farm, and since this date resistant populations of rats have spread to other parts of the country. Warfarin-resistant rats have also been reported in Denmark. Warfarin-resistance in mice is more common and occurs sporadically throughout the country

Warfarin resistance appears to be due to the mutation of a single gene although the exact mechanism is not fully understood. If warfarin continues to be used against a rodent population that contains individuals resistant to the poison, the percentage of the population that are resistant will increase. Warfarin resistance should be suspected if bait continues to be eaten at a high rate, assuming that rodents are not migrating from other areas. When warfarin resistance is encountered an alternative treatment should be employed. Difenacoum is effective against resistant common rats but other anticoagulants should not be used against resistant populations. Calciferol can be used to deal with resistant rats and mice. Calciferol is vitamin D_2 and it interferes with calcium metabolism. Calciferol is combined with warfarin in Sorexa CR and death is caused by the combination of too much vitamin D_2 and too little vitamin K. As the poison operates through 2 different mechanisms the chance that resistance will develop to either is reduced. Alternatively, resistant rodents can be dealt with using acute poisons.

Practical aspects in the use of rodenticides
The choice of an attractive bait to which the poison can be added is very important. Cereal baits such as oats, maize and wheat are best and other sources of food should be eliminated. The baits should be placed in position and a record kept of the number of baiting points and their exact location. Poison baits should be contained within marked bait containers. More baiting points will be needed when treating for ship rats than common rats and many more points are required to deal with mice, as their feeding habits are very erratic.

Where it is impossible to eliminate alternative food sources cereal baiting points may be supplemented by warfarin water baits. The water bait is put in chick founts and should consist of a solution of 0·005% sodium warfarin with 5% sugar added to improve palatability. Other possible sources of water should be eliminated.

At the end of the treatment all unconsumed poison must be removed and a search made for rodent bodies. Dead rats and mice should be handled with waterproof gloves and disposed of by burying or incineration.

Rodenticidal dusts

Poison baits can be supplemented by the use of rodenticidal dusts. The dust is ingested as the rodent grooms itself. Such dusts tend to be less effective against the ship rat, as it holds its body and tail higher off the ground than the common rat and mouse and is suspicious of areas covered by light-coloured dusts.

The dusts available contain warfarin, coumatetralyl or the organochlorines H.C.H. and D.D.T. The dust can be spread on floors and ledges or blown along trunking and down holes, but clearly it has a very limited application in food premises, because of safety considerations. On such premises it should only be used in areas away from open food. The danger from the spread of dust can be much reduced by containing it within shoe boxes into which has been placed crumpled tissue paper. If a hole is cut in each end and an attractive bait put in the box, rodents entering will pick up significant quantities of poison on their bodies. If shoe boxes are used they should be marked 'POISON'.

Trapping

Trapping is rarely a successful method of dealing with a rodent infestation. Traps can play a part in preventing a reinvasion of a premises previously cleared of infestation, although a large number of traps are likely to be needed for that purpose.

The treadle type, break-back trap is to be preferred to the 'prong' type, as it can be baited with cereals, flour or dried fruit. Despite conventional wisdom even mice are more attracted to such baits than to cheese! The traps should be set with their treadles across rodent runs, *i.e.* at right angles to walls, so they can be sprung from either side. As rats exhibit new object reaction rat traps should be baited but left unset for a few days to encourage rats to feed freely from them. This is unnecessary for mice.

Ultrasound

Ultrasound is sound of such a high frequency that it cannot be detected by the human ear. Frequencies above 20,000 Hz come into this category. It is known that loud ultrasonic sound can cause fits in some rats and mice (audiogenic seizures) and devices are on the market designed to prevent rodent infestation by the emission of ultrasound.

Unfortunately, ultrasound is readily absorbed by many materials and thus, sound shadows can be created giving areas free of ultrasound. Furthermore ultrasound can only be propagated over short distances so several sound sources may be needed to protect even a small area. This system is likely to have a limited application and certainly should not be relied upon as an alternative to proper rodent proofing.

7.2.3 Rodent proofing

There is a legal obligation to maintain food premises in such a condition as to reduce the risk of rodent infestation and clearly, adequate rodent-proofing makes good sense. Both rats and mice can gain access through very small holes, mice being able to pass through a 10 mm ($\frac{3}{8}$ inch) gap.

The space beneath outside doors is a common point of entry, and the gap between the base of the door and the threshold should be not more than 6 mm ($\frac{1}{4}$ inch). Worn thresholds should be made good and if necessary the gap beneath the door reduced by planting a metal bar in the threshold. In addition the base of external doors and door posts should be metal-lined to prevent gnawing by rodents. Broken or large-holed airbricks can give rodents access to the wall cavity and subfloor space. Airbricks should be protected by expanded metal sheeting having a maximum mesh size of 6 mm ($\frac{1}{4}$ inch). As common rats resort to drains and sewers these must be maintained in good repair. Gaps around service pipes that pass through walls should be eliminated and central heating pipes should be fitted with sleeves built into the wall. Where the space around the sleeve is more than 6 mm ($\frac{1}{4}$ inch) it should be packed with crumpled wire mesh.

Both rats and mice can climb and may enter buildings at high level. The external climbing of downpipes can be prevented by the use of flat or cone-shaped metal guards projecting at least 250 mm (9 inch) from the pipe. Wire balloons in ventilation pipes will prevent rats climbing such pipes internally and entering roof spaces in that way. It has been found that mice can climb rough textured brick walls and this can be prevented by gloss painting two courses of the brickwork, having first rendered the surface smooth with cement and sand.

Works of rodent proofing should normally be carried out after a treatment to deal with an infestation has been completed. This is to reduce the disturbance to the normal feeding habits of the rodents, but should reinfestation be occurring from outside, then treatment and proofing work will need to be undertaken simultaneously.

Whenever rodent treatment or proofing is carried out hygiene standards at the premises should be reviewed. Particular attention should be paid to the storage of waste food and to any areas where harbourage of pests could occur. Even in a well-proofed building mice may be introduced during deliveries and a pest control contract may be worthwhile considering (see 7.5).

7.3 INSECT PESTS

Many different insects can cause problems in food premises. In particular, various foodstuffs can be infested by insects and mites. Such infestations can thereafter be transported to catering premises, retail shops and the home. No attempt is made here to deal with the different infestations that can arise in food itself. In such cases the advice of the local Environmental Health Officer should be sought. This chapter concentrates on the insects which commonly infest food premises in this country and the methods available for dealing with them.

For most people the control of insect pests means the use of insecticides. Certainly chemical control of insects is common and often very effective but it is not the only method of insect control. Other methods include:

(1) Interference with insect reproduction and growth by the use of hormones.
(2) Physical control, *e.g.* by screening and trapping.
(3) Control by good hygiene.
(4) Biological control through the introduction of natural enemies of the pest.

Methods 1 and 4 are rarely used in catering or retail premises (although see 7.3.4 for the control of Pharoah's ants by hormones) but successful insect control may well involve the other two methods either individually or in addition to chemical control.

7.3.1 Insecticides commonly in use

The brief descriptions of insecticides that follow include details of their acute oral toxicity. These figures have been calculated from the single oral dose in mg/kg of body weight needed to kill 50% of a group of laboratory rats, the LD_{50}. Although these figures give some indication of the comparative toxicity of the insecticides they must be used with discretion. Other factors relating to the use of the insecticide in the field can be important when considering its potential toxicity. The figures are taken from the M.A.F.F. publication '*Contact insecticides used in food storage practice in the U.K. and notes on spraying against stored-products pests*' (I.C. 1977/19).

Extreme care must be exercised in the use of all insecticides in food premises, however potentially toxic or safe they may be. The manufacturer's instructions must be strictly adhered to and where serious infestations occur the services of the local authority or a reputable pest control contractor should be obtained.

Organo-chlorine insecticides
(1) Chlordane
An insecticide with stomach and contact action. It has a good residual effect when used as an emulsion or in an oil-based spray. It is very effective against ants, wasps and cockroaches. It is fairly toxic to mammals with an LD_{50} in rats of 457–590 mg/kg.

(2) D.D.T.
This stomach and contact poison persists in the environment for a very long time. It is not suitable for use in food premises. The LD_{50} in rats is 113 mg/kg.

(3) Dieldrin
A very toxic and persistent chemical. Its only use in the food trade is by skilled operators for the control of Pharoah's ants and Oriental cock-

roaches (German cockroaches are often resistant to dieldrin). In such cases it is usually formulated as a lacquer.

Even in such limited situations it is recommended that whenever possible alternative chemicals of shorter persistence and lower mammalian toxicity are used. The LD_{50} in rats is 46 mg/kg.

(4) Gamma H.C.H.

Gamma H.C.H. is a general-purpose insecticide having strong stomach and contact action as well as some vapour activity. It is used against many pests and some evidence of resistance is available in a number of species including the German cockroach. It is not as persistent as D.D.T. and therefore poses less of an environmental hazard, nevertheless it is gradually being replaced by organo-phosphorous and carbamate insecticides. The name lindane is used when a product contains at least 99% gamma H.C.H. The LD_{50} in rats is 88–91 mg/kg.

Organo-phosphorous insecticides
These tend to decompose more rapidly in the environment than the organo-chlorine insecticides.

(1) Bromophos

A contact and stomach insecticide with a very low mammalian toxicity (LD_{50} in rats 3,750–7,200 mg/kg). It is slow acting but quite persistent, remaining active for at least 3 months. It is used for the control of cockroaches.

(2) Diazinon

Used in sprays and lacquers mainly against flies, ants and dieldrin-resistant German cockroaches. It has a good knockdown effect but is not very persistent. Its effectiveness is increased by the addition of the synergist piperonyl butoxide. It is sometimes formulated with pyrethrins for use in aerosol sprays. The LD_{50} in rats is 150–600 mg/kg.

(3) Dichlorovos

A very toxic product requiring particular care. It rapidly vaporises and can therefore be used effectively against flying insects but because it is very unstable is of limited value in well-ventilated rooms or where a long residual life is required. Dichlorovos is incorporated in plastic resin strips from which it slowly vaporises, so dealing with flying insects. Such strips are suspended from the ceiling but should not be placed close to a heat source or an open window. Impregnated strips normally remain effective from 12 to 14 weeks although they are not very satisfactory in well-ventilated rooms. The LD_{50} is 56–80 mg/kg in rats.

(4) Fenitrothion

A general-purpose contact insecticide. It has very good residual properties and is useful in cockroach control. The LD_{50} is 250–500 mg/kg in rats.

Carbamate insecticides
Carbamates tend to have a high mammalian toxicity.

(1) Bendiocarb
This is a general insecticide used to control Oriental cockroaches, Pharaoh's ants, garden ants and other pests. Some strains of German cockroaches have been found to be resistant to this insecticide. It has a high mammalian toxicity with an LD_{50} of 35–100 mg/kg in rats.

(2) Carbaryl
Carbaryl has a much lower mammalian toxicity than other carbamates. It is formulated as a dust and wettable powder for crawling insect pests and as a bait for wasp control. The LD_{50} in rats is 850 mg/kg.

(3) Dioxacarb
A contact and stomach insecticide used against cockroaches and other crawling insects. It is more persistent than dieldrin where temperatures are higher than 30°C (86°F). The LD_{50} is 80–150 mg/kg in rats.

(4) Propoxur
A contact insecticide with rapid knockdown which can be used against flying as well as crawling insect pests. It has a good flushing effect and is sometimes used to dislodge hidden cockroaches when surveying premises (see 7.3.4). It has an LD_{50} of 90–128 mg/kg in rats.

Pyrethroid insecticides
(1) Pyrethrins
A mixture of 6 insecticidal compounds are found in the flower-heads of the pyrethrum flower (*Chrysanthemum cinerieaefolium*). These pyrethrins are extracted into solvents and have been used in food premises for many years because of their comparatively low mammalian toxicity. They give a very rapid knockdown; treated insects first showing hyperactivity and then paralysis. Some insects can recover but most formulations contain a synergist, usually piperonyl butoxide, which depresses the insects' detoxifying mechanisms. Pyrethrins are unstable in sunlight and a spray deposit is normally only effective for a few days. Unlike synthetic pyrethroids, they have a good flushing effect and can be used to dislodge hiding cockroaches. The LD_{50} in rats is 800 mg/kg.

(2) Synthetic pyrethroids
A succession of poor harvests of the pyrethrum flower coincided with the commercial availability of synthetic analogues based on the natural product. Various synthetic pyrethroids exist and tend to give either a rapid knockdown or a better kill than natural pyrethrins. Therefore, commercial products usually contain two different pyrethroids so both effects are produced.

Several of the synthetic products are considerably less toxic than natural pyrethrins, which are themselves considered a very 'safe' insecticide. In addition the synthetic pyrethroids are quite stable in light and may remain active from 4 to 6 months. A mixture of bioallethrin for knockdown and bioresmethrin for killing action is a common formulation. bioallethrin has an LD_{50} in rats of 500–860 mg/kg and bioresmethrin 9,000 mg/kg.

Inorganic insecticides
Boric acid
Boric acid has been used as an insecticide since the end of the nineteenth century. It acts as a stomach poison and is utilised as a dust or incorporated in baits. It is slow in action but unlike many other insecticides it does not repel insects and remains stable for a very long time, even at temperatures of 30°C (87°F) or above.

It is a white crystalline powder and should be dyed a distinctive colour when used in pest control. Although it has a low toxicity with an LD_{50} of 2,660–5,140 mg/kg in rats it is usually applied in a dust containing 50–100% boric acid compared with organic insecticides containing only a few per cent of the active ingredient. Boric acid should therefore be handled with great care. As little as 5 grams of boric acid is believed to be fatal to children.

Its main use is against cockroaches, who consume the poison in bait or ingest it as dust particles during their normal grooming processes.

7.3.2 Insecticidal formulations
Emulsions (or miscible) concentrates
The insecticide is contained within oil droplets dispersed in a solvent. Emulsifying agents are also incorporated in the product. The emulsion concentrate is added to water before application. Miscible concentrates are those that can be mixed with water or oil.

Water-based emulsion sprays are suitable for use on impermeable surfaces such as plastics and rubber. They are also useful where fire risk would prevent the use of an oil-based spray. They should not, however, be used around electrical installations or on absorbent surfaces such as wood or concrete.

Oil solutions
The insecticide is dissolved in a solvent which then must be diluted with odourless kerosene or technical white oil (T.W.O.) before application. Ready-to-use formulations are available. Oil-based insecticides usually penetrate an insect's cuticle better than water-based products. Oil solutions are not suitable for use on rubber or plastic surfaces.

Wettable powders
These consist of a mineral-based powder to which has been added an insecticide. Emulsifying agents are also incorporated to aid mixing in water. Wettable powders are suitable for use on absorbent surfaces and

can be applied to non-absorbent finishes, although some deposit from the powder may be visible.

Dusts and powders

These are insecticides mixed with an inert mineral powder and are intended for use on horizontal surfaces as a barrier to crawling insects. Their use in food premises is limited to areas where open food is not present.

Lacquers

These are strong solutions of insecticide that have been formulated so that when sprayed onto a clean surface they dry as a hard lacquer. Dieldrin is often prepared as a lacquer. Lacquers are only used against cockroaches and tropical ants.

The method of application is to lay 4-inch continuous bands of lacquer at floor/wall junctions, across door thresholds and around pipes, ducts and doors (see Fig. 9). The purpose is to ensure that insects have to pass over the band during their search for food. Care must be taken to see that they cannot short-circuit the system, as most insecticides do have a repellent effect and cockroaches and ants will avoid them if possible. Although the lacquer should not be scrubbed it does require light washing, as this removes dust and grease and brings fresh crystals of insecticide to the surface. Under ideal conditions lacquer can remain effective for up to two years.

Gel

Good results have been achieved in cockroach control by mixing fenitrothion emulsion concentrate with methyl cellulose (*e.g.* New Polycell) to give a 1% solution of insecticide. 1–5 mm thick deposits of the resultant gel can be applied to vertical surfaces without run off. The gel is applied with brushes or a low pressure spray in bands as in lacquer application. Besides adhering to vertical surfaces it also has the advantage of not washing away so easily as an emulsion or wettable powder.

Aerosol sprays

The insecticide is dissolved in a solvent and a liquefied gas is used as the propellant. The insecticidal solution is released as minute droplets or aerosols. It is possible to obtain automatic devices designed to discharge pyrethrin aerosol sprays into a room at predetermined intervals.

Slow release resin strips

Dichlorvos-impregnated strips can be used to control flying insects (see 7.3.1). They are not suitable where open food is continuously exposed to the vapour.

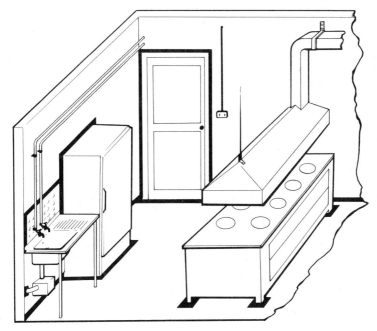

Fig. 9 A kitchen showing where residual insecticide must be applied in continuous bands for cockroach control. (*From M.A.F.F. Advisory leaflet 383 'Cockroaches'*)

Smoke generators

Insecticides (usually gamma H.C.H.) may be combined with combustible chemicals to form smoke generators. When burnt the generators produce a thick white smoke. The insecticide is contained in the smoke and is deposited on the surfaces in the room. This form of insecticidal treatment is unsuitable in rooms where open food is handled.

Thermal vaporisers

Thermal vaporisers are thermostatically controlled electric heating units that are used to vaporise pellets of pure insecticide, usually gamma H.C.H. Thermal vaporisers have been banned in domestic premises in the U.S.A. and are only cleared under the Pesticides Safety Precautions Scheme in Britain where a definite need for their use exists. They cannot be recommended in food premises.

Baits

Baits comprising of an attractive food to which an insecticide has been added can be used. Boric acid is sometimes used against cockroaches in this way. Insecticidal baits are likely to be most effective when no alternative food supplies exist.

7.3.3 Physical pest control methods

Electronic ultraviolet insect control

Insects are attracted to ultraviolet (U.V.) light, which is not visible to the human eye. Many devices are now available which utilise U.V. light to attract flying insects onto an electrically charged grid, where they are killed, their bodies dropping into a collecting tray. This method of flying insect control has considerable merit as it eliminates the need to use pesticides in food premises and ensures that dead and dying insects do not drop onto or into food.

With many different units to choose from, care should be taken to select the one best suited for the situation in question. The effectiveness of a unit depends on two factors. Firstly, its ability to attract insects. It must be remembered that the sun is the greatest producer of U.V. light and the U.V. wattage of the unit must be sufficient to counteract the U.V. in daylight. This usually means that at least 30 watts of U.V. output is required for a unit to be successful; more if a lot of white tiling is present. The U.V. wattage must not be confused with the watt consumption which is also quoted in manufacturers' literature. In large rooms several units may be required and manufacturers' advice on the area covered by a unit varies considerably. A conservative estimate would be that a 30 watt wall-mounted unit would protect 37 sq. metres (400 sq. ft). The second essential requirement is that the unit will deal efficiently with insects when they are attracted to it. Most U.V. devices have the electrocuting grid set in front of the light source. Some have the grid behind the source. The efficiency with which the insects are dispatched depends on the amperage—at least 5 mA is required otherwise recovery may occur. Certain models include a pulsating current to encourage the corpses of larger insects to fall into the collecting trough, rather than stick to the grid, which they are prone to do.

The siting and maintenance of electronic U.V. insect control units is very important. To avoid competing with the U.V. light from the sun, units should be situated as far away from windows as possible. Ideally, the units should be situated 2·4 metres (8 ft) above the floor and in a position where insect activity is likely, *i.e.* where the air is warm, still and food odours are common. Ceiling-mounted units being visible from two sides are to be preferred to wall-mounted units, where they can be accommodated.

Whatever type of equipment is used it should be visible from all parts of the room and not screened by ventilation hoods, ducting *etc.*

As U.V. light is not visible to the human eye it is not possible to determine the continuing strength of U.V. emission from a unit. The U.V. output deteriorates over time and tubes should be replaced, each spring.

Cockroach traps

A number of different cockroach traps have been produced and can be used for controlling cockroach infestations. The use of traps alone is unlikely to prove very effective and their main use is as a surveying tool to determine the presence of cockroaches and as a means of monitoring the effectiveness of chemical treatments.

One such trap is constructed of water-resistant coated cardboard. Inside the trap are bands of fixative gum and a central band of bait consisting of polysaccharides and other substances. The cockroaches become trapped by the gum as they are attracted to the bait.

An alternative type of cockroach trap now available is the Oecos Electro-Roach Trap. Chemical attractants are placed in the trap and cockroaches that have been lured to the trap are subjected to an intermittent electric shock which causes them to fall upon and be retained by a replaceable sticky pad.

7.3.4 Common insect pests in food premises

Cockroach

Over 3,000 species of cockroach exist, most of them living in tropical forests. About 10 of these species are pests of buildings. In Britain 99% of infestations are due to either the Oriental cockroach or the German cockroach, other species only rarely being found. All the species that infest premises in Britain originated in tropical climates, finding their way here in ships and ships' cargo. Although there is some evidence that the Oriental cockroach can adapt to the British climate sufficiently to survive outside, most infestations are centred on heated buildings. Kitchens, bakeries, hospitals and other institutions being commonly infested.

The cockroach is a serious pest in food premises as it has been shown to carry pathogenic bacteria. All cockroaches can pick up and carry bacteria on their bodies and legs. In addition the faeces of cockroaches may contain salmonellae, *E. coli* and other bacteria, as well as the viruses responsible for hepatitis and polio, and the eggs of parasitic helminths. Cockroaches also possess an objectionable odour which emanates from their abdominal scent glands, their salivary glands and faeces. This smell is most persistent and is passed on to any food contaminated by them.

Cockroaches are omnivorous and will thrive wherever food is left uncovered or where food scraps are allowed to accumulate behind fittings or in cracks and crevices. They are nocturnal in habit and this makes it more difficult to assess the extent of any infestation. All species found in Britain have a similar life cycle with only minor variations. The cycle is an incomplete metamorphosis with the young resembling the adult cockroach in everything but size. The eggs are contained within an egg case or ootheca. On hatching, a nymph appears and grows to full maturity through a succession of moults. Adult females can produce several oothecae at intervals of 15–30 days.

Cockroach species found in Britain

(1) Oriental cockroach (*Blatta orientalis*)
Oriental cockroaches thrive in premises where the temperature is between 20 and 28°C (68–83°F). They are strictly nocturnal. An adult will measure 20–24 mm ($\frac{3}{4}$–1 inch) in length and unlike the German cockroach it is a poor climber, as it lacks an adhesive pad between its claws. It is slow to reach maturity and can take 2 years to become fully grown in a cool environment. The oothecae are dropped by the female and take between 6 weeks and several months to hatch. This makes control difficult and means that long-lasting chemicals are required or repeated treatments necessary to deal with nymphs that emerge some considerable time after the initial treatment.

(2) German cockroach (*Blattella germanica*)
The German cockroach is smaller than its Oriental relative, being 10–15 mm ($\frac{3}{8}$–$\frac{1}{2}$ inch) long. It is a good climber and requires a higher temperature, 25–35°C (77–95°F), to thrive together with high humidity. The ootheca is carried by the female until about a day before hatching occurs and this makes it easier to control than the Oriental cockroach.

(3) American cockroach (*Periplaneta americana*)
This large, 28–44 mm (1–1$\frac{3}{4}$ inch) reddish-brown cockroach is only rarely found infesting premises in Britain. This is mainly because it requires a hot environment of at least 30°C (86°F). It is a good climber and has been discovered infesting the drains of buildings that discharge large volumes of hot water. Its oothecae are cemented into crevices.

The treatment of American cockroaches is similar to that required for Oriental cockroaches.

(4) Brown-banded cockroach (*Supella longipalpa*)
About the same size as the German cockroach, *Supella longipalpa* is a common indoor pest in the U.S.A., but only rarely found in Britain. It requires hot conditions around 30°C (86°F) and is rather difficult to control.

(5) Australian cockroach (*Periplaneta australasiae*)
A little smaller than the American cockroach, being 30–35 mm (1–1$\frac{1}{3}$ inch) in length. It is reddish brown in colour with a yellow stripe on the edge of its wing covers. This cockroach has caused damage to plants in heated greenhouses in Britain, including specimens in the Royal Botanic Gardens at Kew.

(6) Surinam cockroach (*Pycnoscelus surinamensis*)
This species too has been found in heated greenhouses in Britain. It is 18–24 mm ($\frac{3}{4}$–1 inch) in length and shining brown or black in colour.

(7) Brown cockroach (*Periplaneta brunnea*)
Like *S. longipalpa* quite common in the U.S.A. but has been found in a few London premises, often being imported to Britain in consignments

of bananas and other tropical crops. It is reddish brown in colour and measures 31–37 mm (1–1½ inches).

The control of cockroaches

Too often the control of cockroaches has been seen as a matter of keeping the numbers down rather than the elimination of the infestation. Certainly cockroaches are a difficult pest to deal with but with care and proper planning eradication can be achieved.

A thorough survey to determine the extent and nature of the infestation is essential. A night-time visit is the best way to obtain the required information. It is usually recommended that the premises should have been in darkness for at least 2 hours prior to the visit and that the inspection be carried out by torchlight. This is done to avoid the rapid scuttling away of cockroaches when the main lights are switched on.

Cornwell, however, suggests that such precautions are unnecessary as cockroaches are disturbed by noise and not by artificial light. Lights may be switched on if this is done quietly. Furthermore, he points out that the time of maximum activity in cockroaches varies with the alteration of day length. In the winter the best time to carry out a night inspection is between 6 p.m. and 9 p.m. and in the summer between midnight and 3 a.m.

When an inspection is carried out the whole premises should be examined for active insects, as should adjoining premises. If a daytime inspection must be relied upon then an aerosol spray of natural pyrethrins can be used to flush cockroaches out of their hiding places. Areas that should be examined with particular care include around refrigerator motors, below cookers, inside heating ducts and in any cracks and crevices. Other evidence of infestation includes faecal spotting, cast skins, dead bodies and deposited oothecae.

The flushing out of cockroaches is a useful survey method but has its limitations. Certainly the insecticidal spray will only dislodge a small proportion of the cockroaches present and tends to be more effective against the Oriental rather than the German cockroach. A more accurate assessment of an infestation may be achieved by using cockroach traps as described in 7.3.3. If traps are used suitable instructions must be given to staff to ensure that they are not interfered with.

Whatever method of survey is used it must provide information on the extent of the infestation and the species involved, as this will influence the treatment chosen. It is unusual for more than one species to be present but not unknown.

The first stage of treatment is to eliminate sources of food by improving hygiene and storing food in pest-proof containers. Perhaps even more important is the removal of any potential water supply, for although cockroaches can survive starvation for many weeks they require constant access to water. Areas where water collects should be looked for and dripping taps repaired. In addition cracks, crevices and other hiding places should be eliminated.

Fenitrothion, propoxur, dioxacarb and bendiocarb are some of the most effective insecticides available for use as sprays against cockroaches. Such spraying must be carried out very conscientiously and can be supplemented by the use of dusts. Dusts should only be used away from open food and where the deposit can remain undisturbed for long periods. Fenitrothion and dieldrin are available as powders although the latter does not retain its potency long in hot ducting. Boric acid powder is very long lasting and is unaffected by hot conditions, although it is rather slow acting. It can also be used in a bait made up of 1 : 1 W/W dry mixture of boric acid dust and porridge oats powder. The addition of boric acid to the water used for floor cleaning at the rate of 0·5 kg/10 litres of water (approximately $\frac{1}{2}$ lb/gallon) is a useful additional measure. If this is done trisodium phosphate detergents must not be used in such a solution as they react with the boric acid.

Fenitrothion or propoxur can be mixed with methyl cellulose to form a gel (see 7.3.2). This will adhere more readily to vertical surfaces which is important when dealing with the German cockroach, and the gel is also less easily washed away during cleaning than an emulsion or wettable powder.

Cockroaches can also be controlled by using lacquers applied in bands around infested rooms (see 7.3.2 and Fig. 9). Lacquers are usually formulated containing dieldrin or diazinon. Dieldrin is much longer lasting but should not be used against German cockroaches, as they tend to be resistant to it.

Hidden oothecae will be unaffected by whatever treatment is carried out and this means that nymphs will hatch out, in the case of the Oriental cockroach 3 months or more after the initial treatment. German cockroaches are less of a problem in this respect as the oothecae are carried by the female until about one day before they hatch. To be successful, cockroach treatment has to utilise insecticides that are sufficiently persistent to deal with nymphs as they emerge and at the same time not be washed away during routine cleaning or, alternatively, several successive treatments must be employed at intervals of 2–3 months.

A treatment for cockroaches cannot be considered complete unless a follow-up survey has been carried out, perhaps 3 weeks after treatment for German cockroaches and 3–4 months after the final treatment for Oriental cockroaches. Cockroach traps are ideal for this purpose. If the success of the treatment is not so monitored, undetected areas of infestation may remain and it will not be long before the problem is as bad as ever.

Garden ant (*Lasius niger*)

Garden ants do not represent a public health hazard but unfortunately are attracted to sweet foods which the workers take back to their nest. In this way they can be a serious nuisance in the kitchen. The most effective way of dealing with this problem is to trace the site of the nest and destroy it by spraying with 0·2% chlordane emulsion. Where this cannot be done lindane dust can be blown into the cracks through which ants are gaining access and the ground around the building sprayed with 0·2% chlordane emulsion.

Pharaoh's ant (*Monomorium pharaonis*)

Pharaoh's ants were introduced into this country early in the nineteenth century and are now widespread throughout Britain. Infestations only occur in permanently heated buildings. The ants are very small, the workers being yellow in colour and measuring 2 mm ($<\frac{1}{8}$ inch). Males are black and 3 mm long, whilst queens are 4 mm in length and yellow/brown in colour. Queens and males are raised throughout the year, nests often containing several queens. The workers are attracted to sweet and high protein foods and forage widely to supply the nest. Once the colony is established new nests are set up. Foraging workers are known to transmit pathogenic bacteria and over the years have proved very difficult to control.

Successful treatment requires careful planning and execution. The extent of the infestation must be determined by baiting with fresh liver. At least one small container holding a quantity of liver should be placed in each room, cupboard and passageway in the premises to be treated. The liver must be replaced with fresh liver daily, for 3 days. During this time the trails used by the workers will be established and treatment can begin well beyond the foraging area. If this is not done the insecticide may have a repellent effect and spread the infestation. So treatment should always proceed towards the centre of the infestation. Treatment should also start on the upper floors, as Pharaoh's ants tend to be more numerous at lower levels. The use of a lacquer is recommended (see 7.3.2 and Fig. 9). Lacquers containing propoxur or dieldrin are very effective against these insects. Following treatment further test baiting with liver should be carried out and any pockets of survivors dealt with. When three consecutive weekly baitings fail to produce any ants then the premises can be considered to be free of infestation.

An alternative treatment that has been found to be successful is the use of the hormone analogue methoprene. This causes the queens to cease laying. Bait containing 0·5% methoprene is used. Adults are not killed but die after their normal life span, about 10 weeks for workers, and the colony becomes extinct. Methoprene is non-persistent and has a low mammalian toxicity.

Whatever method is used to control Pharaoh's ants it must be linked to good hygiene standards to eliminate sources of food.

The Housefly (*Musca domestica*)

Flies can carry bacteria on their feet and on the hairs of their bodies. The fact that they will roam over poorly stored refuse, animal manure and in other insanitary areas means that they can easily contaminate food, if they have access to it. Flies can only consume liquid matter and so they predigest food by salivating upon it.

The Housefly is the commonest fly seen indoors. It is 6 mm ($\frac{1}{4}$ inch) long and is grey with four black stripes on its back. Its life cycle is an example of complete metamorphosis. The larvae or maggots develop from eggs laid in a suitable food material. The larva burrows in the food until it reaches the stage when pupation is to occur. It then seeks a cool, dry spot and forms a pupa. The pupa is an inactive stage in the life cycle and in due course an adult housefly emerges from it. The length of the life cycle is very variable, depending on climatic conditions, but it can be as short as 10 days in a warm environment.

The control of houseflies depends firstly on good hygiene. Hygienic refuse storage is essential if breeding places are to be eliminated and food should be covered when stored, to prevent its contamination by flies. Premises should, as far as possible, be fly-proof. Opening windows should be screened with mesh having a maximum gap of 1·2 mm ($\frac{1}{16}$ inch). External doors should be self-closing or if left open for ventilation purposes be protected with a mesh screen, plastic strips or an air curtain. Within the premises electronic U.V. insect control units are likely to be the best method of dealing with flying pests of all kinds (see 7.3.3). Aerosol sprays of pyrethrins, or dichlorvos-impregnated strips can be used if appropriate.

Rather smaller than the Housefly but quite commonly seen is the Lesser Housefly (*Fannia canicularis*). This fly is particularly associated with animal houses where it will breed in manure. It does, however, resort to other premises but is less attracted to human food than the Housefly. The control methods are the same as for the Housefly.

Blowflies

The Bluebottle (*Calliphora vicina* or *C. vomitoria*), Greenbottle (*Lucilia sericata*) and the Flesh flies (*Sarcophaga* spp.) are serious pests wherever meat is handled. They breed in meat and are often seen resting on sunlit walls during the day. The essential requirement when troubled by these pests is to improve hygiene, eliminating any accumulations of meat scraps and ensuring that waste meat and bones are held in fly-proof containers pending collection. Any walls on which blowflies are known to congregate can be sprayed with a water-dispersable powder containing fenitrothion, and dustbins can be sprinkled with an insecticidal dust. Other fly-proofing precautions should be taken as described in the section on the Housefly.

Wasps (*Vespula* spp.)

There are 6 native species of wasp in Britain. They nest in a variety of places, *e.g.* banks, roof spaces and trees. The queen emerges from hibernation in the spring to build a small nest. She lays eggs and the grubs develop into adult workers, who build up the nest whilst the queen continues to lay eggs throughout the summer. It has been estimated that in a nest with 7 combs 25,000–30,000 wasps may be raised in a season. Towards the end of the summer new queens are produced. These fly and are fertilised by males and then the queens hibernate. All other wasps die with the approach of winter.

There is no evidence that wasps spread disease but towards the end of the summer their diet changes from insects to fruit and sweet foods. It is then that they become a serious pest in the food industry.

Should a wasp problem result from a nest established nearby then the nest should be destroyed and most local authorities will undertake this work. But since workers can travel up to a mile, nest location and destruction will often be impracticable. The premises can be proofed against flying insects as described in the section on the Housefly, although it may be found that air curtains are not so effective against these larger insects. Electronic U.V. flying insect control units will deal effectively with wasps and pyrethrin aerosols can be used.

An old but useful method of control is the wasp trap. This consists of a jam jar containing a quantity of jam or syrup as well as some water to which has been added a few drops of detergent to make the wasps sink.

7.4 THE PESTICIDES SAFETY PRECAUTIONS SCHEME

This non-statutory scheme began in 1957 and today its participants include Government departments, and representatives of the British Agrochemicals Association, the British Pest Control Association and the British Wood Preserving Association. The aim of the P.S.P.S. is to safeguard the health of those who use pesticides, the consumers and users of the final product, as well as members of the public, livestock, domestic animals and wildlife.

Participants in the scheme undertake to notify the Government departments before introducing a new pesticide or form of treatment. The P.S.P.S. specifies the precautions that need to be taken when using a particular pesticide and these are contained in recommendation sheets that can be obtained from the Ministry of Agriculture, Fisheries and Food, Pesticides Branch, Great Westminster House, Horseferry Road, London SW1P 2AE. In addition specified precautions are printed on the product labels. The secretariat of the P.S.P.S. are able to provide additional information and advice to those who require it. Such technical advice concerning pesticides for use in food storage, home kitchen and larder is available from the Joint Secretary, P.S.P.S., Pest Control Laboratory, London Road, Slough, Bucks.

7.5 PEST CONTROL CONTRACTORS

There are now many pest control companies in Britain. Some are national concerns employing large staffs, whilst others are small, local firms. The choice of a contractor is obviously very important as their standard of performance can vary enormously. It is wise to consider contractors who are members of the British Pest Control Association, as members of the B.P.C.A. undertake to ensure that their staff are trained to a prescribed minimum standard. The Association also has a Code of Practice for its members engaged in servicing.

Besides commercial contractors many local authorities will undertake pest control work on a chargeable basis and will often negotiate pest control contracts with local retailers and caterers. Local authority pest control officers are usually very well trained and the charges can be very competitive.

Although the cost of a treatment or the charge for a contract is a consideration, even more important is the need to obtain value for money. The contract charge may be very low but if infestations remain unchecked then it is money wasted. Quotations for pest control contracts can vary enormously, usually because the contracts are too loosely drawn, leaving the contractors to quote to different specifications. Contractors should be asked for quotations based on a clearly written specification of the extent of pest control required. The frequency of visits is important but so is the procedure required should an infestation occur. Contractors should be required to follow up each such incident until the pests are eradicated.

Although the services of a good pest control contractor or local authority are invaluable the food trader should never be tempted to think that their employment in any way limits his own responsibility to ensure a pest-free food business.

Chapter 8

HEALTH EDUCATION AND HYGIENE INCENTIVE SYSTEMS

If outbreaks of food poisoning are to be prevented, it is essential that all in the food industry are well informed about the causes of food-borne infection and their role in its prevention. It is not enough for those who are responsible for the nation's food to simply know the rules, they must understand the reasons for the rules. It is only when people appreciate the basic theory that underlies good food hygiene practice that they are able to apply the principles intelligently to their own situation.

Health education in the food industry is a tremendous, one might even say a daunting, task. It is, unfortunately, the case that many young people leave school without any real understanding of food hygiene. Certainly more should be done in schools to provide basic instruction in this topic, which is very relevant whether a school leaver is destined for the food trade or not. The need for good induction training for all who commence work in the food industry is very great. Unfortunately, such training is not sufficient in itself; health education must be a continuous exercise. Much of what is learnt is quickly forgotten, and new developments in food handling and marketing affect the ways that food hygiene rules need to be applied. So food hygiene education should be a regular feature in any food business. Such education is required at all levels: management, supervisory staff and the food handlers themselves, but the key to success in health education rests with senior management. Example is a fundamental ingredient in food hygiene awareness. If those at the top are seen to be concerned about maintaining good standards their attitude will be reflected throughout the organisation. If, on the other hand, management are prepared to accept poor premises and inadequate equipment, any attempts to indoctrinate staff in good food hygiene practices will be met with justified cynicism.

It must be accepted that not all are fitted to the role of educators, in the sense of delivering a formal lecture or leading a discussion group. But given a sound understanding of the principles of food hygiene, and some instruction on how to pass on such knowledge, many can make a useful contribution to health education in their own organisation. Unfortunately, there are few training opportunities open to food trade managers in this field. Some colleges of technology offer courses in health education, endorsed by the Health Education Council, but these are mainly intended for staff employed in environmental health, social services and the National Health Service. The food hygiene courses offered by the Royal Society of Health and the Royal Institute of Public Health and Hygiene do deal with health education, amongst many other topics.

Whenever assistance is required with food hygiene education the first approach should be made to the local Environmental Health Officer. Most E.H.O.s will be prepared to take part in health education exercises and will often be able to provide films, slides and set up simple demonstrations showing bacterial colonies *etc*. Such visual aids make any talk more interesting and can be used to drive the important points home.

Details of courses, films, booklets and other health education material are given below.

8.1 FOOD HYGIENE COURSES AND HEALTH EDUCATION MATERIALS

8.1.1 Food hygiene courses

Certificate and Diploma in Food Hygiene
Details from The Royal Institute of Public Health and Hygiene,
28 Portland Place, London W1N 4DE.

Both the Certificate and Diploma courses are part-time and are held at local colleges of technology. The qualifications are awarded upon the successful completion of written and oral examinations. The Certificate is a basic qualification in food hygiene and leads on to the more advanced Diploma course.

Certificate in Hygiene of Food Retailing and Catering
Details from The Royal Society of Health, 13 Grosvenor Place, London SW1X 7EN.

This is also a part-time course run at local centres, and involves the sitting of a written and oral examination. This course is designed to allow the student to study, in addition to general food hygiene, one of the following areas in some depth: (a) Bakery (b) Fish and Poultry (c) Grocery (d) Ice cream (e) Meat and Meat Products (f) Milk and Milk Products.

Diploma in Supermarket Retailing
The College of Distributive Trades, Department of Food Commodities, Briset House, 6-9 Briset Street, London EC1M 5SL.

A sandwich course for trainee supermarket managers and includes, amongst other subjects, food hygiene.

Meat Crafts and Hygiene
The College of Distributive Trades, as above.

A part-time course on butchery which includes food hygiene instruction.

Cleaner Food Course

This is a course in basic food hygiene intended for food handlers. It is run jointly by the Institution of Environmental Health Officers and The St John Ambulance Association. The course takes 6 hours, normally in three 2-hour sessions, and is followed by a straightforward examination with multiple-choice questions.

The course is administered from 'Cleaner Food Centres' situated throughout the country and information on the nearest centre can be obtained from the local Environmental Health Department.

8.1.2 A selection of food hygiene films

Key to Cleanliness (16 mm, Colour, 21 minutes)

Produced by J. Lyons and Co. Ltd in 1971. The film is mainly concerned with hygiene in food factories but the basic principles of food hygiene are explained well and it is suitable for showing to all food handlers. It particularly emphasises the need for personal hygiene and the cleanliness of food premises and equipment.

This film has been used widely by environmental health officers and the local health department will probably be able to arrange a showing of it. It is also available for hire or purchase from Guild Sound and Vision Ltd, Woodston House, Oundle Road, Peterborough PE2 9PZ.

The Germ Who Came to Dinner (16 mm, Colour, 22 minutes)

A film produced by The Health Education Council in 1979, and intended mainly for managers in the food trade. It is a very interesting film and includes three case studies of food poisoning incidents, presented by an environmental health officer. It is available on free loan from The Central Film Library, Government Buildings, Bromyard Avenue, London W3 7JB, or the local Environmental Health Department may well have access to a copy.

Food Without Fear (16 mm, Colour, 20 minutes)

Made for Diversey Ltd in 1971. It explains well the growth of bacteria and the need for temperature control. It also covers washing-up techniques. Available on free loan from Guild Sound and Vision, Woodston House, Oundle Road, Peterborough PE2 3PZ.

Hygiene is a Habit (16 mm, Colour, 20 minutes)

The most recent Diversey film. It deals with danger areas in food preparation. Available on free loan from Guild Sound and Vision as above.

Machine Clean (16 mm, Colour, 8 minutes)

Deals with the efficient operation of different types of dishwashers. Available on free loan from Guild Sound and Vision as above.

In Safe Hands (16 mm, Colour, 10 minutes)
Another Diversey film covering the need for food handlers to 'clean as they go' and frequently wash their hands. Available on free loan from Guild Sound and Vision as above.

Food for Thought (16 mm, Colour, 15 minutes)
A Rentokil film concerning catering hygiene. Available on free loan from the Rentokil Film Library, Webber Road, Kirkby, Liverpool L33 7SR.

The Challenge (16 mm, Colour, 18 minutes)
Produced by Rentokil concerning rat infestations. Suitable for those responsible for large-scale food storage. Available on free loan from Rentokil as above.

The Intruders (16 mm, Colour, 16 minutes)
A Rentokil film about cockroach infestations. Available from Rentokil on free loan.

Of Mice and Men (16 mm, Colour, 15 minutes)
1975 Rentokil film about the control of mice. Available on free loan from Rentokil.

Room for Hygiene (16 mm and 35 mm, Colour, 16 minutes)
A Unilever film on basic food hygiene produced in 1961. The 16 mm film is also available in East Bengali, Finnish, Greek, Hindi, Iban, Italian, Portuguese, Sinhalese, Swahili, Swedish, Tamil, Urdu, West Bengali and Yoruba. Available on loan from the National Audio-Visual Aids Library, Paxton Place, Gipsy Road, London SE27 9SR, and the Scottish Central Film Library, 16–17 Woodside Terrace, Glasgow G3 7XN.

A Tale of Two Microbes (16 mm and 35 mm, Colour, 20 minutes)
A Unilever film featuring Frank Muir and June Whitfield. It deals in a humorous way with contamination and the multiplication of bacteria. Available on loan from the National Audio-Visual Aids Library and the Scottish Central Film Library, as above.

Sanitation: Why All the Fuss? and *Sanitation: Rules Make Sense* (16 mm, Colour, 10 minutes each)
Basic food hygiene films for food handlers. Available on loan or to purchase from Training Films International Ltd, St Mary's Street, Whitchurch, Shropshire.

Sanitation: Rodent and Insect Control (16 mm, Colour, 10 minutes)
The role of pests in the spread of disease and how to keep them out of the kitchen. Available on loan or to purchase from Training Films International Ltd, as above.

Dishwashing Machine Operator (16 mm, Colour)
Correct use of dishwashing machines. Available on loan or to purchase from Training Films International Ltd, as above.

Handwashing of Kitchen Utensils and Glassware (16 mm, Colour)
Explains the correct techniques for the use of a three-compartment sink. Available on loan or to purchase from Training Films International Ltd, as above.

Hygiene in Catering (16 mm, Colour, 10 minutes)
Sponsored by Lever Industrial Ltd and shows the investigation of a case of food poisoning at a hotel. An environmental health officer uncovers many instances of negligence in the kitchen. Available on loan or to purchase from Training Films International Ltd, as above.

Care and Cleaning of Kitchen Equipment (16 mm, Colour, 12 minutes)
Shows the correct techniques for cleaning kitchen equipment. Available on loan or to purchase from Training Films International Ltd, as above.

8.1.3 A selection of food hygiene slides and filmstrips
Camera Talks Ltd, 31 North Row, London W1R 2EN produce a number of titles available as both colour slides and filmstrips. Teaching notes can be obtained with the sets and in many cases tape cassette commentaries are available. Titles include the following:

Food Hygiene series
(1) *Preventing Contamination*
(2) *Planning for Hygiene*
(3) *Materials and Methods*

Clean Food: concerned with general kitchen hygiene.

Insect Pest series
(1) *Life History and Characteristics*
(2) *Control Measures*

Food Poisoning: slides showing the causes of bacterial food poisoning.

Lyons Central Laboratories have produced a series of kits for training food handlers. The kits include colour slides and a taped commentary. The kits are available from Guild Sound and Vision, Woodston House, Oundle Road, Peterborough PE2 9PZ. The titles include:

Hygiene for tea bars and trolleys.
Germs from raw food.
Washing up (2 parts).
Storage of perishable foods.
Hygiene for people who serve food.
Personal hygiene for hotel and restaurant staff.

Hygiene in the hotel kitchen.
Hygiene for waitresses and waiters.
Killing germs in the food industry.
Food poisoning and you.
Perishable foods in the kitchen.
Food hygiene regulations for employers, management and supervision.
Food hygiene regulations for people preparing or serving food.
Where germs come from.

Training Films International Ltd, St Mary's Street, Whitchurch, Shropshire produce a number of filmstrips. The filmstrip training materials available include the following titles:

Kitchen sanitation rules.
Insect and rodent prevention.
Sanitation for waiters and waitresses.
Washing kitchen utensils and glassware by hand.

These materials are available as 35 mm or 16 mm filmstrips or as slides with an audio cassette.

Diversey Ltd, Audio Visual Division, 33/35 New Bedford Road, Luton, Beds. Audio-visual programmes available as filmstrips or 35 mm slides with accompanying cassette. Titles include:

Introduction to the science of cleaning.
Why hygiene?—concerning catering premises.
The machine routine—concerning machine dishwashers.
Kitchen clean series—in three parts.
Hygiene—a fact of life—in four parts.

Hospital Caterers Association, Victoria Central Hospital, Mill Lane, Wallesey, Merseyside L44 5UF. Three food hygiene training kits relating to hospital catering are available, comprising of slides, a cassette commentary and instructor's notes. The three kits have been prepared in conjunction with the Institution of Environmental Health Officers and the Department of Health and Social Security, and deal with:

Personal hygiene.
Good catering practices.
Equipment, cleaning and maintenance.

8.1.4 Leaflets, posters and charts

Many leaflets, posters and charts are available from various sources, some of which are given below:

Health Education Council, 78 New Oxford Street, London WC1A 1AH. A number of leaflets and posters obtainable free of charge, including 'Now wash your hands', 'No smoking', *etc*.

Department of Health and Social Security, Catering and Dietetic Branch, Hannibal House, Elephant and Castle, London SE1 6TE. Clean food leaflets in English, Italian, Spanish and Urdu are available, free on request, as are food hygiene posters.

Eaton Enterprises, P.O. Box 34, Walton-on-Thames, Surrey KT12 3JR. Summaries of the Food Hygiene (General) Regulations, 1970, in English, Chinese, Spanish, Urdu and Italian are available to purchase as well as leaflets, notices and posters.

Rentokil Advice Centre, 16 Dover Street, London W1X 4DJ. Wall charts are available free of charge showing flies, cockroaches, rats and mice.

Food, Drink and Tobacco Industry Training Board, Barton Street, Gloucester GL1 1QQ. The Board produce a Guide entitled 'Training for Food Hygiene'. Although mainly intended for the food manufacturing industry its advice on the implementation of food hygiene training can be usefully adapted for the catering and retail sectors.

8.2 FOOD HYGIENE INCENTIVE SYSTEMS

Many attempts have been made to achieve consistently high standards of food hygiene by inducement rather than by the enforcement of rules. All such incentive systems have their limitations, but some have proved to be of value.

In the 1950s many local authorities introduced 'Clean Food Guilds' to which only premises attaining a high standard of food hygiene could belong. Members of the Guild were entitled to display a sign on their premises indicating the achievement of this standard. In recent years the number of local authority sponsored Clean Food Guilds has diminished but from time to time commercial undertakings have operated similar schemes. The British Steel/Egon Ronay Clean Kitchen Award was an example of this approach.

A number of large food businesses have held food hygiene competitions between their branches. The results are usually based on a series of inspections carried out by head office staff over a predetermined period. Naturally the larger the prize the greater the incentive but such a competition can generate very beneficial rivalry between branches.

A further variation on this theme is the construction of a food hygiene league table. At least one local authority has used this approach to good effect. In this case the league positions of different premises were based on the average number of bacterial colonies revealed by swabbing key items of equipment.

PART 2

FOOD HYGIENE IN SPECIFIC
CATERING AND RETAIL TRADES

Chapter 9

CATERING PREMISES

9.1 VARIETIES OF CATERING

There are many forms of catering business ranging from the village tea shop to the large international hotel. All provide meals and/or snacks but the methods of food preparation vary with the type of service provided. As costs have risen and competition grown keener, so there has been a general movement towards methods that give a high output and can be operated by semi-skilled staff. This trend has been encouraged by a growing consumer demand for quick service and the popularity of the snack or light meal rather than the three- or four-course menu. The variety of catering methods is endless, although it is possible to point to a number of types of catering service that are commonly encountered.

Short or called order catering (fast foods)
In this system the food is cooked immediately after the customer has given his order. The food available for use in short order catering is naturally limited to items which can be satisfactorily cooked in the short time available. The most common cooking methods employed are grilling, frying and microwave cooking. The food is purchased ready prepared or preparation is carried out at some stage before the order is given. If preparation has been carried out hygienically and good precooking storage conditions exist this form of catering has much to commend it from a food hygiene point of view. Examples of this system include meals produced at steak bars and much of the food available from public houses.

Advance preparation
When full meals have to be prepared for large numbers prior preparation and cooking often become necessary. Unfortunately, countless outbreaks of food poisoning have been traced to foods prepared and cooked in advance and later reheated for service. The danger does not lie in the advance preparation, but in poor storage between cooking and service and in particular the storage of food at inappropriate temperatures. It must be remembered that the cooking process may not destroy the spores of *Cl. perfringens* or *B. cereus* and therefore, food should be maintained at temperatures above or below those at which such pathogens will multiply. The short-term storage of cooked foods between 65–

80°C (150-176°F) should not give rise to problems and therefore, hot-plate cupboards and bain-maries should be set to maintain food at such temperatures. Where food is not to be served hot, or has been cooked some time in advance, it should be rapidly cooled and maintained at a temperature of below 10°C (50°F) until required (see 9.3.2).

Cook-freeze system
This is really an extension of the advance preparation method but utilising deep freeze storage as a safe means of keeping food until it is required for use. It is of particular value in situations where food would normally be transported hot to the consumer, for example at hospitals. In a cook-freeze system reheating takes place immediately before the food is required, with any transportation occurring whilst the food is in a frozen condition.

Staff in a main production kitchen prepare and partially cook fish and vegetables whilst meat, poultry and some other dishes are fully cooked. The food is then portioned and blast frozen to −20°C (−5°F) and stored at this temperature until required. When needed it is dispatched to a regeneration kitchen where it is quickly cooked and served.

This system allows large numbers to be catered for as fluctuations in demand are evened out. It also allows the best use to be made of skilled staff, with reheating being carried out by unskilled operators. The nutritional value and palatability of the resulting meals should an improvement on those obtained by traditional methods of mass catering.

As far as food safety considerations are concerned scrupulous attention must be paid to hygiene throughout the process, particularly at the portioning stage. Cooking must be thorough and followed by rapid freezing. Final reheating should quickly raise the frozen meals to a temperature of 80°C (176°F) and this can be best achieved in a forced-air convection oven. The use of a microwave oven is less satisfactory because of the problem of 'cold spots' developing during the reheating of frozen foods (see 9.5.2 (h)).

Cook-chill system
The cook-chill catering system consists of the cooking of food followed by fast chilling, storage in controlled low temperature conditions above freezing point, 0°C (32°F) to 3°C (37°F) and subsequent reheating immediately before consumption. This definition is taken from the D.H.S.S. booklet *Guidelines on Pre-Cooked Chilled Food* which should certainly be consulted by anyone considering the commencement of a cook-chill operation.

Cook-chill catering possesses many of the advantages of the cook-freeze system and the regeneration of the meal can easily be accomplished in microwave ovens as frozen food is not involved. However, there is less room for error in the system as only a small rise in storage temperature will bring the food into the temperature range required for the growth of food poisoning bacteria. A cook-chill system therefore requires careful control and regular monitoring.

The principal recommendations made in the D.H.S.S. booklet include:

(a) Initial cooking to be sufficient to destroy the vegetative stages of any food poisoning bacteria present.

(b) The chilling process to start not more than 30 minutes after cooking, and the food to be chilled to 3°C (37°F) within a further period of 1½ hours.

(c) The food to be stored at between 0°C (32°F) and 3°C (37°F).

(d) The chilled food should be distributed under temperature-controlled conditions.

(e) Reheating should raise the food to at least 70°C (158°F) and the food consumed as soon after reheating as possible.

(f) Should the temperature of food rise above 10°C (50°F) during storage or distribution the food should be discarded.

Meals cooked to order
This method remains the essence of good catering and when undertaken by a skilled chef produces the most enjoyable food with few risks to health.

9.2 PRINCIPLES OF CATERING DESIGN

As catering is carried out in a great variety of premises and many different catering systems are employed it is only possible to give general guidance on design considerations. The most significant matters which need to be taken into account when designing any food catering premises are given below.

9.2.1 Size of the premises

To a large extent this depends on how elaborate the menu is to be. The temptation is always to increase the area available for customers at the expense of food preparation and storage space. In areas where rents, rates and other overheads are high it will be essential to maximise the space provided for paying customers. In such cases the size of preparation areas can be reduced by the use of convenience foods.

The only direct legal requirement relating to the amount of space that is required is contained in the Offices, Shops and Railway Premises Act, 1963. This specifies a minimum of 40 sq. ft (3·7 sq. m) floor area and 400 cubic feet (11·3 cu. m) air space for each employee. But as this may include the space occupied by equipment and fittings it is quite inadequate to ensure sufficient space for food preparation to be carried out hygienically and safely. Various attempts have been made to specify non-legal standards of space for food preparation and storage areas. The Department of the Environment and the Department of Education and

Science have issued such guidance for school kitchens and examples of these standards are reproduced below. It should be noted that state school catering involves the provision of only one meal a day and, therefore, this standard would need to be applied to other branches of catering with considerable care.

Approximate floor areas for traditional school kitchens
D.O.E. and D.E.S. guidance

No. of meals	Kitchen floor area (sq. ft/sq. m)
up to 50	300/28
51–100	500/46·5
101–150	570/53
200	720/67
250	820/76
300	920/85
350	1170/108·5
400	1270/118
450	1370/127
500	1550/144

In his book *Principles of Catering Design*, F. Lawson has produced figures and diagrams for guidance on the space required for various food preparation and storage areas. His recommendations are based on the number of meals served per day and an example of these recommendations is given in Fig. 10.

The space available in aisles between equipment and walls *etc.* is important and must be sufficient to allow a good flow of staff and food without danger of accidents. Lawson (op. cit.) states 950–1,050 mm (38–42 inches) as being the minimum space necessary with 1,250–1,350 mm (48–54 inches) clearance being required around hot equipment.

One point which is often forgotten is that the size of the premises can be reduced and cleaning made more difficult by the retention of obsolete or unused equipment. Machinery and fittings that are no longer required should be disposed of.

9.2.2 Layout

Whatever the size and type of catering premises it is essential to ensure that the very best possible use is made of the space available. The more food has to be handled and the greater the distance it needs to be transported the more chance there is of contamination. An orderly progression or flow should be aimed at, starting with the reception of foodstuffs and proceeding to storage, preparation and service, with as little cross-over of flow lines as possible. Furthermore, the layout should be planned to segregate inherently dirty operations, such as vegetable preparation, in areas well away from those where other foods are handled. Sections where cooked food is prepared need particular care when

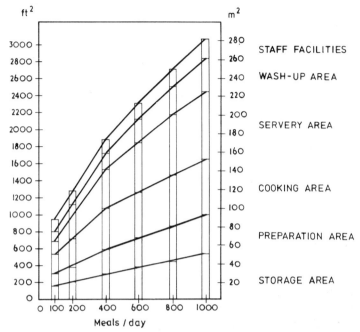

Fig. 10 Areas required for storage, kitchen, servery and staff facilities using conventional methods of food preparation. (*Graph taken from 'Principles of Catering Design' by Fred Lawson*)

they are sited, so as to reduce the risk of contamination to these susceptible foods.

Food preparation areas

The principal decision to be made in connection with the layout of food preparation areas is whether to group equipment around the walls or in central islands. The wall grouping system does lead to economies in the provision of services and makes maintenance easier, as water, gas and electrical supplies need not be sited above the ceiling or below the floor.

The removal of fumes and drainage from equipment on outside walls is also easily achieved. For these reasons wall grouping is often chosen for smaller kitchens. In larger establishments sufficient wall space is unlikely to be available and the grouping of equipment in islands will allow more economic use of space. F. Lawson (op. cit.) considers that island grouping is likely to be practicable where the minimum dimension of the kitchen is 6·5 m (21 feet) and more than 100–150 main meals are prepared at a time. In the very largest premises a further separation of wet equipment (*i.e.* boilers and steamers) from dry equipment can be useful as it allows centralised services such as drainage, water and ventilation to be conveniently arranged. Obviously any form of central island arrangement will require mechanical ventilation with canopies and trunking.

The exact division of the kitchen depends on the nature of the business and design of the premises but the layout of food preparation areas can be conveniently considered under four headings: (a) vegetable preparation (b) meat and fish preparation (c) pastry preparation and (d) general preparation. It will be appreciated that such areas may be provided in separate rooms or be contained within an 'open plan' kitchen.

(a) Vegetable preparation
The removal of soil and peel from vegetables is an inherently dirty operation. It must also be remembered that some spore-forming food poisoning organisms are to be found in the soil, particularly *Cl. perfringens*. For these reasons vegetable preparation should be sited where it can give no risk of contamination to other foods, especially those that have already been cooked.

A double sink is desirable as this allows one bowl to be used for the soaking of vegetables awaiting preparation. In all cases where raw vegetables and salads are prepared a separate vegetable sink should be available. Vegetable preparation sinks should be fitted with a removable sieve to the drainage outlet and so reduce the possibility of blockages due to vegetable peel. Areas around vegetable preparation sinks, peeling and chipping machines are likely to become quickly contaminated with dirt and splashings. For this reason adequate impervious splashbacks are essential as is sufficient space around and beneath equipment to allow easy cleaning. The potato peeler should be sited as near to the vegetable store as possible to avoid the lengthy carrying of potatoes.

(b) Meat and fish preparation
Sufficient easily cleanable working surfaces are important in this area. A separate surface, as well as separate utensils, must be provided for the preparation of cooked meats (see 4.4.1—cutting boards). Where fish preparation is to be carried out a fish slab will be necessary. A nearby sink is also required.

(c) Pastry preparation
In addition to the preparation of pastry and bakery goods, sweets are usually prepared in this area. The necessary equipment includes a marble slab for pastry making, as well as adequate tables and mixing equipment. When used, pastry ovens would be situated nearby.

(d) General preparation
The additional space required for general preparation will vary considerably with the nature of the catering business.

Food storage
In many catering establishments the amount of food storage space available is inadequate. The actual amount and type of space required will depend on the frequencies of deliveries and nature of the business. If meals are prepared from convenience food then less storage space will be

required than would otherwise be the case, but more refrigerated storage may be necessary.

Vegetable stores

In smaller premises a separate vegetable store is seldom necessary and vegetable racks are quite satisfactory. Vegetable stores should ideally be away from daylight but provided with good ventilation. They should be situated in a cool part of the premises easily accessible to the vegetable preparation area.

Dry goods store

This is used for canned and bottled food, cereals, flour *etc.* and the important requirement is that it should, indeed, be dry. Rooms that are subject to condensation are unsuitable as such dampness will result in damage to dry packeted foods and the rusting of cans. Again the temperature should not be too high otherwise insect growth in cereals and dried fruits will be encouraged. A temperature range of 10-15°C (50-59°F) is most appropriate.

Refrigerated storage

Adequate refrigerated storage is an essential requirement to ensure the safe keeping of meat, fish, milk and eggs, as well as products made from these foods. Details about refrigeration will be found in Chapter 5.

Refrigerators should not be sited in larders or food stores as they produce considerable amounts of heat. They should be sited in a cool room, away from other heat sources and provided with adequate ventilation.

Staff facilities

See 12.1.4 and 10.1.5.

9.2.3 Services

Ventilation

Chapter 4 considers some of the general principles involved in ventilation. Here, considerations that apply particularly to catering premises will be dealt with. In all except the very smallest premises mechanical ventilation will be required. Careful planning is essential and the system should be designed to ventilate across the kitchen and away from the dining area. Air inlets should be well away from dustbin areas and sanitary conveniences and positioned to avoid draughts. The extraction outlets should be at high level to deal with steam and vapour and be positioned to prevent short-circuiting of the airflow.

Equipment that produces large quantities of heat, steam or oil fumes should be separately ventilated and provided with a canopy. Grease filters must be incorporated in the system where frying or grilling equipment is in use and arrangements made for their regular cleaning. A spare set of filters is useful, as this allows cleaning to proceed while the replacement filters are used in the ventilation system (see 4.3.2).

Air reconditioners are sometimes seen in kitchens. These consist of canopies through which fume-laden air is drawn. The air passes through an activated carbon filter, which removes cooking odours. The value of such appliances in reducing cooking smells is obvious but their use does not reduce the need for adequate through-ventilation.

Lighting and other electrical services

Good lighting not only makes working conditions safer, more comfortable and efficient, it also shows up dirt and aids effective cleaning. A good standard of lighting, therefore, is essential in catering premises. The levels of illumination recommended for catering premises in the *Code for Interior Lighting* published by the Chartered Institution of Building Services are as follows:

Situation	Illumination in lux	Position of measurement
KITCHENS		
Food stores	150	Floor
General working areas	500	Working surface
STAFF RESTAURANTS		
Canteens,		
Cafeterias,	200	Tables
dining rooms	300	Counter
HOTELS		
Bars, coffee bars	150	Tables
Dining rooms,		
grill rooms,	100	Tables
restaurants,		
general		

All electrical services provided in the kitchen should be waterproof to allow easy and thorough cleaning of the premises.

Gas supply

Gas appliances used in the kitchen should be provided with flexible connectors to the gas supply. If this is done and the appliances are mounted on rollers they may be moved without difficulty. This will aid cleaning. Rollers are available that will carry weights of up to 450 kilos (1,000 lb). Such rollers are fitted with a brake which is applied when the equipment is in a stationary position.

Two types of flexible connector are available:

(1) flexible connections approved to BS 669 which can be used when the surface temperature of the appliance, which may come into

contact with the tube, is not more than 70°C above the ambient temperature and the tube will not be splashed by oil or fat and
(2) bronze or stainless steel corrugated tubing (in accordance with British Gas Technical Specification) for which there is no temperature limitation and which is not affected by splashing with oil or fat. Type (2) is more likely to be necessary in catering premises.

These flexible tubes are usually connected via a bayonet plug-in connector which must be disconnected before the appliance is moved. The result of not providing such flexible connections is to be seen in numerous catering establishments up and down the country. Dirt and grease soon build up on the walls and floor around cooking appliances and it becomes an impossible task to remove it, even given determined staff and long-handled scrapers!

Water supply and drainage
An adequate supply of mains water is required to service all the sinks, dishwashers, wash hand basins and other equipment necessary. Means of supplying constant hot water is also essential whether from a central source or via instantaneous water heaters. Ideally, supply pipes should be chased into the walls to avoid cleaning difficulties. Alternatively the pipes may be carried well clear of the walls to allow cleaning behind them.
For consideration of drainage including grease traps see 4.3.3.

Refuse storage and disposal
Considerable quantities of refuse arise from catering establishments and much of this waste is of a putrescible nature. If not handled properly it will give rise to poor hygienic conditions and encourage rodent and insect pests. It is therefore essential that thought is given as to how refuse will be stored and disposed of. Short-term storage of refuse in the kitchen and washing-up area is usually necessary and a container provided with a close-fitting lid is required. Such bins are often provided with plastic lining sacks and these make refuse handling more convenient and hygienic. If the ultimate means of disposal is collection by the local authority then arrangements for storage between collections is necessary (see 4.3.4). The main choice rests between dustbins, bulk containers and refuse sacks. The choice is largely determined by the system operated by the local authority. If dustbins are used a sufficient number conforming to the relevant British Standard are required, and close-fitting lids are essential. Lids soon become difficult to fit if the dustbin is subjected to rough handling. Such treatment is more likely if material adheres to the inside of the bin and needs to be dislodged by banging the bin. This can easily be avoided if wet refuse is wrapped before being placed inside the dustbin. Dustbins should be stored on a concrete or paved area which can easily be hosed down.
Plastic or paper refuse sacks, being disposable, are more pleasant to

handle than the traditional dustbin but if not protected can be damaged by roaming animals. Wire-guarded holders are available for such sacks or a caged enclosure can be constructed for their storage.

In larger premises it may be economically worthwhile to install a waste compacter and so reduce charges for refuse collection (see 4.3.4).

Waste disposal units
Waste food can be disposed of to a swill collector, but if this is done the occupier of the food business must ensure that the swill collector is licensed by the Ministry of Agriculture, Fisheries and Food. Failure to do so is an offence under the provisions of The Diseases of Animals (Waste Food) Order, 1973. In practice, licensed swill collectors are few and far between and waste food often has to be disposed of via the normal refuse collection system, or a waste disposal unit installed. Such units allow the disposal of macerated food waste to the drainage system. Domestic units are often fitted to the sink outlet but commercial waste disposal units are independent pieces of equipment, separately plumbed and drained.

An electrically driven macerating unit breaks down waste food to a fine mash and it is washed to the drainage system by the water supply provided to the unit. The size of the motor in the unit reflects the size of the cutting ring and varies with the volume of waste to be handled and the type of material to be disposed of. For example, a high powered machine would be required to deal with chop bones. It is important that a machine of sufficient size is used otherwise problems may occur. The following may be used as a guide:

$\frac{3}{4}$ h.p. up to 80   meals/hour
$1\frac{1}{2}$ h.p. 200–300   „   „
3 h.p. 350–500   „   „
$5\frac{1}{2}$ h.p.min. over 500   „   „

Power increased by one step if chop bones *etc.* are to be dealt with.

9.3 FOOD PREPARATION AND COOKING—THE DANGERS

As has been seen in Chapter 3 certain foods are more often associated with food poisoning than others. Foods particularly at risk are those containing meat, fish, milk and eggs, and for this reason they need to be prepared with particular care. This, however, must not blind us to the need to follow good food hygiene practices when other food is prepared. Until quite recently rice was not thought to be a significant food in connection with food poisoning. But now it is known that poorly prepared rice held at the wrong temperature is the most common cause of *Bacillus cereus* food poisoning.

The number of food poisoning incidents would be dramatically reduced if, whenever food is handled, two basic principles were observed, namely the avoidance of cross-contamination and the maintenance of good temperature control.

9.3.1 The avoidance of cross-contamination

It must never be forgotten that raw meat, poultry and eggs may be contaminated with food poisoning organisms. For this reason the only safe rule with these foods is that they must be treated as if they are contaminated. Such raw foods should be prepared with equipment and on surfaces that are not allowed to come into contact with cooked food. After the preparation or handling of uncooked meats, poultry and eggs the food handler must wash his hands and ensure that equipment and surfaces are cleansed and disinfected. Raw foods must also be stored away from cooked products.

It must be realised that some food poisoning organisms (clostridia) survive in soil and may be present on unwashed vegetables. This is the principal reason why vegetable preparation should be segregated from other activities in the kitchen, otherwise cross-contamination is likely.

9.3.2 Temperature control

Chapter 2 explains the physical requirements that have to be met if bacteria are to multiply to dangerous levels. Obviously it is sensible to provide conditions which are not favourable to rapid bacterial multiplication. The one factor that is most easily controlled by the food handler is the temperature of the food. If food preparation is arranged so as to reduce to a minimum the time that food (and particularly food containing meat, fish, milk and eggs) is allowed to spend in the danger zone 10–65°C (50–150°F) then the chances of food poisoning are significantly reduced. Indeed apart from the elimination of food poisoning bacteria at source (*i.e.* from the raw foods) good temperature control is the one single factor most likely to contribute to a drop in food poisoning.

Temperature control has several aspects including: the thawing of frozen food, the size of meat joints and poultry, the cooking, cooling and reheating of food and the temperature of food storage.

Thawing of frozen food

Although there is no need to thaw small food portions such as chops, or fish fillets before cooking, all frozen meat joints and poultry should be completely thawed before cooking commences. Clearly, the larger the joint of meat or size of poultry carcase the longer the thawing time will be. Thawing will also vary with the temperature at which it is carried out. Table 5 indicates thawing times for various sized turkeys at an ambient temperature of 15°C, as recommended by the British Turkey Federation.

However, thawing is usually most safely accomplished in a refrigerator. Care must always be taken in disposing of the drip from thawing meat and poultry as this may be contaminated with pathogenic bacteria.

Size of joints and poultry

When food is cooked by traditional methods heat arrives at the surface of the food by radiation and convection. Details of these processes are given in 9.4.1 and 9.4.2 below. As heat is transferred to the centre of the food, so it is stored and the temperature of the food rises. The speed at which a temperature increase will occur depends on three factors. (a) The thermal diffusivity of the food, *i.e.* the rate at which the food will conduct heat. This value is constant for a given food. (b) The temperature at which the outside of the food is raised to. Clearly the risk of charring limits this temperature. (c) The thickness of the food. There is a very rapid increase in cooking time as the thickness of the food increases, and so the risk that a sufficiently high, safe temperature may not be reached is greater, the larger the mass of food being cooked.

Various recommendations as to the safe maximum size for joints and poultry have been made. Joints of meat not exceeding 2·7 kg (6 lb) have been recommended by B. Hobbs and R. Gilbert in *Food Poisoning and Food Hygiene*. Such comparatively small joints are particularly important in the case of rolled joints where surface contamination will be rolled into the centre.

With regard to the size of poultry it would appear, from work done at the Birmingham College of Food and Domestic Arts, that even the largest turkeys commercially available can be cooked so as to reach a minimum internal temperature of 70°C (158°F). This temperature should ensure the destruction of salmonellae. This is always provided that frozen birds are correctly thawed first. See Table 5 below for recommendations for the cooking of various sized turkeys.

The cooking of food

Foods containing meat, fish and eggs should be so cooked as to ensure that the internal temperature reached is sufficiently high to destroy any vegetative food poisoning cells present. Relatively high temperature cooking is therefore to be preferred and for this reason some methods of cooking are inherently safer than others. Cooking by steam under pressure, roasting, grilling and frying are among the safest methods as a high temperature in the foods is achieved. Whereas boiling, braising and stewing raise the food to lower temperatures and therefore give a lower safety margin. For this reason meat which has been boiled, braised or stewed should never be cooled and reheated but used immediately after cooking.

The destruction of bacteria by heat is achieved by a combination of temperature and time. The higher the temperature the shorter the time necessary to kill the bacteria. In catering it is not practicable to express the amount of heat required for bacterial destruction using the parameters of both temperature and time, as equipment for producing the necessary heating and cooling reduction curves are unlikely to be available. Instead it is normal to express the heat required as a single centre temperature. A centre temperature of 70°C (158°F) can be considered satisfactory, except in the case of small articles of food such as individual meat pies. In such cases the temperature rise will be very rapid and a high temperature will be maintained for only a short time, therefore a centre temperature of 80–90°C (176–194°F) is more apropriate. The use of a meat thermometer can therefore be very helpful in ensuring the safe cooking of meat and poultry. Unfortunately, many such thermometers are not properly calibrated in °C or °F but simply record meat as being 'well done', 'rare' *etc.*

Some guidance to the temperature achieved during cooking can be gleaned from the appearance of the cooked meat. The red colouration of beef and lamb is due to the protein myoglobin. In pork and 'white' poultry meat the myoglobin level is much lower, therefore the meat is whiter. At 60°C the red myoglobin turns to brown meta-myoglobin and therefore the meat possesses a 'cooked' appearance. Certainly meat that appears reddish after cooking has not been raised to a sufficiently high temperature.

TABLE 5

Thawing and cooking of frozen turkeys

(From recommendations by the British Turkey Federation)

Oven ready weights	Minimum thawing time at room temp. or 15°C (59°F)	Minimum cooking times at 177°C (350°F) Gas Mark 4
20 lb	30 hours	3½ hours
25 lb	36 ,,	4½ ,,
30–35 lb	48 ,,	5–5½ ,,
40–45 lb	60 ,,	6–6½ ,,

Note: Giblets should be removed before cooking and the turkey should not be stuffed.

TABLE 6

Approximate oven temperatures and gas mark equivalents

	Gas mark
107°C (225°F)	¼
121°C (250°F)	½
134°C (275°F)	1
148°C (300°F)	2
162°C (325°F)	3
176°C (350°F)	4
190°C (375°F)	5
204°C (400°F)	6
218°C (425°F)	7
232°C (450°F)	8
245°C (475°F)	9
260°C (500°F)	10

The cooling and reheating of meat

Whilst adequate cooking will destroy the vegetative cells of food poisoning bacteria, bacterial spores will, for the most part, be unaffected (see 2.4). Because of the heat resistance of its spores *Cl. perfringens* is often found to be the cause of food poisoning where reheated meat and meat products are implicated. If all meat dishes were consumed immediately following cooking this form of food poisoning would be very rare indeed. The problem arises when such foods are allowed to cool slowly at warm ambient temperatures. During such conditions the spores germinate and rapid multiplication takes place. If the food is then 'warmed through' instead of being subjected to reheating above 70°C (158°F) the danger is compounded, as the numbers of bacteria multiply even further. For these reasons extra care must be taken with meat and poultry dishes which are not intended for immediate consumption. The prime need is for such food to be rapidly cooled immediately after cooking and this certainly cannot be achieved by standing food in a hot, steamy kitchen. The problem is that neither can the dish be placed in a traditional refrigerator as condensation and other problems will occur, possibly having a damaging effect on the other food stored. Ideally, one of the specially designed blast chillers should be used to lower the temperature of the food rapidly. Unfortunately, such equipment is very expensive and may be impracticable in the smaller food business. In this case the meat dish should be immediately removed to a cool well-ventilated room, and allowed to stand. Cooling will be enhanced if a good movement of air is maintained by the use of an electric recirculating fan (see 5.5.2).

Whatever means of preliminary cooling is used the meat must be sufficiently cooled so as to allow it to be placed in a refrigerator within $1\frac{1}{2}$ hours of cooking. This allows advantage to be taken of the lag phase of bacterial multiplication which will occur after high temperature cooking. During the lag phase little multiplication of pathogens will occur (see 2.3.1). If it is intended to reheat the dish at a later stage this must be done thoroughly. Soups and stews should be brought to the boil and allowed to simmer for 15 minutes and meat raised to a temperature of at least 70°C (158°F). On no account should meat or meat products be reheated more than once.

Post-cooking contamination is particularly serious as many harmless organisms which would compete for nutrients with pathogens would have been destroyed during cooking. In such circumstances the multiplication of food poisoning bacteria can be very rapid. This is another important reason to ensure that cooked food is kept well away from raw foods as well as from utensils and surfaces used for the preparation of raw foods.

9.3.3 The use of foods other than meat

Milk

Milk is sometimes supplied to catering premises in small churns or kits. It is important that these are stored under refrigeration and when empty, swilled out before being returned to the dairy for steam disinfection. Transparent plastic displays of milk, known as 'Whirlcools', were very popular at one time. Refrigerated milk is stored in these and continuously agitated by paddles within the machine. Unfortunately samples of milk from 'Whirlcools' were often found to be unsatisfactory when examined by the methylene blue test. Reasons for such failures include inadequate cleaning of the equipment, failure to maintain the milk below 4·5°C (40°F) or because of the practice of topping up with fresh milk instead of emptying every 24 hours.

The modern method of serving milk in the catering trade is the 'Milkpak'. This is a polythene bag of milk contained within a cardboard outer box. The 'Milkpak' is placed in a specially designed refrigerated unit and connected to a tap. Since the 'Milkpak' is disposed of when it is empty it might be expected to be an ideal system, but survey work in some areas has shown that satisfactory results are not always achieved in practice. The main problem would seem to be poor stock rotation at the point of catering sale, often made worse by less than daily production at the dairy. In addition, as few dairies produce 'Milkpaks' the production/delivery chain can be quite long. For these reasons such milk is not always as fresh as bottled milk and caterers should pay careful attention to stock rotation and the coding on 'Milkpaks' received. (See 12.2.5, proposed restrictions on sale of untreated milk.)

Cream and imitation cream
Cream is usually pasteurised and is therefore rarely associated with food poisoning. It is, however, a good medium for bacterial growth and care should be taken to avoid contaminating foods containing cream. Cream should be stored under refrigeration whilst awaiting service.

Imitation creams provide less suitable media for bacteria but organisms can draw nourishment from the foods decorated with such creams, *e.g.* cakes, trifles *etc.* (See 3.4.5.)

Eggs
Raw eggs can be contaminated with salmonellae, particularly duck eggs. For this reason they should be refrigerated and all equipment used in connection with eggs thoroughly cleaned and disinfected before being used for other foods.

Ice cream
Ice cream is required by law to be pasteurised and is therefore a very safe product. However, it can easily become contaminated if not handled correctly. A metal scoop is usually used to dispense loose ice cream and ice cream samples that fail the methylene blue test (a useful guide to the hygiene of the product) usually do so because of poor scoop hygiene. The correct procedure to ensure the cleanliness of the scoop is as follows:

(a) before the day's work commences immerse the scoop in boiling water for 3 minutes;

(b) the scoop should then be stored in either a well of cold tap water which is continuously replaced by a flow of clean water, or in a straight-sided jar of water which must be changed every half hour, irrespective of usage. In the latter case a suitable disinfectant may be added to the water.

9.4 COOKING METHODS

9.4.1 Convection heating

Convection heating is utilised in the traditional oven as well as in the hot cupboard. During convection, heat is transferred by the warmed air molecules to the surface of the food. The speed of cooking depends on the temperature of the air and the quantity of heated air that passes over the food during a given time. In a conventional oven this airflow is brought about by the expansion and consequent reduction in the density of the heated air, causing an upward draught. The flow of hot air and therefore the rapidity of heat transferred can be greatly increased by the incorporation of a fan in the oven. Thus, a forced-air convection oven will cook food significantly faster than a traditional oven (see 9.5.2). Heat transferred during convection will also increase if steam is introduced into the oven, as the latent heat in the steam will be released during its condensation on the food.

9.4.2 Radiation heating

Radiant heat is transmitted directly from the heat source to the food and travels in straight lines. Radiant heat has the advantage that, unlike heating by convection, it immediately begins to warm the food, but it can also more readily cause charring.

9.4.3 Conduction heating

Conducted heat is transferred from a heat source through a material directly in contact with that source. The heat that passes through the base of a saucepan from a gas burner or electric ring is an example of conducted heat. The ability of materials to conduct heat varies and is expressed as their thermal conductivity. Stainless steel is a poor conductor but has the advantage of not being subject to scale build-up. Even a very thin film of scale will seriously reduce the thermal conductivity of a material. A further reduction of heat transfer occurs during the heating of liquids due to the formation of a stationary or laminar layer of liquid near the surface of the cooking vessel. If this layer is broken up by stirring or through the boiling action of the liquid, heat transfer will be increased.

9.4.4 Steaming and pressure cooking

The use of steam at atmospheric pressure and a temperature of 100°C (212°F) releases a substantial amount of heat. This occurs as the steam condenses on the food and the latent heat of vaporisation is released. Steaming also has the advantage of reducing moisture loss in food. Steam under pressure is necessarily produced at a higher temperature and can be used to reduce cooking times and deal with tougher foods.

TABLE 7

The temperature of Steam at increased pressures

Pressure lb/sq. inch	Temp. °F
0	212
5	227
10	239
15	250
20	260

Such temperatures will be achieved only if the air in the vessel is effectively purged before the valve is closed off

9.4.5 Frying

Fat or oil can be raised to the comparatively high temperatures of 160–188°C (320–370°F) and can therefore be used for the rapid cooking of food. During frying part of the fat combines with the food and so imparts a distinctive flavour to the dish. Fats and oils have a limited life as cooking media. With repeated heating they undergo a reaction which leads to rancidity, giving rise to bitter flavours and acrid odours. In addition food residues which remain in the fat will continue to be heated and will eventually become charred. When this occurs the fat will darken and its smoke point will become lowered. This is the temperature at which it will give off smoke.

Well-designed fryers have an insulated cool zone into which food debris can fall and can remain without being repeatedly subjected to high temperatures. But even with a cool zone the fat must be strained and filtered at regular intervals (see 11.1.2).

9.4.6 Microwave cooking

Energy is supplied to the food by very high frequency electromagnetic waves which cause an increase in molecular motion resulting in heat generation. The microwave band ranges from 2 to 100 cm in wavelength but as this overlaps the frequency used in radar the catering frequency is restricted by the Post Office to 2450 MHz, *i.e.* 12 cm wavelength, to avoid interference with telecommunications.

The dielectric properties of foods influence the degree to which they will absorb microwaves. Foods whose electric properties are most absorbent of energy will be most readily heated by microwaves. As the electromagnetic waves enter the food the molecules tend to align themselves with the energy. Since the microwaves are changing polarity every half cycle the food molecules also change direction every half cycle, *i.e.* 4,900 million times a second. The friction caused between the molecules converts the microwave energy to heat. The maximum penetration of microwaves is between 4–5 cm ($1\frac{1}{2}$–2 inches) and beyond this the food will be cooked by conduction.

Microwaves are transmitted through materials like glass, china and paper, without heating them. This property is very useful when handling foods cooked in a microwave oven, as the containers remain cool. However, microwaves are reflected by metals, including aluminium foil, and therefore foil containers must not be used for foods to be cooked by microwaves (see 9.5.2).

9.5 COOKING EQUIPMENT

9.5.1 General considerations

When choosing cooking equipment the maintenance of hygiene must be an important consideration. The design should be simple, avoiding potential dirt traps. Where possible the appliance should be raised 30 cm (12 inches) from the floor and fitted with wheels to allow its movement for easy cleaning. The Gas Council issues annually a list of approved gas catering appliances and the Electricity Council also issue publications on electrical catering equipment. British Standards exist for both gas (BS 2512) and electrical equipment (BS 417). Encouraged by the European Catering Equipment Manufacturers' Association there is a movement towards the use of 'Gastronorm' standard modular sizes in catering equipment. In this system the interior dimensions of ovens, refrigerators, hot cupboards *etc.* are based on standard sized pans and trays. The Gastronorm system aids the efficient use of catering equipment.

9.5.2 Ovens

(a) *Oven range*
This general-purpose equipment comprises of an oven or ovens and a boiling top. The boiling top may include a griddle plate for direct cooking.

(b) *General-purpose oven*
In order to save floor space general-purpose ovens may be stacked one on top of another and separate facilities for boiling provided.

(c) *Forced-air convection oven*
In a conventional oven the hot air is carried to the top of the oven by convection currents. This heated air and steam passes over the food surface only once, before it leaves the oven via the vent. This method

gives a slow transfer of heat which can be increased only by raising the oven temperature, through the burning of more fuel. In a forced-air convection oven a fan is used to continually recirculate the hot gases. The rate of cooking can be regulated, by varying either the airflow or the temperature. The result is more rapid cooking, increased thermodynamic efficiency and the maintenance of an even temperature, allowing successful batch cooking.

(d) *Rotary oven*
In order to even out temperature variations ovens incorporating rotating shelves are sometimes employed.

(e)˙ *Pastry oven*
The baking of pastry requires accurate and even temperature control. To ensure this, pastry ovens are very shallow and are provided with accurate temperature control equipment. Pastry ovens are frequently stacked in tiers to save floor space.

Nowadays the forced-air convection oven is increasingly used for pastry cooking.

(f) *Automatic slow cooking oven*
Recently a new oven designed to cook meat at low temperatures and then hold it until required has appeared on the market. A temperature probe is inserted into the largest joint at the commencement of cooking and a cooking programme selected. When the required centre temperature is reached the oven switches to a non-cooking cycle which holds the meat until required, perhaps hours later. The advantages of this method are said to include an increase in nutritional value of the food and a reduction of shrinkage.

Tests carried out at the Central Public Health Laboratory, Colindale, have shown that, if operated in accordance with the manufacturer's instructions, this oven is no more hazardous than most conventional cooking systems. But strict adherence to the instructions is essential if vegetative pathogens are to be destroyed and spores of *Cl. perfringens* are to be prevented from rapidly multiplying. It is particularly important to note that the 4-hour holding period included in 'rare meat' programmes is essential from a food safety point of view and removal of the meat prior to the completion of the full programme could lead to dangerous levels of pathogens remaining in the food.

(g) *The steaming oven or steamer*
The supply of steam may be from an outside source and regulated by a valve or generated within the appliance. The cooking temperature is determined by the pressure at which the oven is operated. There are three main types of steaming oven. The atmospheric type, the low pressure steaming oven operating at a pressure of $\frac{1}{2}$ lb/sq. inch giving a tempera-

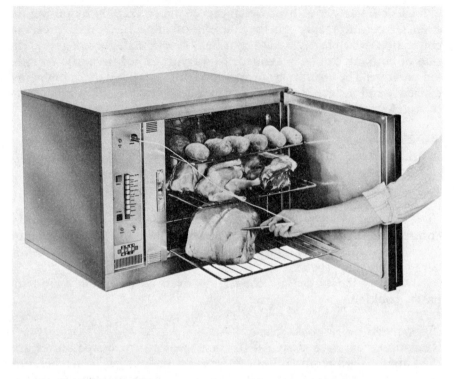

Fig. 11 Alto-Shaam 747 automatic slow cooking oven with centre temperature probe. (*Reproduced by courtesy of Rems Restuarant Equipment Machine Sales Ltd*)

ture of 102°C (216°F), and the true pressure steamer at 5 lb/sq. inch and a temperature of 108°C (226°F) (see 9.4.4).

Steam convection ovens have been developed to obtain the benefits of both steaming and forced-air convection cooking.

(h) *Microwave oven*

Microwave ovens are rated according to their cavity power, which is usually measured by heating a fixed quantity of water for a specific time and measuring the temperature of the heated water.

The cavity of the oven is constructed of mild steel and the dimensions of the cavity are critical as they need to be matched to the waveguide and magnetron characteristics. The door must be constructed to provide an adequate seal to prevent microwave leakage, even after prolonged use. British Standard BS 3456 requires that after the door has been opened and closed 100,000 times the leakage should not exceed 5 mW/cm². The door must also be fitted with three interlock switches to ensure that the opening of the door will switch off the oven. It must be possible to see through the door to gauge the progress of cooking and this is usually achieved by the provision of an aperture, covered with expanded metal

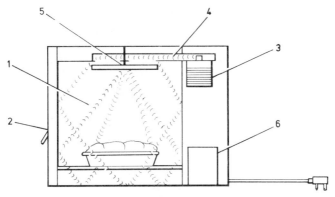

Fig. 12 Microwave cooker component identification

1. Cooking Cavity   2. The door
3. Magnetron   4. Waveguide
5. Mode stirrer   6. Power supply

(*Reproduced by kind permission of Thorn Domestic Appliances (Electrical) Ltd*)

mesh. The diameter of the holes is critical to the prevention of micro-wave leakage.

The magnetron is the unit that produces the microwaves through an interaction of electrical and magnetic fields. The average life of the magnetron is between 3,000 and 5,000 hours. During its life the power of the magnetron will gradually decline and slightly longer cooking cycles will be necessary. The magnetron is connected to the oven cavity by a metal duct known as the waveguide, as it directs the microwaves into the cavity. A metal stirrer is often incorporated just below the outlet from the waveguide. It rotates and its function is to scatter the microwave energy around the inside of the oven cavity. Failure to adequately scatter the microwaves would result in the production of standing waves of energy, causing hot and cold spots in the food. Some ovens also incor-porate a rotating turntable to aid even cooking. A cooling fan is neces-sary to maintain the magnetron at its optimum working temperature and to prevent condensation in the cavity. It is essential that the timer fitted to the oven is sufficiently accurate to deal with foods which require a very short cooking period.

Food must be placed above the base of the oven otherwise the lower surface of the food will be very unevenly cooked. The browning of foods can be a problem, especially small articles such as sausages, as these cook very quickly. Browning dishes are available. These are ceramic dishes with a tin-oxide coating to their lower surface. The dish is placed in the oven for a few minutes and then the food is put inside it. The hot surface of the dish sears the outside of the food and so browns it. To ensure even browning it is necessary to turn the food during cooking. Alternatively the cooked food may be browned under a grill.

The greater the density of the food the longer cooking will take and the quantity of food in the oven also influences cooking time. The cooking period increases with an increase in the quantity of food being heated. Composite foods composed of several ingredients having different densities can be difficult to cook in a microwave oven.

Some microwave units are provided with a defrost cycle to deal with frozen food. A microwave pulse occurs automatically every 30 seconds to steadily break down ice crystals. Ice crystals absorb microwaves much less readily than water in food does and therefore tend to form cold spots, whilst other areas become overheated. Short exposures to microwave energy allows the heat produced to be distributed throughout the food before the next pulse occurs. Where such a facility does not exist microwave cooking of frozen food should be carried out in two stages, to allow the heat to be adequately dispersed throughout the food.

Certain materials are unsuitable as containers for holding food to be cooked in a microwave oven. Untreated polystyrene will melt, as will the wax on waxed paper, and metal containers will reflect the microwave energy and cause damage to the magnetron.

The main advantage of microwave cooking is, of course, its speed and convenience in operation (see 9.4.6).

(i) *Combined microwave and forced-draught convection oven*
This type of oven is very useful for cooking frozen food straight from the freezer. The surface of the food is quickly thawed by the circulating hot air and ultimately given a cooked appearance whilst the interior is rapidly thawed and cooked by the microwaves.

(j) *Infra-red oven*
Infra-red ovens are usually heated by tungsten filaments in quartz tubes. Heat is radiated directly onto food placed beneath the filaments, whilst food above the heat source is warmed by convection and conduction. A fan draws air over the surfaces of the food to prevent overheating. Some infra-red ovens incorporate a refrigeration compressor so that the air in the circulation system can be chilled. This reduces further the risk of charring the surface of the food and allows the rapid thawing of frozen food without risk of burning. The principal advantage of this type of oven is that it allows a rapid warm-up to a high temperature and can be used for many cooking processes.

9.5.3 Boiling equipment

(a) *Boiling tables*
These are used where the boiling space provided on the top of ranges is inadequate or where traditional ranges are not in use.

(b) *Boiling pans*
Boiling pans are used for large quantities of liquid or for boiling batches

of vegetables. They are jacketed containers indirectly heated by air, water or steam. Water to the pans is provided by a swivel arm or direct connection. The pan is emptied either via a pouring lip, by tilting on pivots, or through a stopcock.

9.5.4 Frying equipment

Shallow fat frying is carried out in a pan or on a griddle, whilst deep fat fried food is cooked immersed in 10–15 cm (4–6 inches) of fat or oil. Deep fat fryers are provided with wire trays and stands for drawing off fat (see 9.4.5).

Shallow tilting frypans (Bratt pans) are used extensively in Europe and are very versatile. They may be used for boiling, frying, stewing or braising and can be tilted to allow easy emptying (see Fig. 13).

9.5.5 Grilling equipment

Grilling food involves the use of radiant heat applied from above, in the traditional grill, or a salamander can be used which is capable of applying a flame direct to the top of the food.

9.5.6 Holding units

(a) *Hot cupboards*
These cupboards are heated by gas or electricity and should be capable of maintaining an internal temperature of 70–85°C (160–185°F). They are intended for plate warming and short-term holding of hot food, and must never be used for reheating foods, especially meat.

(b) *Bains-Marie*
Bains-Marie are heated wells which are filled with hot water. Vessels containing cooked food are placed within the well so as to maintain the appropriate temperature. There are several designs but as with the hot cupboard the essential requirement is that the food must be maintained above 70°C (160°F).

9.6 WASHING-UP

Although often looked on as a menial task, washing-up is a vital part of the catering operation. No matter how hygienically food preparation and cooking is carried out it is still very necessary to ensure that the crockery and cutlery used is clean and wholesome. Indeed, the standards of cleanliness of such articles is one of the few indicators that the customer has to enable him to assess the standards of hygiene and care achieved in the kitchen.

9.6.1 Manual washing-up

Satisfactory washing-up by hand requires the provision of two sinks. The first is used to physically remove the dirt and grease and the second

Fig. 13 Shallow tilting frypan or Bratt pan. (*Photograph supplied by courtesy of Zanussi C.L.V. Systems Ltd*)

to disinfect the items to ensure a further reduction in bacterial loading. The procedure should include the following points. Firstly, gross contamination must be removed by scraping food scraps *etc.* into a waste container. This reduces the load on the first sink which should contain hot water of 50-60°C (122-140°F) and an appropriate detergent. The crockery and utensils are washed-up in this sink and then loaded into baskets. Care must be taken to ensure that the pieces are not touching one another, as this will prevent adequate heat-treatment in the second sink. The second sink should contain water at a temperature of 82°C (180°F) and the baskets of crockery and cutlery are lowered into this water. The baskets should remain in the water for $1\frac{1}{2}$–2 minutes. Upon removal the items will air dry, so avoiding the possibility of recontamination by the use of a tea-towel.

The only satisfactory way of achieving the necessary water temperature in the second sink is by the application of local heat. Insulated sinks heated by gas or electricity are usually referred to as 'sterilising' sinks although disinfecting sinks would be more correct. Where a heated sink is not available, the two sinks should be marked 'wash' and 'rinse'. A suitable cationic disinfectant should be used in the 'wash' sink in conjunction with a non-ionic detergent (see 6.4.1 page 65). Rinsing should be carried out in the second sink with clean water at as high a temperature as possible.

Properly carried out dishwashing by hand can achieve good results, but all too often it is skimped and insufficient attention is given to maintaining detergent strength in the first sink and adequate heat treatment in the second. Furthermore, it is a process that has high labour costs and is slow; probably only 600 mixed pieces an hour can be dealt with satisfactorily. For these reasons mechanical dishwashing has found favour in all but the smallest establishments.

9.6.2 Mechanical dishwashing

There are various basic types of mechanical dishwashers.

(a) *Brush type machines*

This type of machine is only occasionally encountered. A motor drives rotating nylon brushes in a sink full of hot water and detergent. Plates are held between the brushes and cups are placed over the ends of the brushes. Cutlery is placed in racks and immersed in the sink, the agitation of the water by the brushes providing the mechanical action necessary for cleaning. Disinfection is then carried out in a heated second sink. The brushes are good at removing hard greasy deposits and the equipment's lack of sophistication makes servicing and dosing relatively easy, but it is a process requiring a high input of labour and is not much quicker than manual washing-up.

(b) *Agitated water machines*

These are open sinks with impellers arranged in the sides of the units. The dirty items are placed in the sinks in baskets and washed by the turbulent action of the water. This is followed by disinfection in a second heated sink. Like the brush-type washers these machines are now obsolete.

(c) *Jet action machines*
In jet action dishwashers the tableware is washed by the action of high pressure sprays. To ensure maximum efficiency the work needs to be loaded at right angles to the jets, and jet design and positioning is crucial to the satisfactory operation of the machine. There are several varieties of jet dishwashers:

(i) Small machines
In this type of equipment the racks of tableware are put into and taken out of the machine by hand. The cleaning cycle comprises of a hot water and detergent wash at 60°C (140°F) followed by a rinse at 82°C (180°F). Three main designs of small dishwashers are available. They are given below in order of increasing capacity.

Washer with integral rack system. These machines are similar to the domestic dishwashers available, having racks fitted inside the machine. As the racks are a fitment they cannot be loaded or unloaded when the dishwasher is in use. Rates up to 50 meals/hour can be dealt with by such a machine.

Hood machines. Separate racks are used and can be loaded or unloaded whilst the machine is in use. They have a semi-circular hood which shuts down over the top of the work. The jets operate from beneath the work and the downward washing action comes from water jets bounced off the inside of the hood.

Door machines. The work is loaded into trays which can be removed from the machine. Jets are positioned above and below the work. There are two main variants of this type of dishwasher. Firstly, the straight-through machine where trays are put in through one door and taken out through a door on the opposite side, and a corner version where the entry and exit doors are at right angles. This latter arrangement can save considerable space in a small kitchen. Such equipment can cope with up to 300 meals/hour.

(ii) Conveyor machines
If a rate of 300 meals/hour is exceeded then a machine with a conveyor feed will be necessary. Such machines have a washing process that occurs over several stages. This is necessary to avoid the heavy soiling of the detergent that would occur during a high throughput of dirty tableware. All or only some of the following stages may be present in conveyor machines, depending on their size.

Pre-wash section. Gross soiling is removed with used water from the washing and rinsing stage. The temperature of the water in this section does not need to be high but a good jet pressure is important. The waste is discharged to the outlet via a strainer.

Main wash section. This section utilises the combined action of detergent and water pressure to carry out the main washing of the tableware.

Power rinse. Water at a temperature of 70°C (158°F) is used to remove detergent and any starchy material still adhering to the tableware.

Hot rinse. A fine spray of water at 82°C (180°F) is used to disinfect the work and ensure rapid dry off.

Air drying section. This section is only necessary in the treatment of plastic ware, as plastic does not retain heat long enough to air dry.

(iii) Rotary machines
These are high rate machines that incorporate a conveyor that runs from the outlet of the machine to the inlet. The clean work is conveyed to a table where unloading takes place. The empty rack is then refilled with dirty crockery *etc.* and placed on the conveyor, which takes it into the machine.

(iv) Flight machines
In very large establishments the speedy loading of the machine is a problem. In the very largest equipment trays are not used, but instead the conveyor is constructed of a continuous train of v-shaped pockets, into which the crockery can be placed while the conveyor continues to move. These 'flight machines' are free standing and the conveyor is carried in the open for a few feet to allow handling of the tableware. Two operators are needed, one to load and the other to unload. The work passes through the following compartments: pre-wash, main wash, second wash, rinse and hot water spray. As the rinse section is in continuous operation there are separate detergent and rinse tanks.

9.6.3 Detergents used in machine dishwashing
A high foaming agent would interfere with jet action, therefore the use of products having low foaming characteristics is important. Alkali-based detergents are effective in removing animal and vegetable fats and therefore various mixtures of sodium carbonate, sodium metasilicate and trisodium phosphate are used. Low foaming wetting agents may be incorporated as well as a chlorinating agent to remove tannin stains from teacups. In hard-water areas such a detergent may react with calcium and magnesium salts, causing scale formation in the jets and a white hydroxide film on crockery and glassware. In such areas water softening is needed or sequestering agents will need to be added to the detergent.

Great care is necessary in detergent selection where very fine china is in use, especially where the decoration is applied over the glaze. Sodium aluminate is often incorporated in detergents designed to protect the glaze on fine china.

To avoid hard-water 'streaks' on plates and glasses a wetting agent may be included in the rinse water to ensure that almost all the moisture drains away before it has a chance to dry on the surface.

The detergent solution is usually recirculated in mechanical dishwashers. Strainers are fitted to prevent large food debris blocking the jets but fat and small particles will pass through the strainers. The strainers must be cleaned regularly and where the machine does not incorporate a pre-wash section food residue should be rinsed off with warm water before loading the machine.

In many small and medium-sized machines the rinse water drains into the detergent tank, excess liquid being lost over a weir to the drain outlet. For this reason it is essential to add detergent to the tank regularly to maintain its strength and also to periodically drain and refill the tank. In fully automatic dishwashers the strength of detergent is electronically controlled. The conductivity of the solution is monitored by a probe mounted in the detergent tank. When a conductivity change is detected, due to a drop in detergent concentration below a pre-set level, the control unit activates a detergent injection device.

9.6.4 Faults encountered in mechanical dishwashing

Greasy crockery
This results from a failure to emulsify all the fat on the tableware. It is due to either insufficient wash water temperature or inadequate detergent dosing. However, care must be taken not to raise the water temperature too much otherwise the removal of certain foods will become even more difficult. A temperature of 60°C (140°F) is about right.

Starch deposits
These are from potatoes and puddings and are particularly likely where some delay has occurred between eating and washing up. Starch is not emulsifiable and an efficient oxidising agent in the detergent is essential.

Chalky crockery
This condition is due to hard-water carbonates or the reaction between alkaline detergents and hard water. Water-softening equipment or a detergent that does not precipitate hardness salts is essential.

Spotted crockery
During rinsing and air drying spotting may occur due to:

(a) over-rinsing in hard water. This removes the surface active agent in the detergent and allows droplet formation, or
(b) inefficient rinsing leaving starch particles *etc.* on the crockery.

Tableware that will not air dry
This can be due to an insufficiently high temperature during the final rinse. A temperature of 82°C (180°F) is necessary, but air drying will always be difficult if washed crockery is stacked in a room of high ambient temperature and humidity.

To achieve the best results from mechanical dishwashers good supervision and maintenance is necessary, as well as accurate thermometers to indicate the temperatures of the wash and final rinse water.

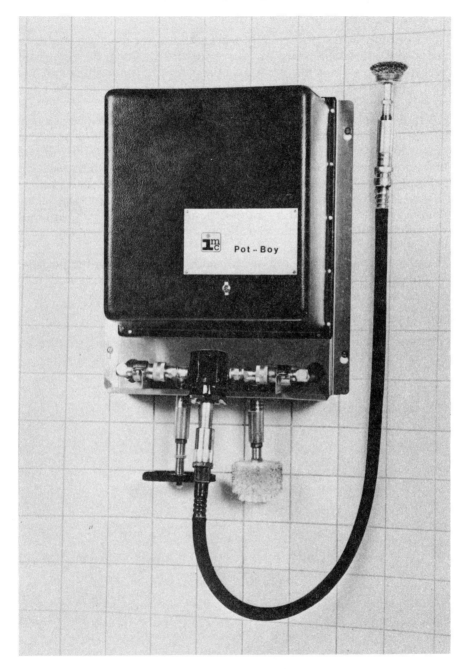

Fig. 14 Rotary pan scrubber. (*Photograph courtesy of Imperial Machine Co. (Peelers) Ltd*)

9.6.5 Pot washing

This is usually achieved manually and in all but the smallest establishments separate facilities are necessary for pot washing. These should consist of deep sinks to accommodate the pans, one for washing and one for rinsing. To assist manual pot washing, rotary pan scrubbers are available, for positioning near the sinks.

A mobile dip tank has been developed to allow the extended soaking of heavily soiled items such as oven tops, baking trays and pots and pans, whilst keeping the pot-washing sinks free for the washing of less dirty equipment. The dip tank can be placed in any convenient position and is provided with a drain cock to allow it to be emptied over a suitable gulley. It is used with a solution of caustic soda or a proprietary decarboniser and can be heated by an electric immersion heater. Overnight soaking of articles will remove stubborn deposits of carbon with little physical work.

Automatic pan washers are on the market and work on the pressure jet principle. Such equipment has wash and rinse sections and may incorporate an extended washing period of up to 15 minutes.

9.6.6 Glass washing

This is often undertaken separately because of the fragile nature of glassware and the possibility of smearing (see 10.2.4).

Chapter 10

THE LICENSED TRADE

The changes in the licensed trade over the past twenty years have been considerable. Most noticeable has been the move towards pressurised brewery conditioned beer, although there has been an orchestrated consumer resistance to this trend, leading to 'real ale from the wood' again appearing in many public houses. In addition the public house has become an accepted place for a meal, as well as a drink. All over the country publicans offer meals ranging from bar snacks to three-course lunches. It is this trend that has caused most food hygiene problems as many premises, poorly suited for food preparation, have been pressed into this use (see 10.1.4).

10.1 THE PREMISES

10.1.1 The cellar

The correct storage of draught beer is important if the product is to retain its quality. The optimum temperature range for beer storage is 13–15°C (55–60°F) and therefore some means of cooling the cellar may be required in the summer and heating may well be necessary in the winter. Temperature control is usually less important in below-ground cellars where temperature variation is not so extreme. In above-ground cellarage adequate insulation of the doors and walls will help to avoid undesirable temperature fluctuations.

Beer is sensitive to odour and can easily become tainted; it is therefore essential that the cellar is kept in a hygienic condition. The floor must be easy to clean and sloped to a trapped gully or sump containing an electric float pump discharging to the sewer. A tap and hosepipe are required to allow washing down in the event of beer spillage. The water in the gully or sump must not be allowed to stagnate and the cellar should not be used for the storage of strong-smelling cleaning materials.

A granolithic surface is usually the most appropriate floor finish in the cellar as it is sufficiently hardwearing to resist the impact of barrels *etc*. Special protection may need to be given to the floor where barrels are delivered via a chute.

The external angles of cellar walls also require protection, as may other wall areas subject to heavy wear. The walls must be kept clean and this can be a particular problem in below-ground cellars, where penetrating dampness and mould growth are common. If mould is allowed to develop unchecked it may be responsible for airborne infection of the beer, giving cloudiness and off-flavours. If the dampness is severe then there is little alternative but to damp-proof (tank) the cellar to render it waterproof. In other cases walls may be painted with an oil-based paint incorporating a mould inhibitor (see 4.2.2 page 42). The ceiling should receive similar treatment. Small areas of mould may be washed clean with a weak bleach solution.

The cellar should be adequately ventilated, as this will reduce dampness and mould growth. Ventilation openings must be kept free of obstruction. Cellar lighting should be provided by moisture-proof electrical fittings because of the high humidity level.

The stillages in a cellar are often constructed of brick, concrete or stone but movable tubular stillages make cellar cleaning easier. A sink with a hot and cold water supply must be provided in the cellar for the washing of beer taps *etc*.

10.1.2 The bottle store

This is often separate from the beer cellar. Stock should be arranged so that the principle of first in, first out can be applied and a container provided for the safe storage of broken bottles.

10.1.3 The bar servery

It is essential that the bar service area is well equipped and organised if the dispensing of drinks is to proceed efficiently and hygienically. Sufficient space must be available and the area kept uncluttered, with adequate provision being made for empty and broken bottles and glasses. The floor behind the bar must be comfortable, easy to clean and non-slip. Vinyl/aluminium-oxide sheeting is often specified for such areas.

A double sink or a single sink and glass washing machine is required, unless washing-up is carried out at a central point. In addition, a wash hand basin must be provided in a convenient position for bar staff. Shelving provided for glassware must be constructed of a material that is easy to clean, as shelving can soon become tacky and requires frequent cleaning.

The ventilation of the bar servery is important, as quantities of cigarette smoke must be dealt with. Unless food is actually cooked in the bar area, when local ventilation is necessary, the extraction system should draw air away from the bar.

The lighting in bars is often subdued, but in the service area it must be sufficient to allow the service of drinks and the washing of glasses to be carried out efficiently.

10.1.4 Food preparation areas

In many public houses the preparation of food has grown without sufficient thought being given to considerations of food hygiene. This has led to food being prepared under poor conditions and frequently to the use of the licensee's domestic kitchen for the preparation of food for sale. This latter situation is never satisfactory, as domestic kitchens are often used for purposes not appropriate to areas where food is prepared for the public, *e.g.* laundering and the feeding of pets. Furthermore, such use of domestic kitchens brings them within the scope of the Food Hygiene (General) Regulations, 1970, and subject to routine inspection; a situation not always welcomed by the licensee. It is best to keep domestic and business food preparation separate; to mix the two causes problems for all concerned.

The exact area required for food preparation will depend upon the menu. If only sandwiches or finger snacks are available it may be possible to set aside an area in the bar servery for such limited preparation to be carried out. Where knife and fork meals are served a separate and properly equipped kitchen is required.

For details concerning general catering hygiene see Chapter 9.

10.1.5 Sanitary accommodation

In the past sanitary accommodation for the customer at licensed premises has been very primitive. Even today the facilities all too often consist of the minimum of sanitary fittings, a wash hand basin supplied with cold water only and no soap or means of hand drying.

Vandalism is a problem in this area and one not readily resolved. The more easily the licensee can keep a watchful eye on the public lavatories the better and for this reason, as well as for the convenience of customers, the sanitary accommodation should be contained within the premises. Where this is not possible a covered way should be provided to link the toilets to the main building.

Adequate ventilation is necessary to prevent the build-up of foul odours and to reduce condensation, which is often a problem in such areas. An intervening ventilated space must be provided between the sanitary accommodation and bars or other food rooms.

The local authority can require a sufficient number of sanitary conveniences to be provided for customers at licensed premises (Public Health Act, 1936—Section 89). A standard frequently applied is given below.

TABLE 8

Provision of sanitary accommodation for the public

	Male	Female
W.C.s	1 per 100 up to 400 then 1 per 250 or part thereof	2 per 100 up to 200 then 1 per 100 or part thereof
Urinals	1 per 25	—

(From B.S.C.P. 3 Chapter VII, 1950)

Guidance on the number of customers who can safely use the premises may be obtained from the Fire Prevention Officer.

Staff sanitary accommodation must comply with The Sanitary Conveniences Regulations, 1964, and The Washing Facilities Regulations, 1964 (see 12.1.4). Where such accommodation is used by both the public and staff, and more than 10 persons are regularly employed to work on the premises, the number of water closets and wash basins must be increased by one for both males and females.

10.2 THE PRACTICES

10.2.1 The handling of beer

There are two basic types of draught beer supplied to public houses, cask-conditioned or sediment beer and stabilised or brewery-conditioned beer. Upon receipt at the licensed premises, cask-conditioned beer must be put on a stillion and left undisturbed for at least 24 hours. This 'fining period' is to allow sedimentation to take place, since the yeast used in fermentation at the brewery has not been completely removed, and serving too early would result in cloudy beer. The yeast also causes secondary fermentation and the production of carbon dioxide which determines the 'condition' of the beer. Too much carbon dioxide will make the beer lively and difficult to serve, whilst too little will make it flat.

When the beer has settled following delivery the cask should be tapped (the best time for tapping will vary with different beers). Tapping involves the insertion of a tap into the cask and it is vitally important that the tap used is thoroughly clean. A period of, perhaps, between 6 and 24 hours is allowed to elapse following tapping before the cask is vented. A vent in the top of the cask is opened and a 'spile' inserted. When a cask is in use the spile must be eased to allow air to replace the beer as it is withdrawn. Wooden spiles should only be used once; spiles made of impervious material should be cleaned and disinfected before being re-used. Whenever a cask becomes empty it should be sealed without delay.

The quality of cask-conditioned beer depends very much on the way it is handled in the cellar and the care taken by the licensee. Airborne mould spores gaining access through the vent can be a serious problem, causing cloudy and poor quality beer. This can be avoided by the connection of the vent to a carbon dioxide line, allowing this gas to enter the cask instead of air from the cellar.

Wooden casks, lined with pitch, are the traditional containers for beer, but cask-conditioned beer is now usually supplied in stainless steel or aluminium casks, as these are much easier to clean.

Stabilised beers are filtered at the brewery and carbonated to the necessary level, before being put into sterile kegs. Such beer can be served immediately after delivery and connection. The fining and venting procedures associated with cask-conditioned beers are thus avoided, as are most of the problems of incorrect handling in the cellar. Stabilised beer may be held at relatively high ambient temperatures, for example in the bar, and cooled prior to serving by an in-line cooler. A top pressure of carbon dioxide or compressed air is used to dispense stabilised beer.

Stabilised beers are delivered in metal kegs. Kegs have a single aperture to which the beer and gas lines are connected by mechanical means and not by friction, as in the case of a cask.

Although most draught beer is supplied in casks or kegs, bulk deliveries in tankers are made to premises where a high volume of sales justifies this. In such premises bulk storage tanks are provided. Bulk tank storage is normally associated with stabilised beer but in some areas sediment beers may be handled in this way. Disposable plastic bag linings may be used in the tank in the case of stabilised beer and this eliminates the need to clean and sterilise the tank between deliveries. In other cases the stainless steel tanks are cleaned via an access hatch, and this cleaning should be carried out as near to refilling time as possible.

The return of overspill beer from drip trays to stock is an objectionable and illegal practice. The use of oversized glasses and measured beer pulls eliminates overspill and reduces spillage behind the bar. The only beer that may be suitable for re-use once it has been drawn from a cask, is that drained from the pipes before cleaning. Such beer must be filtered through filter paper and examined for clarity before being returned to stock.

10.2.2 Dispensing drinks

When serving bottled beers and other drinks the bottle neck must not be immersed in the drink, as this can introduce contamination. It is also undesirable to serve draught beer by allowing the dispense tap to be partially submerged in the drink whilst the glass is filled. Dispense taps quickly build up with yeast and contamination of the beer can occur.

Fruit juice concentrates should only be dispensed from stainless steel or plastic pourers. Chemical poisoning has resulted from fruit juice served through chrome-plated copper pourers.

Optics must be kept clean, especially the releasing arms, and a regular check made for signs of corrosion. The hand operation of optics is more hygienic than the employment of used glasses to lift the releasing arms.

10.2.3 The cleaning of beer lines

The introduction of transparent plastic and nylon pipework has made the inspection and cleaning of beer pipes much easier than it was. The pipework must be cleaned at least once a week.

Cleaning is carried out by drawing a quantity of suitable detergent solution through the system, followed by cold water to rinse away traces of the cleaning fluid. In keg systems the keg is disconnected and a connection is made to a cleaning bottle containing detergent solution.

The beer tap in the bar is opened and gas from the carbon dioxide cylinder forces the cleansing solution through the pipework. The detergent may need to be left in the pipes to soak, before the cleaning bottle is refilled with water and rinsing of the pipework carried out. The installation of a ring main enables the cleaning of several beer lines to be carried out at one time. In some premises a stirrup pump is used instead of gas pressure, in which case the cleaning solution and rinse water is pumped from buckets and not from a cleaning bottle.

An alternative method of cleaning a keg system is to use sponge pellets instead of detergent. The keg is disconnected and the end of the beer line placed in a bucket. The pellet is inserted in the pipe at the dispense end and the pipe connected to a cold water tap. The water pressure forces the pellet along the pipework and out into the bucket. This process is repeated several times.

Where beer lines are in use with beer engines the cleaning solution will be drawn out of a bucket and not from a cleaning bottle. Careful cleaning of the beer engine must be carried out before pulling detergent solution through the system. Beer engines must be stripped down for cleaning, otherwise accumulations of yeast will occur in them.

The beer taps inserted in casks require careful cleaning and this is best done by boiling or soaking in a detergent solution. Keg fittings also soon become dirty and require soaking and brushing to remove dirt.

Automatic beer line cleaning systems are available. This equipment automatically flushes the pipework with clean water, and this is followed by a detergent soak and three rinses. An automatic system can utilise hot and cold water or a cold supply only.

10.2.4 Glass washing

Hygienic glass washing is an essential operation at any licensed premises. In a busy bar glass washing may be skimped if the facilities are not available to do it quickly and well. A fundamental requirement is to have sufficient glasses available at each bar.

One of the problems associated with the washing of beer glasses is that the head of beer is affected by minute traces of the foaming agents found in many detergents. Even thorough rinsing of the glass may leave sufficient traces of the chemical to destroy the head of any beer served in it. For this reason many liquid detergents cannot be used for glass washing and the alternative specialist detergents are very expensive. This sometimes results in dirty glasses being 'washed' in plain water. In soft water areas alkaline detergents can be used, but they are unsuitable if the water is hard, unless water-softening equipment is installed (see 6.4.1).

Glass washing can be carried out using two sinks. One method is to use the first sink for a detergent wash with a suitable detergent and the second to immerse the glasses in hot water at 82°C (180°F) to effect disinfection. The difficulty in maintaining the necessary water temperature in the second sink ensures that this method is rarely used. An alternative two-sink method of glass washing is to wash the glassware in the first sink in a hot combined detergent/disinfectant solution and then rinse in the second sink.

The use of glass-washing machines means that only one sink is required in the bar area. Most glass washers in use rely on the action of revolving brushes to clean the glassware, each glass being manually held in position during the cleaning process. A large number of different machines of this type are available and those with a separate rinsing chamber are to be preferred. Dregs should be disposed of via the sink before glass washing is commenced. The correct detergent/disinfectant solution must be used and this is often supplied in tablet form. A regular check should be made to ensure that the detergent has not been expended. In addition, the brushes must be kept clean and replaced as necessary.

If properly used such brush-action glass washers can produce very good results but they do rely entirely on the thoroughness of the operator who controls the whole process, including the duration of the cleaning cycle. An alternative to the brush-action machine is an automatic glass washer which utilises high pressure water jets to wash, rinse and disinfect a rack full of glasses. The whole cleaning cycle takes two minutes or less and produces excellent results.

If glasses need to be polished disposable paper cloths should be used.

Chapter 11

TAKEAWAY FOOD PREMISES

The rapid rise of the takeaway food shop must be obvious to even the most casual observer. Such premises provide reasonably priced meals for people in a hurry, and this appears to be a growing market.

This form of catering also offers the proprietor many advantages. He can keep his staff costs to a minimum, neither a dining area nor dining furniture is required and there is no washing-up of customers' crockery and cutlery. It is hardly surprising that many people with limited capital venture into the takeaway trade.

Like all branches of the food industry different takeaway trades bring with them their individual food hygiene problems. The range of takeaway premises is now so large that all varieties cannot be individually considered in this volume. Instead, some of the more important takeaway trades are considered here and in many other cases Chapter 9, Catering Premises, together with Part 1, will provide guidance on the hygiene measures that should be taken.

All takeaway premises which cook meat or fish dishes for sale are required to be registered with the local authority under the provisions of The Food and Drugs Act, 1955—Section 16. The local authority may refuse or cancel registration if they are not satisfied with the hygiene standards achieved or if they believe the premises to be unsuitable for such food preparation. There is a right of appeal to a magistrates' court should registration be refused or revoked.

At the time of writing the Institution of Environmental Health Officers is preparing, in conjunction with trade associations, a code of practice for takeaway food premises, and this is likely to be a very useful food hygiene guide for the trade.

11.1 FRIED FISH AND CHIP SHOPS

Fried fish is the original British takeaway food. Charles Dickens refers to a 'fried fish warehouse' in *Oliver Twist* (1838), and from humble beginnings the fish and chip trade has grown into a national institution.

11.1.1 The equipment

The frying range
This is the most significant piece of equipment and basically consists of a number of cooking pans and a combustion chamber, fitted in a welded

steel frame. Chip storage and scoop boxes are provided and fitted with grids through which fat can drain back into the cooking pans. The chip storage box is heated, as are glass-fronted cabinets used for the holding of cooked fish, pies, *etc.* Ranges are available in many sizes and are usually heated by gas, although electricity or oil may be used.

There are three basic types of frying range:

The counter range over which the customers are served. Extraction ducts run below the floor to a suitable flue.

The wall range is not part of the counter but instead it is sited against a wall, with use being made of an existing chimney flue for fume extraction.

The island range is only installed in very busy premises. The frier works on one side of the range and the cooked food is removed from the other side by serving staff.

Whichever range is installed it must be maintained in a clean condition and regularly serviced to ensure its efficiency and safety. The chip and fish storage boxes, grids and utensils must be cleaned at the end of each frying session. Cooking pans require emptying several times a year as minute food particles will form a thin sediment at the base of the pan and burn during cooking, scorching the fat. To clean, the emptied pans should be filled with hot water and washing soda added. This cleaning mixture should be boiled for at least 15 minutes and then the pans rinsed out.

The extraction system

Except in the case of electrically heated ranges which produce no products of combustion, the extraction system must deal with both combustion gases and cooking vapours. The cooking vapours comprise of quantities of steam and droplets of frying media.

It is of very great importance that the extraction system operates satisfactorily, for not only does this avoid unpleasant working conditions within the shop but a poor extraction system can be a fire hazard and cause considerable nuisance to people in the neighbourhood. New installations are likely to require approval under clean air legislation and early discussions should take place with the local Environmental Health Department if a new range is to be installed.

In counter and island ranges the combustion gases and cooking fumes may be removed in the same or in separate ducts. Twin ducting is always to be preferred as the combustible oil droplets are kept away from the hot combustion products.

In an extraction system the fat and oil are collected in a sump, whilst the vapours enter a stack and are propelled into the atmosphere by a fan unit. The sump must be cleaned out at least once a week.

When wall ranges are installed existing chimney flues are often used and a condenser box provided behind the range. In such cases extraction fans are often not fitted, reliance being placed on the draught created by hot combustion products passing up the flue. With electrically heated ranges there are no combustion products and therefore a fan must be installed. When existing chimney flues are used they should be fitted with a flue liner.

The incorporation of a grease filter in the extraction system will considerably reduce the amount of volatiles reaching the main duct. A grease filter will also lessen the risk of fire and the possibility of nuisance from cooking smells. In addition, an activated carbon filter may be incorporated behind the grease filter. Any filters will require frequent cleaning and the ducting itself must be examined and cleaned every six months (see 4.3.2).

Potato peelers
These machines are usually electrically operated and consist of a carborundum-lined chamber, and a disc also lined with carborundum. The disc rotates, pushing the potatoes against the rough surfaces. Cold water is sprayed into the chamber to remove dirt and scrapings. When the mechanical peeling operation is completed the chamber door is opened and the potatoes discharged into a container. Some peeling by hand, as well as the manual removal of eyes, will still be necessary.

The potato peeler must be cleaned daily in accordance with the manufacturer's instructions. In floor-mounted peelers an interceptor tank is often included in the pedestal. In other types an interceptor for peelings must be provided alongside the peeler or in an inspection chamber or gully situated in the yard. Whatever arrangements are made the interceptor must be emptied and cleaned regularly, otherwise the peelings will begin to ferment.

Potato chipping machines
The hand-operated plunger type chipper can be used for small quantities of chips. In most premises, however, an electrically operated chipping machine will be required. Potato chipping machines are potentially dangerous and must be cleaned strictly in accordance with the manufacturer's instructions. Once a day, hot water should be poured through the working parts whilst they are in motion and once a week the equipment should be dismantled for more thorough cleaning.

11.1.2 The processes
Fish preparation
Filleted fish are dipped in a batter mix, seasoning may be added, and the fish are then cooked in the fryer and stored in a heated display box until required.

Very few fish friers buy their fish whole and then prepare them on their own premises. Almost always ready filleted fish, fresh or frozen, are purchased from the wholesaler. If the fish is fresh it should be delivered to the premises in ice and stored at the fish and chip shop under refrigeration (see 14.2).

In the case of frozen fish fillets these are often supplied in blocks, which must be stored in a freezer. Thawing is usually accomplished by leaving the block out overnight. The thawing temperature must not be too high otherwise decomposition of the fish may commence. Commercial electric thawing equipment or 'thawing boxes' are available.

Thawed fish must be used straightaway or kept under chilled conditions until required. An alternative method sometimes used is to only partially thaw the fish and then fry when the fillets can be removed from the block. In such cases adjustments need to be made to the cooking time of the fish.

The preparation of potato chips
Potatoes inevitably bring with them a certain amount of soil and debris. Therefore, they should not be stored in a food preparation area but in a potato store set aside for that purpose. The ideal store would provide dark but dry and airy conditions. The effects of frost must be avoided but so too must warm conditions, for if the storage temperature is over 9°C (49°F) potatoes will sprout readily. Potatoes must be kept away from strong-smelling substances and food, including raw fish.

After peeling and chipping, potatoes are usually stored in tubs of water, to which an antioxidant has been added to prevent discoloration. The potatoes are drained prior to frying.

Many friers blanch chips by frying until they are cooked through, but only slightly coloured. These blanched chips are then quickly browned in the fryer when an order is placed by the customer.

Most friers use raw potatoes but space, equipment and time can be saved if peeled potatoes or peeled and chipped potatoes are bought in. Ready prepared potatoes and chips are sold containing antioxidant to prevent discoloration.

Care of the frying media (see also 9.4.5)
Although animal fats may be used in some regions, there has been a considerable move towards the use of vegetable oils. Animal fats have the disadvantage of a low smoke point and they also tend to break down rather quickly. When fats or oils are continually used they will begin to oxidate rapidly and this produces smoke, acrid fumes, and poor flavours in the food. The frying media also becomes dark and is subject to frothing.

Food particles and scraps of batter that accumulate in the fat or oil become burnt and charred. These scraps speed up the breakdown of the frying media. It is therefore important that the fat or oil is regularly skimmed with a mesh scoop during frying sessions to remove this source of carbon deposit.

The frying media can be filtered to remove such deposits, either through cheesecloths or by using an oil clarifier incorporating a cartridge filter. Filtering will extend the life of the media.

11.1.3 Other foods sold from fried fish shops

Perhaps to compete with the newer forms of takeaway meals, many fried fish shop proprietors have extended the range of foods they offer. It is important that before embarking on any such extension of his trade, a frier should consider the suitability of his premises and equipment to deal hygienically with a new line. Meat pies, chicken portions, including spit-roast chicken, sausages in batter and peas served in cups are some of the more common additional foods found on the menu at fish and chip shops.

Of all these foods perhaps spit-roast chicken poses the greatest potential hazard. Certainly in the 1960s a number of incidents of food poisoning arose following the consumption of chicken cooked in this way. Besides thorough cleaning of the equipment it is necessary to strictly separate the preparation of the raw and cooked chicken. Separate utensils and working surfaces are necessary for this to be achieved. Frozen chickens must be completely thawed out before cooking commences and the rotisserie pre-heated for 30 minutes prior to the chickens being placed within it. Cooking must be thorough, 30 minutes per pound at 204°C (400°F) has been suggested as adequate.

If the chicken portions are not to be sold immediately following cooking they must be quickly cooled and placed under refrigeration within $1\frac{1}{2}$ hours. Refrigerated storage must be maintained until the chicken is required for sale, when thorough reheating should be carried out.

Where hot meat pies and pasties are sold the microwave oven offers many advantages for cooking or reheating these products. Microwave cooking can be quick and thorough and is much more satisfactory than the slow and gentle warming that occurs in some conventional 'hot' pie cabinets (see 9.4.6 and 9.5.2(h)—microwave cooking).

11.2 CHINESE TAKEAWAY FOOD SHOPS

The early 1960s saw the establishment of the first Chinese takeaways in Britain. Often existing fish and chip shops were taken over and the menu extended to include Chinese dishes, to which the British population was becoming rapidly accustomed.

Traditional Chinese cookery encompasses a tremendous range of dishes, with each region in China having its own recipes, spices, sauces and cooking methods. The food served in the majority of Chinese restaurants and takeaways in the West is based on the Cantonese school of cooking. Cantonese cooking involves extensive use of stir frying (see 11.2.3) and utilises chicken stock as a cooking medium.

One of the advantages of takeaway catering is that it can be conducted from fairly modest premises. However, sufficient space must be available to carry out the business in a hygienic manner. In Chinese takeaway premises space will be required for the storage of bulk goods, especially sacks of rice and drums of cooking oil. In addition an area for the precooling of food prior to refrigeration is necessary, as much of the food is pre-cooked and then reheated when required.

11.2.1 The equipment

The Chinese cooker

Chinese cookers are fuelled by gas and are mainly used as fryers. The cooker top is made of iron or steel and has a number of circular holes cut in it, with a double concentric gas ring burner fitted below each hole. Woks, which are circular metal pans with rounded bases, are seated in the holes, and it is in these utensils that most of the cooking is carried out.

A metal shelf is fixed to the back of the cooker and this is used to store various seasonings, within easy reach of the cook.

Chopping block

This is often a section of tree trunk, sometimes surrounded by a band of hide and is used for many purposes including chopping, mincing and crushing. It may be used for the preparation of cooked and uncooked foods and this is a highly dangerous practice. Separate facilities must be provided for preparing cooked and uncooked foods. In any event a tree trunk section cannot be properly cleaned (see 4.4) and should be replaced with a more suitable block or cutting board.

Automatic rice cookers

Although rice may be boiled in saucepans, automatic rice cookers are now frequently used. These are electrically heated and consist of a large bowl, into which rice is placed. Cold water is then added. The rice cooker is switched on and a timer will automatically switch the cooker off after the cooking period has elapsed. The vessel is insulated and will maintain the temperature of the rice (see 11.2.2).

Utensils

A large metal spoon or hok approximately 300 mm (12 inches) long is used in conjunction with the wok. It is used for stir frying, which involves small quantities of food being stirred in hot oil (see 11.2.3). The hok is also used to dip into the various containers of seasoning and to add these to the dish throughout the time it is cooking.

The cleaver knife is another important utensil. It is usually of all metal construction, either tempered or stainless steel, and comes in two weights. The lighter knife is used to cut meats and vegetables, whilst the heavier version can be used to chop bones and the blunt top edge to crush garlic and ginger.

11.2.2 The food

Pork, lamb, mutton and poultry are used in traditional Chinese cooking but not beef. However, most Chinese takeaways do sell beef dishes to cater for the British preference for this meat. The meat and poultry used in such premises is usually frozen and so adequate deep freeze accommodation is necessary. Careful thawing of meat and poultry must be carried out.

Seafood is another important item on the menu at Chinese food shops. Rice, usually American long grain, is used in large quantities and has been the cause of many cases of *Bacillus cereus* food poisoning (see 3.1.4). *B. cereus* is commonly found in raw rice and boiling the rice will not destroy all the spores present. Should the rice then be stored in the temperature range of 15-30°C (59-86°F) germination of the spores will occur, with rapid multiplication of the organisms and the production of toxin. Unfortunately such temperature abuse does sometimes occur, especially in the preparation of fried rice. Previously boiled rice is used for frying and this is sometimes allowed to 'cool' overnight in a warm kitchen, before being used for frying the next day. The result of this practice has been cases of *B. cereus* food poisoning.

Rice should either be fried immediately after boiling or the rice to be used for frying should be kept hot, at above 63°C (145°F), or quickly cooled in shallow trays and placed in the refrigerator within $1\frac{1}{2}$ hours of cooking. Only small quantities of boiled rice should be cooked as required and all cooked rice unsold at the end of the day should be disposed of.

A stock produced by boiling pork and chicken bones is a very important ingredient in many Chinese dishes, and a large stockpot is kept hot throughout the cooking period. Fresh stock should be made every day and maintained at near boiling temperatures.

Many of the vegetables used at Chinese takeaways are canned but fresh beansprouts are often used. Beansprouts are the white shoots of germinating mung or soy beans and can be obtained from specialist producers. They may also be produced on the premises using dried beans. The beans are washed and then soaked in warm water for 2 hours, then rinsed in cold water before being placed in hot water again for 24 hours. During this period they swell and split. They are then placed in a container, covered with a cloth and water added every few hours. The sprouts grow and are harvested when they reach a suitable size. This usually takes one week.

11.2.3 Some Chinese cooking methods

Stir frying
Stir frying is the most frequently used cooking method. The diced or chopped ingredients are tossed in a wok with a small quantity of oil. The cook adds stock and flavourings at appropriate times during the very rapid cooking process. Much of the food is precooked by boiling or roasting before it is stir fried.

It is important that there is no carry over of flavour from one dish to the next and so the wok and hok must be rinsed between the cooking of each meal. Unfortunately, this is sometimes achieved by rinsing in a container of water which quickly becomes dirty and contaminated with food scraps. A sink should be provided in a suitable position for washing the utensils or a specially designed rinsing trough may be fitted to the front of the Chinese cooker and drained to a nearby gully.

Deep frying

Deep frying is usually carried out in a wok containing a large quantity of cooking oil. Meat, poultry, seafood and some vegetables are cooked by this method. Frying is done in two stages. The food is partially cooked and then stored until required, when cooking is completed. It is important that partly cooked foods are rapidly cooled and stored in a refrigerator until required.

11.2.4 Chinese Restaurant Syndrome (C.R.S.)

In 1968 a Dr Ho Man Kwok wrote to an American journal and described symptoms that he and others had experienced, 15–20 minutes after beginning a meal in a Chinese restaurant. The symptoms, included numbness at the back of the neck, extending to the arms and back as well as palpitations.

Many suggestions were put forward for the cause of C.R.S. (or Kwok's disease as it was dubbed) but it was eventually found that monosodium glutamate (M.S.G.) was responsible. M.S.G. is naturally present in many protein foods and is added to some other foods as a flavour enhancer. Minute quantities of M.S.G. are used in manufactured foods but research showed that an individual had to consume about 3 grams of the substance before any symptoms occurred.

The actual cause of the symptoms appeared to be the considerable quantities of M.S.G. that were sometimes added to clear soup in Chinese restaurants, in the United States, the soup being consumed on an empty stomach. C.R.S. has not appeared in Britain as the Chinese in this country include much less M.S.G. in their dishes than their counterparts did in the United States.

11.3 THE SALE OF HOT DOGS AND HAMBURGERS

These traditional American takeaway foods are now well established in Britain. The hot dog consists of a hot frankfurter sausage served in a soft roll, to which onions are sometimes added. Frankfurters are available frozen, vacuum packed or canned and must be cooked in simmering water for 10 minutes. Once cooked they are stored in a bain-marie at 70–82°C (158–180°F) until required. Temperature control of the sausage before and after cooking is important, as is the use of tongs for handling the frankfurter.

American hamburger patties are made from 100% beef, without any binder or seasoning. They are usually cooked on a griddle and seasoning added. Meanwhile the base of a soft bread roll is toasted. The patty is then placed on this, garnished with salad and the top of the roll placed in position, the resulting hamburger usually being served in an insulated container, complete with napkin.

In such takeaway premises the basic principles of food hygiene must be adhered to, and the simplicity of the operation should make good hygienic conditions easy to achieve.

11.4 DONA KEBABS

Dona kebabs are to be seen in certain parts of the country, particularly in London, serving both restaurant and takeaway trades. They are usually associated with Greek or Turkish restaurants and comprise of a large quantity of raw minced beef or lamb, up to 45 kg (100 lb) in weight, which has been seasoned and hand-moulded around a steel spit. The kebab is put into position on a special cooker which has a radiant heat source on one side. The spit and kebab slowly rotate and the outside of the kebab is cooked. The outer cooked meat is removed by slicing with a sharp knife and is served on Greek bread, leaving the raw meat beneath exposed for further cooking.

The whole process is highly questionable from a food hygiene point of view. Firstly, the hand moulding of minced meat around the spit requires the very highest standards of personal and equipment hygiene. Refrigeration of the raw kebab is essential until it is required for cooking and the very size of the product may make this difficult.

Once the cooking of the kebab has begun, the cooker should not be turned off. However, there is a strong temptation to switch the gas supply off if the demand drops, in order to avoid overcooking the outside of the meat. If this is done the temperature of the surface of the kebab will drop to the level necessary for maximum bacterial growth.

The safety of the product also depends on the skill of the operative in avoiding cutting into the raw core of meat. If he fails in this respect not only will the customer be served with raw or undercooked meat but the knife will be contaminated, and this contamination may be transferred to subsequent slices. The other principal danger arises from left-over meat at the end of trading. In no circumstances should it be used the following day but must be disposed of. For this reason it is better to produce and use several smaller kebabs, rather than one large one.

Some environmental health departments have produced codes of practice for the preparation and sale of dona kebabs and one such code is given below. Certainly anyone considering the sale of this product should make early contact with his local Environmental Health Officer.

Recommendations for preparation and cooking of dona kebabs
1. Ensure that only fresh minced meat is used.
2. When mince has been prepared or delivered, place in cold store until required.

Fig. 15 Dona kebab

3. When required, remove from cold store, mix with other ingredients and form into shapes required. (Ensure that the working surfaces and hands of the operator are clean.)
4. Return to cold storage to set (keep away from other foods).
5. Remove from cold storage and place spit in cooker.
6. Commence cooking on vertical grill immediately.
7. Never turn gas off whilst cooking.
8. Ensure that outside of kebab is thoroughly cooked before cutting thin slices.
9. Ensure that knife used for slicing is kept clean.
10. Do not cut too many slices of meat for keeping in bain-marie. (N.B.—some restaurants cut a quantity of slices in advance to meet peak demand.)

11. Temperature of bain-marie must be maintained at 63°C (145°F) or higher.
12. Do not attempt to reheat any sliced meat that has been allowed to cool.
13. Any meat remaining, either sliced or on the spit, at the end of the day's trading must be thrown away.
14. Do not attempt to use any meat (cooked or uncooked) left over from the previous day's trading.
15. Clean all equipment thoroughly every day.
16. The premises should have efficient and accessible fire-fighting equipment.
17. Ensure that vertical grill is regularly serviced as per manufacturer's instructions.

Chapter 12

GROCERY STORES AND SUPERMARKETS

Since the last war there have been enormous changes in the retailing of food. Two trends in particular can be identified; firstly, the movement from the small counter-service grocer to the self-service supermarket, superstore and latterly hypermarket, and secondly, the development of out-of-town shopping.

It was in the 1950s and 60s that the self-service movement gathered momentum with the rise of the supermarket. A supermarket is usually defined as having a minimum of 186 sq. metres (2,000 sq. ft) of selling space, although 370 sq. metres (4,000 sq. ft) is probably more realistic nowadays. This trend to larger retail units has led to the development of superstores with sales areas of 1,858 sq. metres (20,000 sq. ft) or more, all on one level. Superstores are usually developed on the outskirts of a town, provided with ample car parking and offer a wide range of non-food, as well as food items for sale. Hypermarkets with sales areas of 2,300–3,700 sq. metres (25,000–40,000 sq. ft) or more have been a feature on the continental retailing scene for some years, but so far only a few have been built in Britain.

This retailing revolution has brought about a reduction in the number of small grocery stores, and most of those that remain have become self-service. In response to the challenge from the large retail chain stores, small grocers have banded together in voluntary symbol groups, *e.g.* Spar, Vivo, Mace, Centra *etc*. These symbol groups are either controlled by the retailers themselves or owned by a number of wholesalers. The retailer is committed to purchasing through the group which, being sure of his custom, is able to offer goods at a lower price. The local retailer also benefits from national advertising and can obtain finance to modernise and extend his shop.

The main alternative to the symbol group system open to the small trader is cash and carry wholesaling, designed to reduce delivery costs and thereby improve the trader's competitive position.

In all general food shops, whatever their size, the food hygiene considerations remain the same. A wide range of foodstuffs, requiring different methods of handling and storage, must be supplied to the customer in optimum condition. This requires knowledge about the needs of various foodstuffs and good organisation to ensure the proper rotation of stock.

12.1 THE PREMISES

The general principles of hygienic construction and layout are contained in Chapter 4.

12.1.1 Goods reception and storage

Even the smallest store receives large quantities of goods during deliveries. If the goods reception area is not designed to accept the goods quickly and allow their rapid transfer to the stockroom or display shelving the premises will quickly become cluttered. Such conditions make the maintenance of good hygiene and safety standards difficult and add to the problems of stock rotation. Some congestion during delivery times is almost inevitable, but if this cannot be dealt with quickly, this congestion will be added to when the next delivery is made and very soon proper stock control will be impossible.

What is required is adequate space to allow the goods to be sorted and quickly transported to retail display or storage. Doors should be wide and passageways kept unobstructed. Obviously any change in floor level is to be avoided if at all possible, as it makes goods handling more difficult. Furthermore, reliance upon lifts and conveyors means that mechanical failures can disrupt the whole procedure.

The racking used in a stockroom should be constructed of a material that can be easily cleaned. There must be sufficient space beneath the bottom shelf to allow easy floor cleaning. A space should also be kept between the shelving and any adjoining walls, to allow for cleaning and inspection for signs of infestation.

The stock should be arranged to ensure that the oldest goods will be used first and care should also be taken to keep soaps and other heavily scented products well away from foods liable to tainting.

12.1.2 Food preparation areas

In areas where food is prepared a very high standard of finish is required. Chapter 4 discusses materials suitable for use in food preparation areas. In addition, sinks and handwashing facilities are required where food preparation is carried out. Particular care should be taken over the siting of wash hand basins as these should be as near to the working areas as possible, if frequent use is to be made of them.

When food preparation areas are designed it is important that they should be planned to allow the separation of cooked and uncooked foods (see 9.3.1).

12.1.3 Retail sales area

Easily cleanable surfaces and equipment are essential. In areas where open food is handled by staff, as opposed to a self-service situation, *e.g.* delicatessen counters, hand-washing facilities are necessary and sinks for equipment washing are usually required.

12.1.4 Staff facilities

Good sanitary accommodation is required for staff. Under the provisions of The Sanitary Conveniences Regulations, 1964 (S.I. 966), one w.c. is deemed adequate where the number of persons employed on the premises does not regularly exceed five at any one time, or where no-one is employed on the premises for more than two hours. In other cases accommodation must be provided in accordance with the following scales.

Scale (q)
for females and males, where urinal accommodation is not provided:

Number of persons of each sex regularly employed to work in the premises at one time	Number of water closets
1–15	1
16–30	2
31–50	3
51–75	4

Scale (b)
for males where urinal accommodation is available:

Number of male staff	Number of water closets	Units of urinal accommodation
1–15	1	–
16–20	1	1
21–30	2	1
31–45	2	2
46–60	3	2
61–75	3	3

In addition, where over ten females are employed, means for the disposal of sanitary dressings must be provided.

Wash hand basins must be provided in accordance with the Washing Facilities Regulations, 1964 (S.I. 965), viz.

Number of persons regularly employed at any one time (or where separate accommodation for the sexes is required, number of such persons of each sex)	Number of wash hand basins
1–15	1
16–30	2
31–50	3
51–75	4

Note: these wash hand basins are in addition to any that may be necessary in food preparation and service areas.

The sanitary accommodation must be separated from any food room by a ventilated space, entered through self-closing doors.

Where staff eat meals on the premises adequate facilities must be provided. A staff room with chairs, tables and means of making tea and coffee would be the minimum facilities required.

It is unfortunately the case that staff rooms are often the dirtiest areas in a food shop, because no single person is given responsibility for keeping them clean. The danger of infestation exists if food scraps are allowed to accumulate in this area.

12.1.5 Waste disposal

For general comments on refuse storage and disposal see 4.3.4.

In supermarkets the disposal of cardboard can be a particular problem. In some areas the local authority or private contractors will make a special collection of cardboard and all that is necessary is for it to be neatly stacked in a dry area, until it is collected. Where very large quantities of cardboard need to be disposed of a baling press may be installed and this will considerably reduce the volume of material to be handled. An alternative is the installation of a smokeless incinerator, and if this is considered, early contact should be made with the local Environmental Health Department for advice on the provisions of the clean air legislation that will apply.

12.1.6 Lighting

The levels of lighting recommended for shops in the Code for Interior Lighting published by the Chartered Institution of Building Services are as follows:

TABLE 9

Situation	Illumination in lux	Position of measurement
SHOPS		
Conventional with counters	500	Counters—horizontal
Conventional with wall displays	500	Display—vertical
Self-service	500	Vertical on displayed merchandise
Supermarkets	500	,, ,, ,, ,,
Hypermarkets	500	,, ,, ,, ,,
	1000	Horizontal on working plane
WAREHOUSES AND STORES		
Loading bays	150	Identification labels
Small material, racks	300	,, ,,

12.2 THE FOOD

12.2.1 Fresh meat

Chapter 13 covers butchery in some detail. In many supermarkets meat jointing is carried out in a section divorced from the retail sales area, with the meat then being packed in transparent film and displayed for sale in open-topped chill cabinets. Such prepacked meat should be coded and strict stock rotation enforced.

12.2.2 Bacon, cooked meats, pies and sausages

Where whole sides of bacon are received at the store the muslin wrapping should be removed before they are hung in the bacon chiller. Storage at 3°C (37°F) is ideal. It must be remembered that, although the curing of bacon has an inhibiting effect on bacteria, bacon is an uncooked product and therefore knives and slicers used for preparing bacon must not be used for cooked meats. The cut faces of bacon should be covered to maintain freshness and reduce discoloration. Bacon should be stored away from strong-smelling products, as it is easily tainted (see 13.2.3 bacon slicers).

Particular care must be taken with cooked meats as they are likely to be eaten without further cooking and therefore any contamination with pathogenic bacteria could have serious results. The equipment and surfaces with which cooked meat comes into contact must be regularly cleaned and disinfected. Cooked meats should be maintained at chill temperatures, 5°C (40°F) or below at all times, and handled with serving tongs. It is essential that cooked meats are stored, sliced and displayed in such a way that they cannot come into contact with raw foods, or be contaminated by utensils or surfaces that have been used in the handling of uncooked products. As with all perishable products stock rotation is important and the aim should be to sell cooked meats within six days of receipt at the shop (see 13.2.2 food slicers).

Meat pies also require chilled storage but if the temperature is too low the quality of the pastry will be adversely affected. The ideal temperature is 7–10°C (45–50°F). Meat pies should be sold within 48 hours of delivery.

Sausages are a very perishable product and should be maintained at all times below 5°C (40°F) and sold within 72 hours of delivery. Being an uncooked product loose sausages must be kept separate from cooked meat products (see 13.3.4 concerning the manufacture of sausages).

Most manufacturers of prepacked meat pies and sausages code their products in accordance with the Bacon and Meat Manufacturers' Association scheme. This coding indicates the last acceptable day for delivery to the retail store, and consists of a series of numbers. For the purpose of understanding the code any letters that appear should be ignored as these are for factory identification. These letters will be followed by the numbers 01–52 which denote the week of the year and a day number. The key for the day number is as follows:

3   Monday
4   Tuesday
5   Wednesday
6   Thursday
7   Friday
1   Saturday
2   Sunday

For example a product coded 10 6 would be acceptable at delivery (in 1981) up to and including Thursday 5th March. The retailer should calculate the shelf life from the actual date of delivery to his premises (see also 12.3 date coding).

Continental sausages are becoming increasingly popular in this country and they are a very different product to the familiar British sausage. There are two basic types of continental sausage. Firstly, the dry sausage, which includes the salamis. Most dry sausages have been smoked and this smoking is the only form of cooking to which the sausage is subjected, with the temperature not exceeding 32°C (90°F). The flavour and indeed, the stability of the product depends on the fermentation of the meat by lactic acid-forming bacteria, giving a low pH of 4·8–5·4 (see 2.3.6—pH). In addition, the sausage has a nitrite level of approximately 20 p.p.m. and a maximum water content of 30%. Under such conditions food poisoning bacteria will not grow, although the total count of bacteria may be as high as 10^8 organisms/gram but these are harmless lactic acid bacteria. Such 'dry' sausages can be stored at ambient temperatures and have a shelf life of 6 months.

The other type of continental sausage is the 'semi-dry' sausage and these include frankfurters, cervalets and bolognas. These are smoked at the higher temperature of 58°C (136°F) but less time is allowed for fermentation, therefore the ultimate pH is higher than in the case of 'dry' sausages. Such products should be stored at 5°C (40°F) or below, when they will have a 2–3-week shelf life.

12.2.3 Vacuum packed products

Increasing use is being made of vacuum packs, particularly for cooked meats, bacon and cheese. It is important to realise that vacuum packed products remain perishable and have a limited life.

There are two principal methods of vacuum packing cooked meats. Packs may be pasteurised after filling, to destroy vegetative bacteria, and such products are suitable for storage at ambient temperatures, with a shelf life of 14 days after production. Alternatively, vacuum packs may be unpasteurised. In this case strict hygiene measures during production, coupled with continuous temperature control at 5°C (40°F) or below are relied on to give a 13-day shelf life. Packs requiring refrigeration must be so marked and all vacuum packed products should be date stamped. Packages showing signs of leakage must be disposed of.

The vacuum packing of food extends its shelf life and inhibits the growth of any aerobic organisms present. The danger exists that the anaerobic pathogens, *Clostridium botulinum* and *Clostridium perfringins*, may develop under such conditions, without any accompanying spoilage occurring. Fortunately *Cl. perfringins* requires a temperature above 15°C (59°F) to multiply but this is not the case with *Cl. botulinum*, which will develop at much lower temperatures (see 3.1.6). Adequate salt and nitrite concentrations will inhibit toxin production by clostridia but modern taste demands mild cured meats and the lower concentration of salts may reduce their inhibiting effect on these bacteria. Furthermore, the pathogenic facultative anaerobe *Staphylococcus aureus* will grow in low oxygen conditions and is very salt tolerant. Given temperatures of above 7°C (45°F) it will grow, producing toxin. The chilling of non-pasteurised vacuum packed cooked meats and mild cured bacon at 5°C (40°F) or below is therefore essential (see 12.2.5—vacuum packed cheese).

12.2.4 Fresh fish

See Chapter 14.

12.2.5 Dairy foods (see also 3.4.4)

Milk

To sell milk a retailer requires a licence under the provisions of The Milk (Special Designation) Regulations, 1977, as amended. This licence is obtainable from the local authority and is renewable at five-yearly intervals. Current licences expire on 31st December 1985 (or in case of Farm-Bottled Untreated Milk Distributors Licences, 30th April 1985). In addition to being licensed a retailer of milk must register with the local authority under the provisions of the Milk and Daires (General) Regulations, 1959.

Milk can be sold in four designations, viz.: untreated, pasteurised, sterilised and ultra heat treated. Because of its implication in outbreaks of food poisoning the sale of untreated milk is being restricted. It seems likely that sales of untreated milk from shops, schools, hotels and other catering establishments and institutions will not be permitted after 30th April 1985.

Both untreated and pasteurised milk should be stored under refrigeration. The retailer should understand the coding system adopted by the dairy and take care to ensure proper rotation of stock. Sterilised and ultra heat treated (long life) milk does not require storage at chill temperatures and should not occupy valuable space in the refrigerated cabinet.

Cream

All major producers of fresh cream pasteurise their product but they also tend to credit it with a shelf life of a week or more. The display of a perishable product over such a long period means that good temperature control is essential. Fresh cream should be stored at 5°C (40°F) or below and the stock adequately rotated.

Cheese

Where cheese is cut on the premises care must be taken to keep the cheese cutter in a clean condition. Staff handling raw meat must wash their hands prior to serving unwrapped cheese.

Cheese is now often sold in vacuum packs and if unopened, such packs have a life of 3 months or more. Some moisture may develop within the pack but will rapidly disperse if the cheese is unwrapped for a few minutes prior to use.

Butter

Rancidity is the main problem in butter and results from the breakdown of butter fat into glycerine and fatty acids, including the volatile butyric acid, which produces the characteristic rancid odour. Rancidity is a natural process but is speeded up if the butter is exposed to high temperatures or strong light. Refrigerated storage is therefore important, as is good stock rotation.

12.2.6 Bakery goods

Although bread is too dry a product to be associated with food poisoning it must be kept in clean, well-ventilated premises and the stock be properly rotated if complaints about staleness and mould growth are to be avoided.

The stock rotation of cakes is also important, and those containing custard, or fresh and imitation creams will require refrigeration. All unwrapped cakes should be displayed behind 'sneeze barriers' and served with tongs.

Returnable delivery trays should be brushed free of crumbs and tidily stored until returned to the bakery.

12.2.7 Canned goods

Canned food is protected by a combination of cooking and the exclusion of air from the product. This ensures a relatively long shelf life. Canned food should be stored in a cool, dry place as dampness will soon cause cans to rust. Despite the stability of the product a regular rotation of stock is important as the quality of the food within a can will deteriorate in time. Furthermore, some acid fruits will strip the internal lacquering from the can and allow minute quantities of tin to be released into the syrup. Canned rhubarb poses particular problems in this respect and should not be held over from one season to the next.

Certain canned meats used for slicing at the retail shop or catering premises are only subjected to low temperature processing, in order to maintain their appearance and succulence. Such 'pasteurised' canned meats include large hams and pork shoulders. They must be stored under refrigeration and are usually so marked.

The use of a Stanley, or similar knife, to cut through cardboard outers of canned goods should be forbidden. It is all too easy to perforate a can, with a subsequent complaint about the spoiled contents.

A watch should be kept for leaking, blown or damaged tins and these should be disposed of or the advice of the Environmental Health Department sought.

12.2.8 Cereal products

A dry storage area and good stock rotation is required for cereals. An old packet of a cereal product may well develop an insect infestation and this can rapidly spread and contaminate the rest of the stock.

12.2.9 Frozen food

Chapter 5 gives details about refrigeration and frozen food. In particular, section 5.6 gives practical guidance on the use of refrigeration equipment. That general advice is supplemented here by specific measures appropriate to the use of open-topped storage/display cabinets.

The essential requirement when handling any frozen food is to keep it as near to its optimum temperature of $-18°C (0°F)$ as possible, throughout goods reception, storage and display. Even a small deviation from this temperature will affect the quality of the food.

Cabinets complying with B.S. 3053 should be used and must be sited away from sunlight or other heat sources. The cabinet should be on a level floor to allow the drainage of condensate and the air grille kept free of obstruction. To maintain the frozen food at the correct temperature the cabinet must be loaded to ensure that all food is enclosed in an envelope of cold air, which is constantly drawn over the cooling coils. Any food stored above the load-line will not be so maintained and the tidy loading of the cabinet is important to ensure the correct flow of cold air around the stock. The use of cabinet dividers helps to maintain the packages in an orderly fashion. Cabinets should not be situated in areas prone to draughts as air turbulence will allow air at ambient temperatures to be drawn into the cabinet. If this happens there will be an excessive build-up of frost on the coils and on the top packets of food.

Display cabinets require frequent cleaning and particular care should be taken to remove detached price tickets and labels as these can easily block drainage channels and air grilles. It is strongly recommended that one person is charged with the stocking and cleaning of frozen food display cabinets.

For the sale of loose ice cream see 9.3.3. If wrapped or loose ice cream is sold registration with the local authority under Section 16 of the Food and Drugs Act, 1955, will be necessary.

12.2.10 Fruit and vegetables

The handling of vegetables inevitably brings with it a certain amount of soil. Certain food poisoning bacteria (clostridia) are found in soil and therefore it is important that the handling of vegetables is kept separate from the handling of other open food. Fruit requires careful handling because it is a delicate commodity and it may not be cooked or even washed before it is consumed. The practice of allowing customers to select their own fruit from a display prior to it being weighed and priced is not recommended.

Waste fruit and vegetables must be disposed of regularly to prevent any encouragement to pests or problems of smell nuisance. Fruit and vegetable waste should be stored in a dustbin with a lid and not in a cardboard box.

12.3 THE DATE CODING OF FOOD

For many years most major food manufacturers have given their products a date code to enable them to control stock and deal more effectively with any complaints and problems that might arise during storage and sale. Originally, the meaning of most of these codes was only apparent to the manufacturer or to others who were aware of the key to the code. The codes were in fact specifically designed to prevent the consumer selecting the 'freshest' product whilst leaving slightly older, but perfectly satisfactory products, on the supermarket shelves. However, secret date coding made the job of the retailer and the Environmental Health Officer more difficult when trying to prevent stale food being displayed for sale. Indeed, the 1960s and 1970s brought to light many cases of out-of-code products being displayed for sale. The 'sale or return' system operated by some bakery van salesmen became infamous with out-of-date products being passed on from one shop to the next. Pressure mounted for open date coding of perishable products and this will now become legally required on 1st January 1983, when The Food Labelling Regulations, 1980 (S.I. 1980 No. 1849), come fully into effect.

The regulations require foods to be marked with a 'best before' date, or in the case of perishable food having a maximum life of six weeks, a 'sell by' date, followed by an indication of how long the product can be expected to retain its specific properties, if properly stored.

Foods exempted from the requirements include fresh fruit and vegetables, alcohol beverages with an alcoholic strength of 10% by volume or more, frozen food and food which will retain its properties for more than 12 months or 18 months from 1984 (this would include most canned products), and flour confectionery and bread normally consumed within 24 hours of purchase.

In fact, many food manufacturers now use an open date coding system and more will no doubt adopt such systems before 1st January 1983.

However, even with the protection of open date coding the retailer should keep a close watch on the stock delivered to his premises, for he is responsible for the condition of any food he displays for sale. Where manufacturers continue to use secret codes before 1983 the retailer must make sure that he is aware of the key and so is able to break the code and check on the freshness of his stock. It is often a wise precaution for the retailer to code perishable products himself, indicating the date he received delivery of the goods.

12.4 FOOD COMPLAINTS AND UNSOUND FOOD

Complaints concerning food sold from any shop are likely to arise from time to time. Some will be serious, others will be flippant or even malicious; all should be treated seriously and complainants dealt with courteously.

When the fault lies with the retailer, in his methods of handling, storage *etc.*, then he needs to take appropriate action to put right the situation that led to the complaint. Where the fault lies elsewhere, at the food manufacturing stage perhaps, it is in everyone's interest that the matter is fully investigated. In such cases the retailer should, ideally, refer the matter to the local Environmental Health Officer for a full investigation to be carried out. An alternative course of action is for the retailer to take the matter up with the wholesaler, manufacturer or whoever is responsible and to insist on a written report on the incident. Certainly the return of the product for credit to the manufacturer's representative when next he calls is not the way to handle a justified consumer complaint.

Occasionally a retailer may be faced with a consignment of food which he is doubtful about, or his freezer may have broken down and the food is beginning to soften. In such cases, where he needs an expert opinion on the safety of food, he should not hesitate to call in the Environmental Health Officer for his advice. If the officer believes the food to be unsound he will probably issue a voluntary surrender certificate, which will assist the retailer in any subsequent insurance claim. In the case of a freezer breakdown it is also useful to obtain an engineer's report to substantiate any claim.

All food subject to complaint or suspected of being unsound must be segregated from the rest of the stock and appropriately marked.

Chapter 13

BUTCHERY PREMISES

The traditional butcher's shop is still to be seen in towns and villages throughout the land, although changing shopping habits and public taste are leading to a revolution in this conservative trade. Perhaps the most noticeable change is the development of butchery sections in large supermarkets. In such shops the work of jointing and preparation is usually carried on away from the public's eye, in the meat department. The meat is then wrapped in transparent film and displayed in refrigerated cabinets in the sales area, already labelled, weighed and priced.

The consumer's taste has an important effect on a trade where the avoidance of waste is a prime consideration. Certain cuts are no longer popular and the sale of faggots, which utilise lungs and trimmings, has also declined. Alternative means of avoiding waste are now employed, for example beefburgers, steakettes and 'economy' sausages.

The other great influence on the meat trade is the growing ownership of home freezers and many butchers are equipping and organising themselves to profit from this trend.

Meat and poultry are implicated in 70–80% of all outbreaks of food poisoning where a cause is determined. A significant quantity of meat is contaminated with food poisoning bacteria before it reaches the butcher's shop. Salmonellae are a particular problem in this respect (see 3.1.1) but clostridia can also be found on raw meat. In a poorly organised and run butchery many opportunities exist for cross-contamination, and where cooked as well as fresh and frozen meats are sold the consequences of poor handling can be very serious indeed. All who work in the meat trade must be aware that the very nature of the raw product they handle is such that strict attention must be paid to food hygiene.

13.1 THE PREMISES

13.1.1 Size and layout

As with many other food businesses insufficient space in a butcher's shop can be the underlying cause of poor food hygiene. In addition, where meat processing equipment is in use, cramped conditions can expose those working on the premises to serious dangers. The siting of a bandsaw in an already overcrowded preparation room can make effective cleaning of the room very difficult, as well as posing a definite risk to the machine operator. Unfortunately this type of makeshift arrangement is seen all too often.

The most important layout consideration is the need to strictly separate cooked and uncooked meats in preparation areas, refrigerated storage and retail display. This is not at all easy in the average butcher's shop and considerable thought needs to be given to this point. Care must also be taken when considering the siting of wash hand basins. These need to be situated in a very convenient position if proper use is to be made of them by staff, who will inevitably handle both cooked and uncooked products in the course of a day.

A development that has occurred in some areas is the sale of fruit and vegetables from small butcher's shops. This is an undesirable trend as the presence of unwashed vegetables on the premises introduces an additional potential source of contamination. If these two trades are to be carried on in close proximity to one another, then prepacked fruit and vegetables should be sold.

13.1.2 Structural considerations

In common with other food premises the basic requirements are for impervious, easily cleanable wall and floor surfaces and a slightly absorbent but smooth ceiling (see Chapter 4). However, the nature of the meat trade does raise some particular problems. The main difficulty arises out of the need to provide a non-slip as well as a hygienic floor. The safety of the floor is obviously important in any trade, but where sharp implements and dangerous machinery are in constant use the need to avoid slippery conditions becomes paramount. In the meat trade a certain amount of blood and fat will reach the floor and even on 'non-slip' surfaces will represent some degree of hazard. The traditional method of dealing with this problem is to use sawdust as a floor dressing. This soaks up any blood and adheres to particles of fat, so reducing the risk of slipping. Unfortunately, the use of sawdust does pose a contamination danger to the meat and in addition it is soon carried to all parts of the premises on the soles of shoes, and deposited in many places that are difficult to clean. Furthermore, sawdust may be used to reduce cleaning time, with the dirty sawdust being swept up daily and thorough floor washing occurring only once a week.

In meat preparation areas a compromise must be reached, which ensures a safe working environment but does not make the hygienic preparation of food more difficult to achieve. Firstly, a good non-slip floor must be provided. Vinyl/aluminium oxide sheeting is perhaps as good as anything in butchery sections. In areas of high risk, for example where a band-saw operator stands, strips of self-adhesive mineral-grained tape can be applied to the floor. These are very slip-resistant but are not easy to clean and so should be used sparingly. If, after such precautions have been taken, sawdust is necessary small quantities should be used, but only in areas where blood and fat are likely to fall onto the floor, such as around the block. The sawdust used must be clean and should be damped down at the end of the day, prior to sweeping up and disposal. Sawdust removal should be followed by thorough cleaning of the floor (see also 4.2.1).

The walls behind chopping blocks are liable to be damaged during the jointing of meat. In such a situation ceramic tiles quickly become chipped and require replacement. Stainless steel or aluminium sheeting are the best materials to protect the wall in such areas.

Ceilings should be smooth to allow easy cleaning. The ceiling above a chopping block sometimes becomes contaminated with small particles of meat and may need frequent cleaning.

13.1.3 Ventilation

Good ventilation in meat preparation areas is important and particularly so if any cooked meat products are prepared on the premises. The overall temperature of the preparation areas should not be above 10°C (50°F). Rooms in which refrigerator motors are situated also require good ventilation.

13.1.4 Sinks and wash hand basins

A large deep sink is required, sufficient in size to accommodate bulky items such as detachable coldroom shelving and the mincer barrel. If a domestic-size sink is the only facility available, buckets of warm water will be used for such cleaning jobs. This water quickly becomes contaminated and will not be changed frequently enough, because of the length of carry involved. Very hot water is required at the sink to ensure the removal of grease and fat from equipment being washed.

Careful consideration should be given to the siting of wash hand basins. Experience shows that staff will not use handwashing facilities if they are not readily accessible. Where both cooked and uncooked meat is prepared or sold good handwashing facilities are particularly important. Staff will inevitably handle both types of meat and the use of tongs and greaseproof paper does not reduce the need for frequent handwashing. In such circumstances a wash hand basin is really required at the counter as well as in the preparation area.

13.1.5 Refrigerated storage

One of the essential requirements in a butcher's shop or meat department is adequate refrigerated storage space. Walk-in chillers and freezers are usually provided and these may be built into the premises in traditional materials, or alternatively a modular coldroom may be constructed. Modular units can be modified or extended as future needs arise.

The chiller unit should be capable of operating at temperatures between −2 and 0°C (28–32°F). Adequate hanging space must be provided to allow the proper circulation of air around any meat in the chiller. The traditional wooden slatted shelving is absorbent and impossible to clean satisfactorily. Shelving should be plastic coated metal slatting or constructed of chrome-plated steel wire.

The freezer unit must be capable of holding meat at $-18°C$ (0°F). Frozen meat is frequently stored on the floor of the freezer but this is a very poor practice. Vinyl duckboarding should be used to keep frozen meat off the floor and to allow an adequate circulation of air around it.

Clearly visible thermometers should be provided to all coldrooms and these can be supplemented by an audible alarm, to indicate any excessive rise in temperature. The lighting provided in a coldroom usually consists of a single bulkhead light which casts shadows, making cleaning of the area very difficult. At least two lighting points are required.

Care must be taken in all refrigerated storage to ensure that cross-contamination does not occur. A particular danger can be the risk of drip from fresh meat and offal contaminating cooked meats, if these are stored below the raw products. When cooked meats are stored in the same coldroom as fresh meat they should be kept on shelving specifically designated for that purpose and away from any possibility of contamination.

A common misuse of coldrooms is to utilise the roof for the storage of discarded items, often giving it the appearance of a junk yard. The objects quickly become festooned in cobwebs and covered with dust. Equipment no longer required should be disposed of and not retained 'just in case'.

13.1.6 Refuse storage and disposal

Chapter 4 deals with the basic types of refuse storage facility, but in butchery premises there is the additional problem of the disposal of bones and meat scraps. Bones are often stored in the chiller until collection and as long as there is sufficient space and they are kept in a covered container, this is a satisfactory arrangement. The main danger is that the storage of bones or meat scraps during the summer months will attract the attention of blowflies, unless scrupulous attention is paid to hygiene in the refuse area (see 7.3.4, page 100 for advice on precautions against fly infestation).

13.1.7 Lighting and staff facilities
See 12.1.6 and 12.1.4.

13.2 THE EQUIPMENT
13.2.1 Chopping blocks and cutting boards

The traditional wooden butcher's block is still seen in most family butcher's shops, as well as the meat departments of large stores. It is constructed of small squares of wood, bonded together with moisture-resistant resins and held in a wooden frame. Hardwood is used, usually maple, hornbeam or beech. Some blocks are single faced whilst others are reversible. Wooden surfaces are not to be recommended in food preparation areas for the reasons given in 4.4 (see page 46 and Fig. 4) but the wooden block is such a part of the butcher's established practice that it will be many years before it is replaced by more hygienic equipment.

Cleaning a wooden block is a difficult task because if too much water is used the wood will swell and the block crack. As new blocks are very expensive, there is a natural reluctance to use very much water or detergent and disinfecting solutions on them. This means that rather inefficient dry methods of block cleaning, devised by the meat trade over many years, are employed.

The Food Hygiene Code of Practice No. 8 *Hygiene in the Meat Trades* recommends that wooden blocks should be cleaned by a scraper or wire brush dipped in a detergent/disinfectant solution or with very hot water, containing 4 oz of washing soda to a gallon of water. The surface should then be dried off and salt may be rubbed into the block to assist drying. In fact, what often happens is that the edge of the meat cleaver is used to remove fat from the block during the day. At the end of trading the block is wiped over with a damp cloth and sawdust is rubbed into the block to dry it. The block is then scrubbed with a wire brush and brushed with a soft brush to remove any bits. Salt is rarely used on the block as any residue would tend to darken meat subsequently placed on it.

This cleaning process is often made worse by the equipment used for the purpose. All too often the damp cloth used for wiping is a piece of none-too-clean mutton cloth. Whilst the difficult-to-clean wire brush is sometimes merely tapped against a hard surface to remove debris, before being put away for use the following day. It is difficult to see how a totally satisfactory cleaning procedure can be devised for a wooden butcher's block. Certainly, sawdust should not be used on the block, all cleaning equipment should be cleaned and disinfected after use and if a cloth is used it should be wrung out in a disinfecting solution.

It is worth noting that, when badly worn, wooden blocks can be resurfaced by specialist firms.

A number of synthetic materials are now available for use as chopping blocks. They include high molecular weight polythene 100 mm thick (4 inches), 50 mm (2 inches) synthetic rubber boards and 12 mm ($\frac{1}{2}$ inch) P.V.C. sheeting. All these materials can be easily cleaned and disinfected, and are recommended to replace the traditional wooden block.

Chopping blocks, whatever their construction, should not be used for the cutting of cooked meats. Separate cutting boards should be used for this purpose, as well as separate utensils (see 4.4.1).

13.2.2 Gravity feed food slicers

Gravity feed food slicers are widely in use for the slicing of cooked meats. Older machines may be enamelled and in such cases the paintwork soon becomes chipped and the slicer looks unattractive. Modern slicers are constructed of aluminium or stainless steel.

As it is used for cooked meats it is particularly important that the slicer can be thoroughly cleaned. The machine should be easily dismantled and particular attention should be paid to the cleaning of the blade, and blade casing (where food debris is often trapped), as well as the feed chute and handle.

The gravity feed food slicer should not be used for both cooked meats and bacon slicing. In use the slices should be discharged onto clean greaseproof paper placed on the delivery tray. With meat liable to crumble, *e.g.* corned beef, the meat is often collected in the operator's hand rather than being allowed to fall onto the tray. Such meats should be chilled prior to slicing to make the slices more resilient, so allowing them to be discharged onto the tray without damage.

13.2.3 Bacon slicer

These horizontal feed machines require careful cleaning. Like the gravity feed slicers they are potentially dangerous and should only be used and cleaned by properly trained personnel. The manufacturer's cleaning instructions should be closely followed. The booklet *The Safe Use of Food Slicing Machines* (SHW 14), produced by the Department of Employment and Productivity, gives useful guidance on the safe cleaning of such

Fig. 16 Bacon slicer with guard lowered. *Difficult-to-clean areas: the gripper (A); last slice device (B) and collection tray (C)*

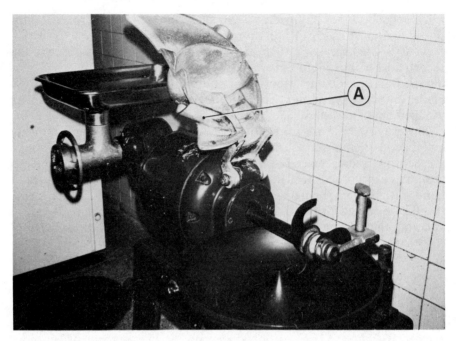

Fig. 17 A combined mincer and bowl chopper. *Hood raised to show difficult-to-clean area behind plough (A)*

Fig. 18 Mincer barrel with plate, cutters and worm removed. *Showing accumulation of dried meat (A)*

equipment and the local Environmental Health Department may well be able to supply a copy.

Particularly difficult-to-clean parts on bacon slicers are the spiked clamp, and the last slice device.

13.2.4 Mincer

The mincer can be used in a variety of operations, including the production of mince and sausage meat. As with all food machinery a mincer should be chosen that has been designed with hygiene in mind. The worm and cutter plates should be easily removable for cleaning and the plunger or feed stick should be made of an impervious synthetic material, not wood.

The mincer barrel is the most difficult part of the machine to clean, particularly the area below the vertical feed tube where dried meat can easily accumulate. Unfortunately, many butchers do not possess the correct shaped brush necessary to effectively clean the barrel, but attempt cleaning with a piece of mutton cloth wrapped around a steel.

Poor trade practices include the mincing of suet to avoid dismantling the cutters for proper cleaning, and the overnight storage of the mincer barrel in the chiller to allow it to continue in use the following day without cleaning. It is essential that the mincer is dismantled at least daily to allow thorough cleaning to be carried out.

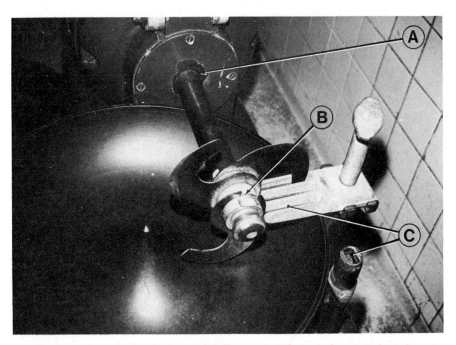

Fig. 19 Bowl chopper showing potential dirt traps. *Where shaft passes through casing (A); blade seating (B) and locking device (C)*

13.2.5 Bowl chopper

Bowl chopping machines are used in the preparation of sausage fillings and again are potentially very dangerous pieces of equipment. Sometimes crevices exist where the cutting blades are set in the revolving shaft and food debris can accumulate in these gaps.

13.2.6 Sausage fillers

The mincer, with appropriate attachment, can be utilised for sausage

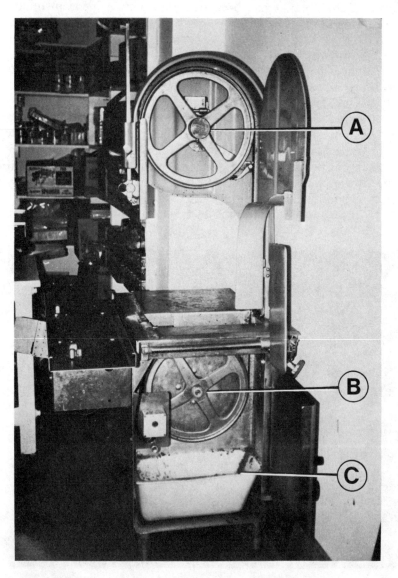

Fig. 20 Band-saw with guards open and table removed. *Difficult cleaning areas: behind top (A) and bottom (B) pulleys and the collecting bucket (C)*

filling but where a considerable trade in small goods is carried on a purpose-made filler can be invaluable. There are two basic types, horizontal and vertical machines.

Horizontal fillers are smaller and cheaper, but the gearing is often rather coarse and the filling uneven. There is a tendency for the washer fitted to the plunger head to wear quickly and for the meat to feed back. The vertical filler has a larger capacity and can be power-operated. Again there is a need to replace the seal to the piston at regular intervals to avoid meat passing into the base of the cylinder. Cylinder, piston and nozzles require thorough cleaning.

13.2.7 Band-saws

These are increasingly seen is use. They are very difficult to clean as the dust they produce is sticky and adheres very firmly to the machinery. The guards provided to prevent access to the pulleys and the band must be opened regularly and the whole area thoroughly cleaned. It is particularly difficult to clean the area behind the pulleys.

With some band-saws it is necessary to remove the working top before the lower guard can be opened to allow cleaning around the bottom pulley. This is a very poor feature as it discourages the frequent cleaning behind the pulleys and emptying of the waste bucket, which is so essential if the band-saw is to be maintained in a hygienic condition. When a band-saw is chosen machines of this design should be avoided.

As with other potentially dangerous machines it is important that manufacturers' cleaning instructions are strictly adhered to.

13.3 THE PROCESSES

13.3.1 The sale of fresh and frozen meat

This is the foundation of the butchery trade and it is essential that it is carried on hygienically. The source of the meat is important and the retailer should ensure that his suppliers' vehicles and staff are clean and hygienic.

All too often meat delivery vehicles are seen to be in poor condition with meat sometimes being carried on the floor or on wooden duck-boards. Food Hygiene Code of Practice No. 8, *Hygiene in the Meat Trades*, deals with the hygienic transport and delivery of meat. The cleanliness of those delivering meat and the adequacy of their over-clothing and head covering will reflect the attitude of the meat wholesaler towards food hygiene. Any failure in this direction may indicate an approach which tolerates poor conditions at the slaughterhouse or wholesale depot.

When displayed for sale meat joints should be protected from possible airborne contamination by 'sneeze barriers' and large wholesale cuts must not be hung where members of the public or staff have to push by them. A refrigerated retail unit is to be preferred to the display of meat at ambient temperatures and precautions should be taken to screen meat in window displays from the direct rays of the sun.

The sale of New Zealand lamb and other frozen meat does present some additional handling problems. It is not possible to joint hard frozen meat with a cleaver, so partial thawing is required. This thawing must be carried out in the chiller. If it is intended to sell the meat in a frozen state, to accommodate the home freezer trade, a band-saw is required to allow the meat to be jointed whilst still frozen.

13.3.2 The evisceration of poultry

The Poultry Meat (Hygiene) Regulations, 1976 have considerably increased the controls on the production of poultry meat. The effect, as far as the retail butcher is concerned, is that legal restrictions have been placed on the sale of poultry from premises other than licensed poultry slaughterhouses. Apart from poultry coming from an approved slaughterhouse and bearing the E.E.C. health mark, birds can only be legally purchased from a poultry producer (*i.e.* one who raises as well as slaughters poultry) and in addition the following requirements must be met:

(a) in the case of wet plucked birds, either whole-bodied or eviscerated, these can be purchased from a producer within the same or an adjoining local authority area.
(b) dry plucked, whole-bodied (New York Dressed) poultry may be purchased from any producer as long as each bird has a label attached, showing the name and address of the producer.

The evisceration of poultry can be a very dirty operation and should be carried on away from other food preparation. A separate synthetic cutting board should be used and the board and knives washed and disinfected after evisceration has been completed. The operative must wash his hands thoroughly before and after eviscerating poultry. Should the bird's intestine break during dressing, thorough cleaning up must be carried out immediately and evisceration only be recommenced when this has been done. The dressed bird should be chilled immediately after evisceration and inedible offal and feathers disposed of.

13.3.3 Preparation of game

Shops licensed under the Game Act, 1831, may sell game in the appropriate seasons. Game birds are usually displayed in the window whole and complete with feathers. Once a sale is made, plucking and dressing is carried out at the rear of the premises and the completed bird collected later. With regard to evisceration similar considerations apply to game as to domestic poultry. In addition game birds, as well as unskinned rabbits and hares, must be displayed in such a way that they will not come into contact with meat and neither will their blood drip onto other food.

As game is shot the flesh will often be bruised and decomposition can set in quickly.

Venison poses particular problems. It is usually delivered to the retail shop eviscerated, but with the hide intact. The hide is particularly difficult to remove and is often very dirty. The evisceration of the deer has been carried out in the field, often by people not experienced in dressing techniques. Thus, the meat suffers from more contamination than is the case in meat from animals killed at a slaughterhouse.

After skinning, venison is usually hung for up to two weeks in a cool place. It is important that it *is* kept cool during this period and away from other meat.

13.3.4 Sausage production

The fresh sausage produced in the United Kingdom is an almost unique product. The ingredients are lean meat, fat, rusk, seasonings, preservative and water. They are mixed and minced or chopped, before being filled into casings. The small intestine of a pig may be used for large sausages and sheep's intestines for small sausages. These natural casings are supplied to the butcher cleaned and salted and are soaked and rinsed in cold water before use. Although salted, natural casings carry many bacteria and can begin to decompose quite rapidly. An alternative is the use of reconstituted casings which are made from comminuted callogen from animal sources, for example the underlayer of beef hide. They are supplied in a dry state and are therefore easy to store, and take up moisture from the sausage-meat on filling. Besides their keeping quality, reconstituted casings also produce a uniform shape of sausage, which presents a more attractive appearance.

The bacteriological quality of the ingredients is vitally important in sausage production as mixing, mincing and chopping spreads any contamination present throughout the product. For many small traders sausage production is a means of using up unsold meat and scraps otherwise difficult to dispose of. Thus, there is a temptation to include meat less fresh than it should be. This temptation must be resisted, otherwise a product with a high bacterial count and a very short shelf life will be produced. Meat intended for sausage manufacture should be stored under hygienic conditions in the chiller.

Care should also be taken with the rusk, which will itself carry a considerable microbiological flora. The rusk bin should not be continually topped up but stock rotation should ensure that the rusk used is fresh.

During the making of sausages it is important to keep the temperature of the mixture down to below 10°C (50°F) throughout the process. This is not easy, as the action of mincing and chopping generates considerable heat. Certainly the operation should be carried out in a cool room, and where a bowl chopper is in use flaked ice can be used instead of water to very good effect. If the sausages are made with the aid of a mincer only, the water should be chilled. The practice of putting the mixture through the mincer twice to produce a finer, more even texture in the sausage-meat should be avoided as this causes a considerable warming of the mixture and will result in sausages with a poor keeping quality.

Rapid cooling of the finished sausages is important. They require storage in a chiller having a low humidity and good air circulation. However, the humidity should not be too low or the air movement too brisk, otherwise dehydration and weight loss occurs (see also 13.4).

13.3.5 Cooked ham

Butchers usually purchase brined gammons. The gammon is boned and excess fat removed. It is placed in a press and usually cooked in an insulated cooker. The temperature is raised to 82°C (180°F), the lid sealed down and the heat turned off. The cooking then continues for 12–14 hours, after which the hams are removed from the cooker and taken out of the moulds. The rind is trimmed off, the ham cooled and then dressed with breadcrumbs.

The correct cooking period is obviously important, as is careful handling following removal from the cooker. Post-cooking contamination is all too possible, unless the operation is carried out with clean hands and implements and well away from raw meat and poultry.

The rapid cooling of the ham after cooking is also an important requirement. Hams in presses can be cooled under a cold water spray (see 9.3.2—cooking and cooling of food and also 13.4).

13.3.6 Tongue

The tongues are cured by injection or brine immersion. They are then cooked by simmering. Ideally the skin and hyoid bone should be removed as soon as sufficient cooking has been done to allow this. The tongue should not be cooled but skinned as hot as possible and then placed in a former and the cooking completed; which takes approximately 3 hours in the case of ox-tongues.

In practice tongues are often skinned after the completion of cooking, and if proper formers are not available they may be pressed into empty liver tins weighted down with scale weights or other heavy objects. Again post-cooking contamination is a very real possibility, and must be avoided by the very highest standards of personal and equipment hygiene (see also 13.4).

13.4 REGISTRATION OF PREMISES USED FOR THE PREPARATION OF SAUSAGES OR COOKED MEATS

All premises used for the manufacture of sausages or cooked meats must be registered with the local authority under the provision of Section 16 of The Food and Drugs Act, 1955. The local authority have the right to refuse or cancel a registration under this section if they are not satisfied with hygiene arrangements. A person aggrieved by such a decision has the right of appeal to a magistrates' court.

Chapter 14

WET FISH SHOPS

Recent years have seen a decline in the wet fish trade with more filleting and other fish preparation being carried out at factories, where it can be mechanised. This has led to the sale of fish, often frozen, through super-markets at the expense of the traditional wet fish shop.

14.1 THE PREMISES, EQUIPMENT AND GENERAL HYGIENE

Chapter 4 deals with the fundamental requirements for hygienic prem-ises and equipment and is applicable to the wet fish trade. Ease of cleaning of both premises and equipment is particularly important as cleaning must be regular and thorough if a stale fish odour is to be avoided.

As far as equipment is concerned good refrigerated storage and dis-play slabs are necessary. An ice maker should also be available as wet fish is best kept in ice.

Where poultry and game is sold from the same premises as fish, a separate area should be reserved for any evisceration or other prepara-tion necessary and separate cutting boards and knives provided (see 13.3.2).

Flies can be a particular problem in the fishmonger's shop and the precautions given in 7.3.4, page 100, should be taken. In addition the offal bucket must be emptied and scrubbed out at least once a day. Fish offal should be stored in bins with close-fitting lids and the bins must be emptied and washed out frequently. Where fish is delivered in returnable metal or plastic fish boxes they should be washed out as soon as they are empty, then dried and stored away from the shop. Specialised detergents are necessary in the fish trade to deal with the removal of scales and slime on fish boxes and other equipment. Soaking in a 1% solution of sodium metasilicate prior to washing has been found to give good results. Non-returnable fish boxes must be disposed of without delay and not pressed into service for other purposes.

14.2 THE DISPLAY AND SALE OF WET FISH

The source of a retailer's fish is of prime importance. Supplies must be obtained from a wholesaler who is able to deliver from the port to the shop with the minimum of delay and under good refrigerated conditions.

Fish begin to spoil from the moment they are caught. Bacteria in the gills and digestive tract, and on the surface of the fish are transferred to the flesh during handling. These bacteria will ultimately bring about the decomposition of the fish. Careful gutting and washing will remove some of the bacteria present but many will remain. The Torry Research Station estimate that, with careful handling and storage in ice, it takes 15–16 days for cod and haddock to spoil sufficiently to warrant condemnation. For herring, six days is the maximum acceptable life.

The smell of stale fish is due to small quantities of trimethylamine (T.M.A.). Trimethylamine oxide is found in varying amounts in all marine fish and when acted on by certain bacteria is converted to trimethylamine, producing the characteristic stale fish smell.

Besides having an unpleasant smell, stale fish appears dull, the flesh is limp and pits under pressure whilst the eyes are sunken and lack any lustre. In ungutted fish the abdominal cavity becomes distended and may show a green discolouration.

The ideal storage temperature for wet fish is $0°C$ ($32°F$). Fish begins to freeze at $-1°C$ ($30°F$) and freezing will damage the flesh. If fish is stored in melting ice it will be maintained at its optimum temperature. In the sale of wet fish there is no substitute for the liberal use of clean, crushed ice. The fish should be displayed on a bed of ice, with additional ice packed around it. Approximately $\frac{1}{2}$ kg of ice is required for $1\frac{1}{2}$–2 kg of fish. The use of ice in this way chills the fish much more rapidly than a refrigerated unit would and in addition prevents the fish drying out. However, chill display cabinets are very useful in slowing down the rate at which the ice melts. Transparent up-stands around the display will stop draughts drying the fish out.

The storage of fish at low temperatures is an important measure in preventing scrombrotoxic fish poisoning (see 3.2.4).

14.3 SMOKED FISH

The smoking of fish results in the deposition of chemicals in the flesh, as well as some drying of the fish. Although this does have a preservative effect this is very limited and smoked fish will keep only a little longer than fresh fish. Smoking is carried out to develop a particular taste, not to protect the product from decomposition.

Smoked fish are brined and sometimes dyed before smoking, they then may be either cold or hot smoked. In cold smoking the temperature of the smoke chamber is usually below $30°C$ ($86°F$) and is insufficient to cook the product, which must therefore be cooked by the consumer. Hot smoked fish products are eaten without further cooking.

Smoked fish should not be stored directly on ice but placed on a refrigerated slab or on trays laid on a bed of ice (see also 14.6).

14.4 FISH ROES

Hard roe is obtained from the female fish and soft roe from the male. Roes are washed and then boiled in salted water. It is important that post-cooking contamination is avoided. Cooked roes should be displayed away from raw food and handled with separate utensils.

14.5 SHELLFISH

Shrimps and prawns are supplied to the retailer boiled and peeled. As peeling occurs after cooking strict personal hygiene is essential at the processing plant. Many prawns are supplied frozen, and problems have arisen with imported prawns having high bacterial counts and showing signs of decomposition upon thawing.

Cockles and whelks are cooked shortly after gathering. Cockles, being bivalves, can become seriously contaminated if they are harvested in sewage-polluted waters (see 3.4.3). Cooking after gathering has not always been sufficient to prevent the illness of consumers (see 3.2.2).

Shellfish that are eaten raw pose the greatest health risk. Mussels sometimes come into this category, although they are usually steamed or boiled. The oyster, however, is always eaten raw and supplies must be obtained from an officially approved source, where purification by chlorination, ultraviolet light or ozone has been carried out.

14.6 BOTULISM AND FISH

Botulism is an extremely serious form of food poisoning, caused by the consumption of minute traces of a toxin produced by the bacterium *Clostridium botulinum* (see 3.1.6). One type of *Cl. botulinum*, type E, is found in the marine environment and has resulted in cases of botulism following the consumption of sea foods.

Fortunately, the toxin responsible for botulism is easily destroyed by cooking but smoked fish eaten without further heat treatment can pose a risk, unless carefully handled. Smoked salmon is of particular concern because much of this product sold in Britain is obtained from the Pacific coast of North America or the seas around Japan. *Cl. botulinum* type E has been found in both areas.

Changes in processing and marketing may have reduced the safety margins in smoked salmon. The modern taste is for a less heavily salted and smoked product and the lower concentration of salt and reduced effects of smoking may be insufficient to prevent the growth of *Cl. botulinum*. Furthermore, vacuum packing of smoked salmon is now carried out and the environment that such packaging provides favours *Cl. botulinum*, which is a strict anaerobe. Vacuum packing will suppress the growth of aerobic bacteria giving *Cl. botulinum* an opportunity to grow without, perhaps, any accompanying signs of spoilage.

The most important control measure that can be taken against botulism from fish and fish products is good refrigeration. The lowest recorded temperature at which *Cl. botulinum* type E will grow is 3·3°C (38°F) and therefore smoked fish, especially vacuum packs, should always be kept below 3°C (37°F). Vacuum packs should be marked with this maximum storage temperature and a 'sell by date'.

In recent years concern has arisen over evidence of a relatively high incidence of *Cl. botulinum* at commercial trout farms in Britain and abroad. Trout has never been implicated in botulism in Britain, but it has elsewhere. The risk is greater with hot smoked trout, not intended to receive further cooking before consumption. In all cases trout should be maintained at below 3°C (37°F) and sold as quickly as possible, smoked trout within five days of smoking.

Chapter 15

FOOD AND DRINK VENDING MACHINES

The use of automatic food and drink vending machines has grown tremendously over recent years. Their value in bus and railway stations, air terminals and similar places is obvious, but they are also a very convenient way of providing drinks and snacks in places of work. Indeed with microwave regenerating ovens they can offer a varied menu, 24 hours a day, which is very useful where shift work is undertaken.

Vending machines may be purchased or hired. If the machine is purchased by the occupier of a premises it will be cleaned and stocked by an employee. If it is rented the occupier will usually arrange for cleaning and loading, whilst the hire company will carry out routine maintenance. Other vending machines are owned by vending companies whose personnel clean and stock the machine, usually on a daily basis. Whatever arrangement is in operation it is important that the person carrying out cleaning and filling is properly instructed in the necessary hygiene measures and in stock rotation.

On occasions problems of copper poisoning have followed the consumption of fruit juices dispensed from vending machines. Investigations have revealed corrosion of various copper parts including storage tanks, pipework, water-cooling coils and carbonators. It is therefore essential that regular maintenance and examination of vending machines is carried out by a competent service engineer.

15.1 CONSTRUCTION OF VENDING MACHINES

All parts of the machine that come into contact with food must be easy to clean. Funnels, mixing bowls and delivery pipes should be easily removable so that they can be replaced with clean equipment during the service and taken away for thorough cleaning elsewhere. The doors must be tight fitting and well sealed to prevent the entry of dust and pests. Ventilation louvres should be insect-proofed, and a self-closing door provided at the delivery point. Machines containing syrup-based products are most likely to become infested, garden ants being a particular problem.

Any illumination situated within the machine should be so positioned as to prevent an undesirable temperature rise in the food compartments.

When the vending machine is refrigerated it must be fitted with an automatic shut-off device, which will stop further sales should the temperature rise unduly. In addition a thermometer, clearly visible from outside the machine, should be fitted.

15.2 VENDING MACHINE TYPES

15.2.1 Beverage machines

Simple drinks dispensers
Each ingredient required is separately fed into a cup following the pressing of a button. Thus, to obtain a white coffee with sugar, three buttons are pressed and then the hot water is obtained from a nozzle. As there are no parts of the machine where wetted drink powders can accumulate, good standards of hygiene are easy to maintain. If the boiler is hand filled the water must be changed daily.

In-cup system
The cups already containing all the necessary ingredients, *i.e.* coffee, dried milk and sugar, are loaded into the machine. After selection the cup drops to the service point and hot water is automatically added, mixing the ingredients.

This type of machine is very easy to clean and refill, as there are no mixing bowls or delivery tubes. The main disadvantage is the higher unit cost when compared with beverages supplied from a post-mix machine.

Post-mix machines
These are the commonest form of beverage machine and also the most difficult to clean. Post-mix simply means that the ingredients are prepared with water in a mixing bowl, after the insertion of a coin. In such machines hot beverages are often combined with the vending of refrigerated fruit juices.

The operation of a post-mix machine is as follows. Upon the insertion of a coin the ingredient motors deliver measured amounts of coffee, milk powder *etc.* into a mixing bowl where it is mixed by the swirl action of water at 80–85°C (176–185°F). The water continues to flow after the ingredient motors have stopped, so that all traces of powder are rinsed out of the bowl and into the cup. The drink passes through piping to a delivery nozzle in the cup station. Any overflow from the cup runs via a drainage outlet to a waste bucket.

The sophistication of post-mix machines varies, some having separate mixing bowls for all the beverages dispensed to prevent any carrying over of flavour from one drink to the next. Many include separate bowls for chocolate and soup as these powders are strongly hygroscopic and are more likely to adhere to the bowl and pipework than other beverage powders.

The ventilation of a post-mix machine is very important as any build-up of water vapour will produce damp powders and therefore a difficult cleaning problem. In addition, humid conditions also favour bacterial growth.

'Floating powder' is a problem in all post-mix machines and if the ventilation system is not adequate serious difficulties can arise. Whenever powder is dispensed from the ingredient container to the mixing bowl a small quantity becomes airborne. This 'floating powder' is drawn out through the extractor fan, but if the conditions within the unit are very humid the fan outlet will quickly block and damp powder will settle inside the machine. The amount of 'floating powder' can be reduced by avoiding very fine ingredients.

When inspecting a post-mix vending machine it is therefore important to ensure that the ventilation outlet is not obstructed in any way and that the extractor fan is free of damp powder. All drink-contact parts must be kept clean and the waste bucket regularly emptied. Product containers must be examined for damp powder, which will partially block their outlets and milk powder should be checked for signs of rancidity.

Vending machines are now available which brew fresh leaf tea or fresh coffee rather than utilise instant powders, so giving an improved flavour. The tea or coffee is allowed to brew in a special brewer unit for approximately 15 seconds before being dispensed into the waiting cup. A scraper automatically removes the used tea leaves or coffee grounds from the brewer unit or, if filter paper is used, the filter paper roll advances to present a fresh paper for each cup brewed. A separate waste bucket is provided for the used tea leaves or coffee grounds and the discarded filter paper. This bucket and the brewer unit itself requires careful cleaning.

15.2.2 Food vending machines

Column vending machines
This is the simplest form of food vending machine. Upon insertion of a coin the item at the bottom of the column can be removed through a drawer, and then all remaining items drop down one place. The familiar chocolate bar dispenser is an example of a column vending machine.

Compartment machines
These comprise of a number of compartments each with a glass door. One door can be opened and the item of food removed, once a coin has been inserted.

Rotary drum and shelf machine
This type of vending unit overcomes the limited capacity of the compartment machine. The compartments in a particular rotating shelf contain one item of food or type of plated meal. These machines may consist of many rotating shelves. Each time a purchase is made the drum will rotate to the extent of one compartment. Such equipment is often refrigerated

and used in conjunction with a microwave oven for reheating plated meals.

Hot can merchandisers

The hot can merchandiser provides a hot meal in a one-portion can, with a ring-pull top. The same vending machine also supplies a disposable bowl from which the food is consumed. All the cans in the machine are maintained at a temperature of above 63°C (145°F) by the circulation of hot air. A temperature of about 68°C (155°F) is probably most acceptable, as temperatures above this will burn the fingers of customers.

The internal surfaces of the machine which come into contact with the cans must be easy to clean, as cans occasionally weep. Stock rotation is important and the product should not be held in the machine for more than 7 days, otherwise separation of the foods will occur and palatability will be reduced. The marking of cans with their date of loading is a useful precaution.

15.3 MICROWAVE REHEATING

Where microwave reheating is to be used in conjunction with food vending, the provision of appropriate value-time tokens with each meal is probably the best way of ensuring adequate reheating. Research must be undertaken to determine the correct time required for safe reheating. The size of meals, particularly the thickness of portions (they should not exceed 4 cm, *i.e.* 1½ inches), must be strictly controlled. (See 9.4.6 and 9.5.2 (h)—microwave cooking and 9.1—cook/chill.)

15.4 SITING OF VENDING MACHINES

Vending machines should be sited away from direct sunlight and on smooth flooring that can easily be cleaned. The machine should either be situated with its back flush to a wall or there be a sufficient gap between machine and wall to allow thorough cleaning all round the equipment. Where a bank of vending units are sited together, care should be taken to ensure that the temperature of one machine will not adversely affect the operation of any other machine.

Adequate litter bins should be provided on the site and all machines and banks of machines should have displayed the name and address of the machine operator.

15.5 CLEANING OF VENDING MACHINES

It is essential that thorough cleaning of vending machines is carried out by properly equipped operatives. Detailed cleaning instructions should be displayed on a plaque inside the machine and a record kept of each cleaning and servicing visit.

Detailed cleaning recommendations are contained within Food Hygiene Code of Practice No. 7, *Hygiene in the operation of coin-operated food vending machines* (available from Her Majesty's Stationery Office).

The Code of Practice recommends that the frequency of cleaning and disinfection should be at least daily for machines dispensing milk drinks and similar liquids, every 48 hours for machines dispensing other liquids, and every 72 hours in the case of other foods. The proviso is made that cleaning and disinfection should be carried out each time restocking occurs, however frequent that may be.

In food vending machines the operator should ensure that food items have not fallen from their shelves or compartments and become lodged in other parts of the machine.

It is strongly recommended that detachable funnels, mixing bowls and delivery pipes should be replaced with clean equipment at each visit and taken away for thorough cleaning and disinfection. Stock must be properly rotated and individual food items and meals should be coded to give a 'sell by date', after which time they should be destroyed. Bulk containers of ingredients should not be continually topped up, but require periodic emptying and cleaning.

If the vending machine is temperature controlled the operating temperature should be carefully checked during the cleaning routine.

Appendix A

ORGANISATIONS CONCERNED WITH FOOD AND FOOD HYGIENE

Health Education Council,
78 New Oxford Street,
London WC1A 1AH.

Institution of Environmental Health Officers,
Chadwick House,
Rushworth Street,
Blackfriars,
London SE1 0RB.

Royal Institute of Public Health and Hygiene,
28 Portland Place,
London W1N 4DE.

Royal Sanitary Association of Scotland,
62 Virginia Street,
Glasgow G1 1TX.

Royal Society of Health,
13 Grosvenor Place,
London SW1X 7EN.

Scottish Institute of Environmental Health,
Hon. Sec. Mr M. Halls,
c/o P.O. Box 4,
Paton Street,
Galashiels TD1 3AS.

Refrigeration

British Frozen Food Federation,
Honeypot Lane,
Colsterworth,
Grantham,
Lincs NG33 5LY.

British Refrigeration and Air Conditioning Association,
Phoenix House,
Unit C,
Phoenix Way,
Heston,
Middx TW9 9ND.

Food Freezer and Refrigerator Council,
25 North Row,
London W1R 2BY.

United Kingdom Association of Frozen Food Producers,
1 Green Street,
Grosvenor Square,
London W1Y 3RG.

Cleaning and pest control

British Association of Chemical Specialities,
93 Albert Embankment,
London SE1 7TU.
(Assn of manufacturers of disinfectants, detergents, polishes and maintenance products.)

British Pest Control Association,
93 Albert Embankment,
London SE1 7TU.

Contract Cleaning and Maintenance Association,
142 The Strand,
London WC2R 1HH.

Meat

Bacon and Meat Manufacturers Association,
18–19 Cornwall Terrace,
London NW1 4QP.

Meat and Livestock Commission,
Queensway House,
Queensway,
Bletchley,
Milton Keynes MK2 2EF.

Meat Research Institute,
Langford,
Bristol BS18 7DY.

Scottish Federation of Meat Trades Associations,
Craigie House,
Craigie Knowles Road,
Perth PH2 0DQ.

Fish

Humber Laboratory,
Ministry of Agriculture, Fisheries and Food,
Wassand Street,
Hull HU3 4AR.
(Provides technical advice on the handling and processing of fish.)

National Federation of Fishmongers Ltd,
2 Queensway,
Redhill,
Surrey.

Scottish Federation of Fishmongers,
24 George Square,
Glasgow G2 1EE.

Shellfish Association of Great Britain,
Fishmongers Hall,
London Bridge,
London EC4R 9EL.

Torry Research Station,
Ministry of Agriculture, Fisheries and Food,
135 Abbey Road,
Aberdeen AB9 8DG.
(Research concerning handling, processing, preservation, storage and distribution of fish. Technical advice available.)

Other foods

British Food Manufacturing Industries Research Association,
Randalls Road,
Leatherhead,
Surrey KT22 7RY.
(Research on problems associated with manufacture, packaging and storage of foodstuffs. Much information restricted to member companies.)

Campden Food Preservation Research Association,
Chipping Campden,
Glos GL55 6LD.
(Research on canning, freezing and drying. Much information restricted to member companies.)

Delicatessen and Fine Food Association Ltd,
5 Fairfield Avenue,
Staines,
Middx TW18 4AB.

Flour Milling and Baking Research Association,
Chorleywood,
Rickmansworth,
Herts.

Catering

British Hotels, Restaurants and Caterers Association,
13 Cork Street,
London W1X 2BH.

Catering Equipment Distributors Association,
397 Bradford Road,
Huddersfield,
Yorks HD2 2QY.

The Electric Catering Centre,
45 St Martin's Lane,
London WC2NE 4EJ.

Hotel and Catering Industry Training Board,
P.O. Box 18,
Ramsey House,
Central Square,
Wembley,
Middx HA9 7AP.

Licensed trade

National Association of Licensed House Managers,
9 Coombe Lane,
London SW20 8NE.

National Union of Licensed Victuallers,
2 Downing Street,
Farnham,
Surrey GU9 7NX.

Scottish Licensed Trade Association,
10 Walker Street,
Edinburgh EH3 7LA.

Takeaway foods

National Federation of Fish Friers,
289 Dewsbury Road,
Leeds LS11 5HW.

Take Away Food Federation (U.K.) Ltd,
34 John Adam Street,
London WC2N 6HW.

Retail food sales

British Multiple Retailers Association,
1-19 New Oxford Street,
London WC1A 1PA.

Institute of Grocery Distribution,
Letchmore Heath,
Watford WD2 8DQ.

Scottish Federation of Grocers and Wine Merchants Associations,
153 Constitution Street,
Edinburgh EH6 7AD.

Vending machines

Automatic Vending Association of Britain,
31 Great Queen Street,
London WC2B 5AA.

Appendix B

SHORT TRADE DIRECTORY OF MATERIALS AND EQUIPMENT

CHAPTER 4

Activated carbon filters

Machine Control Ltd,
Blatchford Road,
Horsham,
Sussex.

Grease filters

Ozonair Engineering Co. Ltd,
Aylesford,
Kent ME20 7NB.

Grease traps

Wade International (U.K.) Ltd,
Adanac Works,
Bluebridge Industrial Estate,
Halstead,
Essex CO9 2HZ.

Cutting boards

Cookley Board,
Formula Housing Research Ltd,
300 Slade Road,
Erdington,
Birmingham B23 7UP.

Darvic H.P. Board,
I.C.I. Plastics Division,
Welwyn Garden City,
Herts.

Whiteside Board,
James Whiteside & Co.,
3 Leathermarket,
Weston Street,
London SE1.

Floor covering (vinyl/aluminium oxide)

Altro Ltd,
Caxton Hill,
Hertford,
Herts SG13 7NB.

Ozonators

Wallace and Tiernan Ltd,
Priory Works,
Tonbridge,
Kent TN11 0QL.

Paints (mould-inhibiting)

Silexine Paints Ltd,
80 Abbey Road,
Barking,
Essex IG11 7BY.

Vanguard Paints Ltd,
Cranleigh Road,
Porchester,
Hants.

Refuse compactor

Imperial Machine Co. (Peelers) Ltd,
Harvey Road,
Croxley Green,
Herts WD3 3AX.

Wall cladding

Cobex Cladding Systems,
Stoney Brothers & Co. Ltd,
Brantham Division Industrial Products,
Brantham,
Manningtree,
Essex CO11 1BR.

Darvic Sheeting,
I.C.I. Plastics Division,
Welwyn Garden City,
Herts.

Stericlad Sheeting,
Harbour Road,
Oulton Broad,
Lowestoft NR32 3LZ.

CHAPTER 5

Blast chillers and rapid cooling cabinets

Foster Refrigerator U.K. Ltd,
Oldmeadow Road,
Kings Lynn,
Norfolk PE30 4JU.

Imperial Refrigeration and Air Conditioning Ltd,
Stephen Street,
St Annes-on-Sea,
Lancs.

Freezer temperature alarm

M.C.A. Electronic Controls Ltd,
Arnside Road,
Waterlooville,
Hants PO7 7UP.

Electronic thermometers

Comark Electronics Ltd,
Rustington,
Littlehampton,
West Sussex BN16 1BR.

Digitron Instrumentation Ltd,
Merchant Drive,
Mead Lane,
Hertford.

Kane-May Ltd,
Burrowfield,
Welwyn Garden City,
Herts AL7 4BR.

CHAPTER 6

Brushes (that can be heat disinfected)

W. T. Clark & Co. (Brushes) Ltd,
Industrial Estate,
Coleshill,
Birmingham B46 1H7.

Vikan Hygienic Brushes,
Red Ball House,
Victoria Road,
Portslade,
Brighton BN4 1XZ.

Contact plates

Sterilin Ltd,
43–45 Broad Street,
Teddington,
Middx TW11 8QZ.

Dip slides

Gibco Bio-Cult Diagnostics Ltd,
Washington Road,
Paisley,
Scotland.

Tillomed Laboratories Ltd,
Henlow Trading Estate,
Henlow,
Beds.

Disinfecting cloths

Wipex Products Ltd,
17 Weymouth Mews,
London W1N 3FQ.

Disposable cloths

Diversey Ltd,
Weston Favell Centre,
Northampton NN3 4PD.

Glover and Wood Ltd,
New Victoria Works,
Jack Lane,
Leeds LS11 9SY.

Millipore kit

Millipore (U.K.) Ltd,
Millipore House,
Abbey Road,
London NW10 7SP.

P.G.C. system

Partome Germ Control Ltd,
18A Queen Square,
Bath,
Avon.

Pressure jet cleaners

Automations International (Distributors) Ltd,
Kleen-King Division,
11 Bath Road,
Heathrow,
Hounslow,
Middx.

Psimat Ltd,
Newtown Road,
Henley-on-Thames,
Oxfordshire.

Vacuum cleaners, sweepers etc.

Cimex Ltd,
Cray Avenue,
Orpington,
Kent BR5 3PX.

Nilfisk Ltd,
Newmarket Road,
Bury St Edmunds,
Suffolk IP33 3SR.

CHAPTER 7

Cockroach trap (electric)

Oecos Scientific Ltd,
9 Southfield,
Welwyn Garden City,
Herts.

Electronic ultraviolet insect control units

Eastmead Electronics Ltd,
Bridge Road,
Camberley,
Surrey.

Rentokil Ltd,
Felcourt,
East Grinstead,
Sussex.

Henry Simon Ltd,
P.O. Box 31,
Stockport SK3 0RT.

Wellcome Industrial (Pesticides),
Berkhamsted,
Herts HP4 2DY.

CHAPTER 9

Food waste disposal units

Imperial Machine Co. (Peelers) Ltd,
Harvey Road,
Croxley Green,
Herts WD3 3AX.

W. and G. Sissons Ltd,
Calver Bridge,
Sheffield S30 1XA.

Mobile heated dip tank

D.F.P. Supplies Leeds,
20 Parkways Avenue,
Oulton,
Leeds LS26 8TW.

Pan scrubbers

Imperial Machine Co. (Peelers) Ltd,
Harvey Road,
Croxley Green,
Herts WD3 3AX.

CHAPTER 10

Glasswashers (revolving brush type)

The Glassmaster Co. Ltd,
119–121 Warwick Road,
London SW5 9EF.

Reckitt Industrial,
P.O. Box 20,
Cressex,
High Wycombe,
Bucks HP12 3TL.

Automatic glasswashers

Jiffi Ltd,
Avonberg Industrial Estate,
Long Mile Road,
Dublin 12.

Automatic beerline cleaning

Cleanaglas Electric Washer Ltd,
Eelmoor Road,
Farnborough,
Hants GU14 7BR.

CHAPTER 13

Anti-slip flooring tape

3M United Kingdom Ltd,
3M House,
Wigmore Street,
London W1A 1ET.

Synthetic blocks

Darvic H.P. 12 mm ($\frac{1}{2}''$),
I.C.I. Plastics Division,
Welwyn Garden City,
Herts.

James Whiteside & Co,
3 Leathermarket,
Weston Street,
London SE1.

BIBLIOGRAPHY

GENERAL WORKS

Aston, G. and Tiffney, J. (1977) *A Guide to Improving Food Hygiene*. London: Northwood Publications Ltd.

City of Canterbury (1976) *Thought for Food*. Environmental Health Department.

Hobbs, B. C. and Gilbert, R. J. (1978) *Food Poisoning and Food Hygiene*. 4th Edition. London: Edward Arnold.

Martin, C. R. A. (1978) *Practical Food Inspection*. 9th Edition. London: H. K. Lewis.

Scottish Home and Health Department (1964) *The Aberdeen Typhoid Outbreak 1964: Report of the Departmental Committee of Enquiry*. (Chairman Sir David Milne) Cmnd. 2542. Edinburgh: H.M.S.O.

BACTERIOLOGY AND FOOD POISONING

Ayres, P. A. (1975) Mussel poisoning in Britain with special reference to Paralytic shellfish poisoning. *Environmental Health*, Vol. 83, No. 7.

Ayres, P. A. (1979) Food poisoning risks associated with foods other than meat and poultry—Shellfish. *Health and Hygiene*, Vol. 3, No. 1.

Beneson, A. S. (Editor) (1981) *Control of Communicable Diseases in Man*. 13th Edition. Washington D.C.: The American Public Health Association. (U.K. Distributor: H. K. Lewis.)

British Association for the Advancement of Science (1977) *Salmonella The Food Poisoner*. Report by a study group.

Frazier, W. C. (1967) *Food Microbiology*. 2nd Edition. New York: McGraw-Hill.

Gilbert, R. J. and Roberts, D. (1979) Food poisoning risks associated with foods other than meat and poultry—Outbreaks and Surveillance Studies. *Health and Hygiene*, Vol. 3, No. 1.

Parry, T. and Pawsey, R. (1973) *Principles of Microbiology for Students of Food Technology*. London: Hutchinson Educational Ltd.

Perry, J. (1974) Food poisoning from fried rice. *Environmental Health*, Vol. 82, No. 3.

Robinson, D. A., Gilbert, R. J. and Skirrow, M. B. (1980) Campylobacter enteritis. *Environmental Health*, Vol. 88, No. 7.

Rothwell, J. (1979) Food poisoning associated with foods other than meat or poultry—Milk and dairy products and ice cream. *Health and Hygiene*, Vol. 3, No. 1.

Seiler, D. A. L. (1979) Food poisoning associated with foods other than meat or poultry—Bakery products. *Health and Hygiene*, Vol. 3, No. 1.

Watercress Working Party (1966) *The Hygienic Production of Watercress*. The Public Health Laboratory Service.

World Health Organisation (1979) *Environmental Health Criteria 11 Mycotoxins*. Geneva: W.H.O.

DESIGN AND CONSTRUCTION

Graham-Rack, B. and Binstead, R. (1973) *Hygiene in Food Manufacturing and Handling*. 2nd Edition. London: Food Trade Press Ltd.

Meat and Livestock Commission (1973) *Floors and Walls of Slaughterhouses and Meatworks*. Technical Bulletin No. 1.

REFRIGERATION

Food Freezer and Refrigerator Council *Teaching Notes on Refrigeration and Food Freezing*.

U.K. Association of Frozen Food Producers *UKAFFP Code of Recommended Practice for the Handling of Quick Frozen Foods*.

PEST CONTROL AND CLEANING

Cornwell, P. B. (1968) *The Cockroach Volume 1*. London: Hutchinson.

Cornwell, P. B. (1976) *The Cockroach Volume 2*. London: Associated Business Programmes Ltd.

Davis, R. A. (1961) *Control of Rats and Mice*. Bulletin No. 181. Ministry of Agriculture, Fisheries and Food. London: H.M.S.O.

Hickin, N. E. (1964) *Household Insect Pests*. London: Hutchinson.

Jenson, A. G. (1965) *Proofing of Buildings Against Rats and Mice*. Technical Bulletin No. 12. Ministry of Agriculture, Fisheries and Food. London: H.M.S.O.

Local Government Training Board (1977) *Insect Control. Reference Manual for Pest Control Personnel*.

McLaughlin, T. (1969) *The Cleaning, Hygiene and Maintenance Handbook*. London: Business Books Ltd.

Ministry of Agriculture, Fisheries and Food (1976) *Control of Rats and Mice. Reference Manual for Pest Control Personnel*. Local Government Training Board.

Ministry of Agriculture, Fisheries and Food (1977) *Cockroaches*. Advisory Leaflet 383.

Ministry of Agriculture, Fisheries and Food (1977) *Contact Insecticides used in Food Storage Practice in the U.K. and Notes on Spraying Against Stored Products Pests*. IC 1977/19.

CATERING PREMISES

Department of Health and Social Security, Ministry of Agriculture, Fisheries and Food, and Welsh Office (1972) *Hygiene in Microwave Catering*. Food Hygiene Code of Practice No. 9.

Department of Health and Social Security (1974) *Hygiene*. Health Service Catering Manual. Catering and Dietetic Branch.

Department of Health and Social Security (1980) *Guidelines on Pre-Cooked Chilled Foods*. H.M.S.O.

Fereday, P. B. and Bates, M. P. (1978) An investigation into the thawing, roasting and cooking of large turkeys. *Environmental Health*, Vol. 86, No. 4.

Glew, G. (Editor) (1973) *Cook/Freeze Catering: an Introduction to its Technology*. London: Faber and Faber.
Hughes, H. L. (1979) A survey of temperature control procedures during catering operations. *Environmental Health*, Vol. 87, No. 8.
Lawson, F. (1973) *Principles of Catering Design*. London: The Architectural Press, 9 Queen Anne's Gate, London.
Pyke, M. (1974) *Catering Science and Technology*. London: John Murray.

THE LICENSED TRADE

Association of Public Health Inspectors (1973) *Hygiene in Public Houses and Licensed Premises*. Code of Practice No. 14.
Metropolitan Borough of Bury. *Licensed Premises—A Code of Practice*. Environmental Health Department.
Miles, J. G. (Editor) (1978) *Innkeeping—A Manual for Licensed Victuallers*. 8th Edition. Brewing Publications Ltd.
Weston, J. R. (1971) *Hygiene in Public Houses*. Aston University Project. Unpublished.

TAKEAWAY FOOD PREMISES

Bertram, P. (1975) *Fast Food Operations*. London: Barrie and Jenkins.
Dowling, S. J. (1975) *The Chinese Food Trade*. Aston University Project. Unpublished.
Fox, D. L. and Wilson, H. D. (1971) *Study of Indian/Pakistani and Chinese Food and Food Practices*. Paper to Environmental Health Officers Association (Tyneside Branch). Unpublished.
Mattosian, R. and Kingcott, E. W. (1977) The Dona Kebab—A possible food poisoning hazard. *Environmental Health*, Vol. 85, No. 3.
Williams, J. R. (1972) *The Fried Fish and Chip Trade*. Aston University Project. Unpublished.

BUTCHERY PREMISES

Department of Health and Social Security and Ministry of Agriculture, Fisheries and Food. Food Hygiene Codes of Practice, No. 5 *Poultry Dressing and Packing* (1961). No. 8 *Hygiene in the Meat Trades* (1969).
Gerrard, F. (1976) *Sausage and Small Goods Production*. 6th Edition. London: Northwood Publications Ltd.

WET FISH SHOPS

Atkinson, R. G. and Bailey, N. F. (1979) *The Student's Guide to Fish and Fish Inspection*. Environmental Health Officers Association.
Department of Health and Social Security and Ministry of Agriculture, Fisheries and Food. Food Hygiene Codes of Practice No. 3 *Hygiene in the Retail Fish Trade* (1960) and No. 4 *The Hygienic Transport and Handling of Fish* (1960).
Ministry of Agriculture, Fisheries and Food. *Torry Advisory Notes 1–81*. Torry Research Station.

VENDING MACHINES

Ashworth, R. M. (1974) *Hygiene of Vending Machines*. Aston University Project. Unpublished.

Department of Health and Social Security and Ministry of Agriculture, Fisheries and Food (1967) *Hygiene in the Operation of Coin Operated Food Vending Machines*. Food Hygiene Code of Practice No. 7.

LEGISLATION

Food and Drugs Act, 1955.
Food and Drugs (Control of Food Premises) Act, 1976.
Milk and Dairies (General) Regulations, 1959 (S.I. 277).
Ice Cream (Heat Treatment *etc.*) Regulations, 1959 (S.I. 734).
Food Hygiene (General) Regulations, 1970 (S.I. 1172).
Poultry Meat (Hygiene) Regulations, 1976 (S.I. 1209).
Milk (Special Designation) Regulations, 1977 (S.I. 1033).
Milk (Special Designation) (Amendment) Regulations, 1980 (S.I. 488).
Food Labelling Regulations, 1980 (S.I. 1849).

INDEX